JUDGING THE JUDGES
PENTECOSTAL THEOLOGICAL PERSPECTIVES
ON THE BOOK OF JUDGES

JUDGING THE JUDGES

PENTECOSTAL THEOLOGICAL PERSPECTIVES ON THE BOOK OF JUDGES

LEE ROY MARTIN

CPT Press
Cleveland, Tennessee

Judging the Judges
Pentecostal Theological Perspectives on the Book of Judges

Published by CPT Press
900 Walker ST NE
Cleveland, TN 37311
USA
email: cptpress@pentecostaltheology.org
website: www.cptpress.com

Library of Congress Control Number: 2018903478

ISBN-13: 978-1-935931-71-3

Copyright © 2018 CPT Press

All rights reserved. No part of this book may be reproduced or translated in any form, by print, photoprint, microfilm, microfiche, electronic database, internet database, or any other means without written permission from the publisher.

Cover illustration, 'Jael and Sisera', by Jacopo Amigoni, c. 1739, oil on canvas.

Dedicated
To My Wife
Karen

Contents

Preface ix
Abbreviations xi

1   Introduction: The Relational God of Judges 1
2   God at Risk: Divine Vulnerability in Judges 10.6-16 9
3   Tongues of Angels, Words of Prophets: Divine
    Communication in the Book of Judges 35
4   Yahweh Conflicted: Unresolved Theological Tension
    in the Cycle of Judges 57
5   Power to Save!?: The Role of the Spirit of Yahweh in
    the Book of Judges 75
6   'Where are all his wonders?': The Exodus Motif in the
    Book of Judges 109
7   Judging the Judges: Searching for Value in these
    Problematic Characters 135

Bibliography 155
Credits 165
Index of Biblical References 166
Index of Authors 172

PREFACE

The essays in this collection represent my ongoing theological interpretation of the book of Judges. In my previous book, *The Unheard Voice of God: A Pentecostal Hearing of the Book of Judges*,[1] I examined the three major speeches of God that are found in Judges 2.1-5; 6.7-10; and 10.6-16. During my research, I was affected most powerfully by the realization that God is passionate both in his anger and in his compassion. The three speeches of God reveal the suffering of God, his vulnerability, the risk that he accepts when he enters covenant, and his desire that his people know him and relate to him. God admits to feeling abused and manipulated. Yahweh is not a distant, detached God; rather, Yahweh is a responsive, relational God. Pentecostal prayer, preaching, and worship all presuppose this kind of relational God. My years in the pastorate, ministering to wounded people, have taught me the value of God's relationality. This monograph, therefore, expands on the passionate relationality of God as it surfaces in Judges. It is a continuation of my interest in the role of God within the narrative of Judges.

I could not have completed this ten-year project without the support of my family, my church, and my colleagues at the Pentecostal Theological Seminary. I am grateful for the encouragement of Seminary presidents Steven Land, Lamar Vest, and current president Michael Baker. The administration and board of trustees have provided travel funds and research leaves that have assisted me greatly. David Han, our Vice President for Academics, has worked diligently to support the faculty and maintain a research-friendly environment at the Seminary.

I appreciate colleagues and students at the Seminary who have shared my passion for the difficult task of integrating academics

---

[1] Lee Roy Martin, *The Unheard Voice of God: A Pentecostal Hearing of the Book of Judges* (JPTSup 32; Blandford Forum, UK: Deo Publishing, 2008).

and spirituality, and I have benefited from ongoing dialogue with the entire faculty and with each of my students. I am especially grateful for the continuing friendship of John Christopher Thomas, who reads my work carefully and who engages me in lively dialogue every day. Our offices are located within shouting distance of each other in the Centre for Pentecostal Theology.

My greatest supporter is my wife Karen, who reads my manuscripts and makes helpful corrections. I also give thanks for my children and grandchildren: Stephen, Michael, Kendra, Marilyn, Caleb, and Joshua. They have given me reason to construct sound theology that will sustain the spirituality of the Pentecostal–Charismatic movement. We read in Judges, '[T]here arose another generation after them, which did not know the LORD or the works that he had done for Israel' (2.10).[2] I am trusting that, by the help and grace of God, the same will not be said of our coming generation.

---

[2] Unless stated otherwise, all biblical quotations are the translations of the author.

ABBREVIATIONS

AB	*Anchor Bible*
ASV	American Standard Version (1901)
BA	*Biblical Archaeologist*
BAR	*Biblical Archaeology Review*
BAGD	F.W. Danker et al., *A Greek-English Lexicon of the New Testament and Other Early Christian Literature* (Chicago: University of Chicago Press, 3rd edn, 2000).
BDB	Francis Brown, et al., *The New Brown, Driver, Briggs, Gesenius Hebrew and English Lexicon: With an Appendix Containing the Biblical Aramaic* (trans. E. Robinson; Peabody, MA: Hendrickson, 1979).
BDF	F. Blass, A. Debrunner, and R.W. Funk, *A Greek Grammar of the New Testament and Other Early Christian Literature* (Chicago: University of Chicago Press, 1961).
BSac	*Bibliotheca Sacra*
BR	*Bible Review*
BZ	*Biblische Zeitschrift*
CBQ	*Catholic Biblical Quarterly*
CHALOT	W.L. Holladay and L. Köhler, *A Concise Hebrew and Aramaic Lexicon of the Old Testament* (Leiden: Brill, 2000).
CSB	Holman Christian Standard Bible (2004)
DCH	David J.A. Clines, *Dictionary of Classical Hebrew* (8 vols.; Sheffield: Sheffield Academic Press, 1993).
DRA	Douay-Rheims Version (1899 American edn)
EJT	*European Journal of Theology*
EP	*Ekklesiastikos Pharos*
ESV	English Standard Version (2001)
GKC	W. Gesenius, E. Kautzsch, and A.E. Cowley, *Gesenius' Hebrew Grammar* (Oxford: The Clarendon Press, 2nd English edn, 1910).
HALOT	L. Köhler and W. Baumgartner, *The Hebrew and Aramaic Lexicon of the Old Testament* (2 vols.; Leiden: Brill, Study edn, 2001).
HBT	*Horizons in Biblical Theology*
ICC	International Critical Commentary
Int	*Interpretation*

ITC	International Theological Commentary
JANES	*Journal of the Ancient Near Eastern Society*
JBL	*Journal of Biblical Literature*
JETS	*Journal of the Evangelical Theological Society*
JPS	Jewish Publication Society Holy Scriptures (1917)
JPT	*Journal of Pentecostal Theology*
JPTSup	Journal of Pentecostal Theology Supplement Series
JSOT	*Journal for the Study of the Old Testament*
JSOTSup	Journal for the Study of the Old Testament Supplement Series
JTS	*Journal of Theological Studies*
KJV	Authorized King James Version (1769 ed.)
LA	*Liber Annuus: Annual of the Studium Biblicum Franciscanum Jerusalem*
LSJ	Henry George Liddell, *et al.*, *A Greek-English Lexicon* (Oxford: Clarendon Press, 1940).
KB	Ludwig Köhler and Walter Baumgartner, *Lexicon in Veteris Testamenti Libros* (Leiden: Brill, 1958).
LXX	Rahlfs, *Septuaginta* (1935)
NAB	New American Bible (1991)
NAC	New American Commentary
NASB	New American Standard Bible (1977)
NAU	New American Standard Bible (1995)
NCBC	New Century Bible Commentary
NIBC	New International Biblical Commentary
NICNT	New International Commentary on the New Testament
NICOT	New International Commentary on the Old Testament
NIDOTTE	W. Van Gemeren (ed.), *New International Dictionary of Old Testament Theology and Exegesis* (5 vols.; Grand Rapids, MI: Zondervan, 1997).
NIV	New International Version (1984)
NJB	New Jerusalem Bible (1985)
NKJV	New King James Version (1982)
NRSV	New Revised Standard Version (1989)
OTE	*Old Testament Essays*
OTL	Old Testament Library
PNEUMA	*PNEUMA: The Journal of the Society for Pentecostal Studies*
RevExp	*Review & Expositor*
RSV	Revised Standard Version (1973)
RTR	*Reformed Theological Review*
RV	English Revised Version (1885)
SJOT	*Scandinavian Journal of Theology*

TDOT	G.J. Botterweck *et al.* (eds.), *Theological Dictionary of the Old Testament* (15 vols.; Grand Rapids, MI: Eerdmans, 1974-).
TJ	*Trinity Journal*
TLOT	E. Jenni and C. Westermann (eds.), *Theological Lexicon of the Old Testament* (3 vols.; Peabody, MA: Hendrickson Publishers, 1997).
TNK	Jewish Publication Society TANAKH (1985)
TWOT	R.L. Harris, G.L. Archer, and B.K. Waltke (eds.), *Theological Wordbook of the Old Testament* (2 vols.; Chicago: Moody Press, 1999).
VT	*Vetus Testamentum*
VTSup	Vetus Testamentum Supplements
VUL	Latin Vulgate (Weber edn, 1983)
WTJ	*Westminster Theological Journal*
WW	*Word & World*
ZAW	*Zeitschrift für die alttestamentliche Wissenschaft*

1

Introduction: The Relational God of Judges

Recent studies have recognized the intricacies and subtleties woven into the fabric of Judges, but the nuanced presentation of God in the book has yet to be explored fully. The character development of Yahweh in the narrative of Judges depicts his interior struggles as he is faced with Israel's offenses against his graciously offered covenant. On the one hand, he obligates himself to comply with his previous pronouncements – his promise to the patriarchs and his vow to keep covenant. On the other hand, he is angered by the Israelites' affronts to the covenant and is compelled to punish their transgressions. Yahweh's inner conflict is heightened further when his compassion is awakened by the cries of the Israelites, who plead for salvation from the suffering and oppression brought on by Yahweh's judgment. However, the long-recognized cycle of sin-punishment-cry-salvation is not static, deterministic, or mechanical. As the schema begins to unravel, it serves as a platform for displaying a carefully constructed portrayal of Yahweh's conflicted passions. The typical overly simplistic interpretations that see Judges primarily as a polemic for Davidic monarchy, an explanation for the continued presence of the Canaanites, or as justification for the exile fail to account for the meticulous theological shadings of Yahweh's characterization in Judges.

The Deuteronomy Tradition

The complex characterization of God in Judges includes theological components from both Deuteronomy and Exodus.[1] Given the placement of Joshua and Judges as the first two books to follow Deuteronomy, it would not be too great a stretch to see Joshua as a depiction of life under the blessings (Deut. 28.1-14) and Judges as life under the curses (Deut. 28.15-68).[2] In addition to the basic Deuteronomistic formula of reward/punishment, Judges utilizes other language that is found in the earlier book of Deuteronomy. If Israel would obey Yahweh's commandments, their enemies would be defeated, and the peoples of the earth would fear them (Deut. 28.7), but if they would not 'hear' Yahweh, then they would be defeated by their enemies (Deut. 28.25), oppressed and plundered (Deut. 28.33). Foreshadowing Israel's behavior in the book of Judges, Moses warned, 'if your heart turns away, and you will not hear, but are drawn away to worship other gods and serve them, I declare to you this day, that you shall perish' (Deut. 30.17-18). Speaking for Yahweh, Moses predicts Israel's treason: '[they] will forsake me, and break my covenant that I have made with them' (Deut. 31.16). He adds the following mournful note:

> For when I bring them into the land which I swore unto their fathers, that flows with milk and honey, they will eat and will fill themselves and become fat; then will they turn unto other gods, and serve them, and spurn me, and break my covenant (Deut. 31.20; cf. Judg. 2.1-5).

Deuteronomy warns that if the Israelites are unfaithful to their covenant obligations, they 'will be only oppressed and crushed all the time' (Deut. 28.33; cf. Judg. 10.8). Therefore, Yahweh's actions in Judges bring upon the Israelites the retribution which they

---

[1] See Walter Brueggemann, 'Social Criticism and Social Vision in the Deuteronomic Formula of the Judges', in Patrick D. Miller (ed.), *A Social Reading of the Old Testament: Prophetic Approaches to Israel's Communal Life* (Minneapolis, MN: Fortress Press, 1981), pp. 73-90. Brueggemann calls for a re-appraisal of the Deuteronomistic retribution theology of deed–consequence in light of its use in Judges in conjunction with the salvation theology of the exodus.

[2] In classic literary terms, Joshua is a romance and Judges is a tragedy; cf. Leland Ryken, *The Literature of the Bible* (Grand Rapids, MI: Zondervan, 1974), p. 23.

deserve and which Yahweh had threatened.[3] This retribution is manifested in the first part of the well-known cycle of Judges, in which Israel's sin leads to punishment through subjugation to the enemy (Judg. 2.14-15).

Furthermore, the Deuteronomic threat of exile becomes an imminent possibility in Judges 6 when the Midianites invade the land and force the Israelites into mountain refuges. Then, by mentioning the 'exile from the land' (18.30), the narrative highlights the possibility that the land can be lost. It is evident, therefore, that God is capable of delivering on his earlier threat (Deut. 28.36-68) to expel the Israelites if they should continue to be unfaithful to the covenant.

The Exodus Tradition

Along with the theology of Deuteronomy, which points to the exile and which promises retribution, Judges displays clear correspondences to the theology of Exodus. The exodus tradition appears in Judges in at least three ways. First, Israel's salvation from Egypt is mentioned repeatedly in Judges. In Yahweh's first speech (Judg. 2.1-5), he reminds the Israelites that he had delivered them from the land of Egypt and had led them into the land of promise. He reminds them further of his promise never to break his covenant. In the second speech (6.7-10), he again recounts the exodus from Egypt and his driving out of the Canaanites. Yahweh's third speech (10.6-16) is intensely passionate and quite surprising, and it marks a profound turning point. Once again, he mentions the exodus from Egypt, and he reminds the Israelites of all the other acts of salvation that he has performed on their behalf, but he refuses to save Israel. In effect, he proposes to break the covenant and abandon his people in contradiction to his earlier promise. Second, Yahweh's acts of salvation in the book of Judge are modeled after the paradigm of the exodus. In the second half of the cycle of Judges, the oppressed Israelites 'cry out to Yahweh'; and, because of his

---

[3] Retribution is a motif that appears early in Judges (1.7) and that is emphasized in the story of Abimelech, which concludes with this pronouncement: 'Thus God repaid the evil of Abimelech, which he had done to his father by killing his 70 brothers' (9.56).

covenant loyalty and his compassion, Yahweh saves them from their enemies. Third, in Judges, Yahweh speaks and acts in accordance with his self-revelation to Moses in Exod. 34.6-7:

> And Yahweh passed before him, and exclaimed, 'Yahweh, Yahweh, a merciful and gracious God, slow to anger, and abounding in covenant loyalty and faithfulness, keeping covenant loyalty for a thousand generations, forgiving iniquity and transgression and sin, yet by no means clearing the guilty, but visiting the iniquity of the parents upon the children and the children's children, to the third and the fourth generations' (Exod. 34.6-7)

In this most intimate revelation to Moses, Yahweh discloses the tension between mercy and justice, a tension that exists within Yahweh's own character. Yahweh's inner conflict as it emerges from Exod. 34.6-7 is explored by Walter Brueggemann, who writes, 'There is no one like Yahweh, who while endlessly faithful, hosts in Yahweh's own life a profound contradiction that leaves open a harshness toward the beloved partner community'.[4] In the book of Judges, Israel's chronic idolatry offends Yahweh's justice and provokes his anger (2.12, 14, 20; 3.8; 10.7); but Israel's cries and groans evoke Yahweh's compassion (2.18; 3.9; 3.15; 4.3; 6.6).[5]

The depth of Yahweh's passion for Israel is evident in Judges 10. For the fifth time in the book, Israel cries out to Yahweh for deliverance from an enemy (10.10); but, on this occasion, Yahweh declares that his patience has been exhausted by Israel's unfaithfulness. Therefore, he will not save them again (10.13). A ray of hope

---

[4] Walter Brueggemann, *Theology of the Old Testament: Testimony, Dispute, Advocacy* (Minneapolis: Fortress Press, 1997), p. 288.

[5] The intertextual connections to Exodus 34 extend beyond Yahweh's self-revelation in 34.6-7. After hearing Yahweh's disclosure, Moses implores Yahweh to forgive the Israelites (34.9), and Yahweh responds by affirming his covenant. Then, in Exod. 34.9-17, Yahweh utters several words and phrases that can be linked directly to the book of Judges: 'I make a covenant' (Exod. 34.10; cf. Judg. 2.1); 'marvels' (Exod. 34.10; cf. Judg. 6.13); the 'work' of Yahweh (Exod. 34.10; cf. Judg. 2.10); 'I am driving out …' (Exod. 34.11; cf. Judg. 6.9); 'beware lest you make a covenant with the inhabitants of the land' (Exod. 34.12; cf. Judg. 2.2); 'lest it be for a snare' (Exod. 34.12; cf. Judg. 2.3); 'you shall destroy their altars' (Exod. 34.13; cf. Judg. 2.2); 'you shall worship no other god' (Exod. 34.14; cf. Judg. 3.6; 6.10); 'lusting after their gods' (Exod. 34.15; cf. Judg. 2.17); and '[do not] take their daughters to marry your sons' (Exod. 34.16; cf. Judg. 3.6); 'you shall make no molded gods' (Exod. 34.17; cf. Judg. 17.3, 4; 18.14-18).

appears, however, for in v. 16, he groans with compassion: 'he was deeply distressed by Israel's suffering'.[6] The Hebrew text of Judg. 10.16b (ותקצר נפשו בעמל ישראל) is rendered by the KJV, 'and his soul was grieved for the misery of Israel', and by the NRSV, 'and he could no longer bear to see Israel suffer', which represents the traditional consensus interpretation. Although the exact wording of the translations and commentaries may differ, they agree that Judg. 10.16b is an expression of Yahweh's compassion toward the Israelites in their suffering.

Despite Yahweh's passionate devotion to Israel and his concern for Israel's survival, Yahweh does not immediately raise up a deliverer. Moreover, he reduces the level of his involvement with Israel. Yahweh's alienation and detachment from Israel continue to be registered all the way from ch. 10 to the end of the book of Judges. Even though Yahweh is 'distressed' by Israel's suffering, he does not return to full engagement with his people.

Divine Relationality

Yahweh's decision to withdraw and let the Israelites fend for themselves leads to ambiguity regarding the role of Yahweh in the latter half of Judges. In the first half of the book of Judges, the role of God is clear – when the Israelites sin, he hands them over to an enemy for discipline; and, when they cry out to him, he raises up a judge who delivers them. Following Yahweh's withdrawal in Judg. 10.13, however, the role of God becomes ambiguous as the tension surrounding God's anger and God's compassion intensifies.[7] The silence of God is continued from Judges into 1 Samuel, where we are told 'the word of Yahweh was rare in those days' (1 Sam. 3.1).

---

[6] It was this text that first made me aware of the deep passions of God in Judges.

[7] The kind of ambiguity that we find in Judges illustrates the function of Scripture to generate dialogue and discernment within the community of faith. The Bible does not answer all of our questions, but it shows us how to discern the way forward in community. See Chris E.W. Green, *Sanctifying Interpretation: Vocation, Holiness, and Scripture* (Cleveland, TN: CPT Press, 2015).

The tension between Yahweh's mercy and Yahweh's justice results from his relationality.[8] Yahweh does not react to Israel mechanically or automatically; instead, he reacts contextually and relationally. The attributes of Yahweh that are listed in his self-revelation to Moses are not abstract philosophical qualities. They are relational attributes: 'merciful and gracious ... slow to anger ... covenant loyalty and faithfulness ... forgiving ... yet by no means clearing the guilty' (Exod. 34.6-7). Each of these attributes requires the existence of an object who stands in relationship to Yahweh. Yahweh is merciful and gracious to a certain person, at a certain time, and in a certain place. These attributes do not exist in a vacuum; they are responses to an 'other'. Yahweh is 'slow to anger' in response to Israel's sin. Yahweh is 'abundant in covenant loyalty' (חסד) toward the parties with whom he is joined in covenant.

Yahweh's relationality generates his willingness to enter into covenant, and the covenant provides the context for the expression of Yahweh's relational attributes. In both Exodus and Deuteronomy, the covenant is central to Yahweh's relationship to Israel. On the part of Yahweh, the covenant is a 'self-imposed obligation'[9] (Exod. 23.32-33; 34.12, 15; Deut. 7.2; Josh. 9.15; Judg. 2.2), which issues from divine choice, not necessity.[10] Yahweh freely choses Israel to be his people, and Israel is the recipient of Yahweh's affection, without regard to their deservedness.[11] 'God's actions flow out of his own commitment, freely made, rather than as compensation for Israelite merit'.[12] Studies of Judges have focused almost entirely on the actions of Israel, but Yahweh is the initiator and sustainer of the covenant relationship; he is the major actor. The existence of the covenant, both in its origins in Exodus or its challenges in Judges, is not dependent on the actions of Israel, but on the actions of Yahweh. As the suzerain, Yahweh is free to revoke the treaty at

---

[8] For a theological explication of God's relationality, see Clark H. Pinnock, 'Divine Relationality: A Pentecostal Contribution to the Doctrine of God', *JPT* 5 (2000), pp. 3-26.

[9] Kutsch, 'ברית', *TLOT*, I, pp. 258-59.

[10] John Goldingay, *Old Testament Theology: Israel's Faith* (Downers Grove, IL: InterVarsity Press, 2006), p. 186.

[11] Gerhard von Rad, *Old Testament Theology* (2 vols.; New York: Harper, 1962), I, p. 129.

[12] Frederick E. Greenspahn, 'The Theology of the Framework of Judges', *VT* 36 (1986), pp. 385-96 (395-96).

any time, but despite the fact that he is the superior party, he declares that he will never break the covenant.

Yahweh's covenant, freely offered, and Yahweh's faithfulness, steadfastly given, offer powerful assurance to the Israelites; but still the covenant is not a one-sided affair;[13] it demands obedience. The corollary to the fact that Yahweh is free and Yahweh is faithful is that if Israel will be faithful, Israel will be free. Goldingay reflects on the double-sided loyalty expected of the covenant:

> The covenant means that Israel's security depends originally on Yhwh's sovereignty and commitment and not on Israel's fickleness, but that Israel's commitment is an absolutely necessary corollary of Yhwh's commitment to Israel. It is not exactly that Yhwh's commitment to Israel is conditional on Israel's commitment. Rather, it demands it.[14]

The covenant, therefore, provides the framework for the relationship between Yahweh and Israel, and the covenantal requirement of mutual faithfulness creates the context for the display of Yahweh's relational attributes.

Conclusion

The essays that follow will explore the complex characterization of God in the book of Judges. At the heart of these studies is the relational nature of God and the tension inherent in God's own self between his compassion and his justice.[15] The relational character of God is manifested in Judges through his covenant loyalty. Unfortunately, the book of Judges does not have a happy ending; but Judges is not the end of the story.

---

[13] So Walther Eichrodt, *Theology of the Old Testament* (2 vols.; Philadelphia: Westminster Press, 1961), I, p. 37.

[14] Goldingay, *Israel's Faith*, p. 188.

[15] The relational character and internal life of Yahweh, displayed in Judges through narrative, is poignantly portrayed through poetry in Hosea. See Walter Brueggemann's exceptionally insightful study, 'The Recovering God of Hosea', *HBT* 30.1 (2008), pp. 5-20.

2

GOD AT RISK: DIVINE VULNERABILITY IN JUDGES 10.6-16

Introduction

> Then Yahweh said to the Israelites, 'Was it not from the Egyptians and from the Amorites and from the Ammonites and from the Philistines – and when the Sidonians and Amalek and Maon oppressed you, you cried unto me, and I saved you from their power? But you have forsaken me and served other gods; therefore, I will not save you again. Go and call upon the gods that you have chosen. They will save you in the time of your distress' (Judg. 10.11-13).

Judges 10.6-16 reports quite a shocking dialogue between Yahweh and Israel. Suddenly and without warning, Yahweh refuses to rescue the Israelites. In spite of their confession and their repentance, Yahweh declares that his patience has been exhausted. He had saved them time after time, but He will not save them again. The cycle of Israel's rebellion had been repeated four times earlier in the book of Judges. It would not be repeated quite the same again. The unique perplexity of this passage and its sudden appearance in Judges should cause it to be the object of much scrutiny, but it has not received significant attention by biblical scholars.

In this study I will offer a brief overview of the book of Judges and the cycle of rebellion. I will then outline the striking features of ch. 10 and discuss the passage's strategic role within the overall structure of Judges. Next, I will discuss the apparent conflict between the anger of God and the compassion of God that is central to the importance of Judges 10. Finally, I will suggest that an underlying theo-logic of ch. 10 (and all of Judges) is that God has chosen to enter into a genuine relationship with his people,[1] and that a genuine relationship causes God himself to be vulnerable to abuse, neglect, and personal injury. As soon as the Lord chose to enter into the covenant, he submitted himself to a position of personal risk.

Overview of Judges

The book of Judges consists of three major sections: 1) an introduction (1.1-3.6); 2) the stories of the judges (3.7-16.31); and 3) a conclusion (17.1-21.25).[2] The introduction offers both a theological reflection on the cause of the events that are found in Judges, as well as a short summary of those events. The second section of the book sets forth the stories of the major judges along with brief accounts of the minor judges. The conclusion consists of two complex narratives that do not relate directly to any of the judges, but are set within the historical time period that belongs to the judges.

The first section of Judges (1.1-3.6) may be further divided into two parts, in the nature of a dual introduction. The first introduction (1.1-2.5) summarizes the completion of the conquest after the death of Joshua. Chapter 1 begins with accounts of tribal victories but concludes with quite a long list of failures. The angel of the Lord appears in ch. 2 and rebukes Israel for failing to expel the inhabitants of the land as God had commanded them. Their failure to complete fully the conquest is interpreted by the angel as a violation of their covenant with Yahweh. According to the angel, the Israelites' root problem was their refusal to hear and obey God's word: 'You have not heard/obeyed (שמע) my command' (2.2).[3] The charge is repeated three more times in Judges: 'They would not hear/obey the judges' (2.17a); 'They have not heard/obeyed my

---

[1] Terence E. Fretheim, *The Suffering of God: An Old Testament Perspective* (Overtures to Biblical Theology 14; Philadelphia: Fortress Press, 1984), p. 35.

[2] D.W. Gooding, 'The Composition of the Book of Judges', in *Eretz-Israel, Archeological Historical and Geographical Studies Xvi* (Jerusalem: Israel Exploration Society, 1982), pp. 70-79.

[3] On the meaning of שמע, see H. Schult, 'שמע', *TLOT*, II, pp. 1375-80.

voice' (2.20); 'You have not heard/obeyed my voice' (6.10).[4] The Israelites were disobedient to the clear commands of God and would suffer because of their stubbornness.

A second introduction begins with Judg. 2.6, which recounts the death of Joshua and Israel's subsequent apostasy. This second introduction focuses on the idolatry that resulted from cohabitation with the Canaanites, and Canaanite religion is described as a constant test for Israel. The introduction concludes with a preview of the cycle of rebellion that will be repeated throughout Judges. The pattern consists of the following elements: 1. Israel did what was evil in the sight of Yahweh, forsaking Yahweh and serving other gods (2.11); 2. God became very angry with Israel (2.14); 3. God gave Israel over to the power of the enemy who oppressed them (2.14-15); 4. Yahweh raised up judges, but Israel would not hear/obey the judges (2.16-17); 5. Yahweh would have compassion on Israel on account of their suffering, and he would deliver them through the leadership of the judge (2.18); 6. After the judge died, the Israelites would relapse into idolatry, with each generation growing worse than the one that preceded it (2.19). The text states from the outset that Israel's spiritual state would spiral downward throughout Judges. Israel's failure, therefore, is presented from two distinct perspectives. First, they failed to drive out the Canaanites; and second, they committed idolatry. These two sins are distinct, yet they issue from one basic source, which is Israel's refusal to hear/obey the voice of God.[5]

The second major section of Judges (3.6-16.31) forms the greater part of the book and consists of a series of salvation narratives whose main characters are called *judges*. These narratives follow the basic pattern or cycle that is detailed above. The narratives, however, are more explicit with regard to several elements, and utilize a variety of expressions when naming the elements of the pattern. For example, the narratives include Israel's cries to God for help (3.9; 3.15; 4.3; 6.7; 10.10). Also, the first four narratives

---

[4] In addition to the four accusations, the question of Israel's obedience is mentioned two other times: 2.17b and 3.4. The theme of hearing/obeying is also found four times in the concluding chapters of the book: 18.25; 19.25; 20.3; and 20.13.

[5] James D. Martin, *The Book of Judges: Commentary* (New York: Cambridge University Press, 1975), p. 135.

conclude with the words 'and the land had rest' (3.11; 3.30; 5.31; 8.28). Furthermore, in the case of Othniel, Gideon, Jephthah, and Samson, it is said that the 'Spirit of Yahweh' came upon them (3.10; 6.34; 11.29; 13.25; 14.6; 14.19; 15.14). Thus, the pattern is generally the same, but each narrative includes unique details and variations on the theme.

The major judges (those who appear in the longer narratives) are Othniel, Ehud, Deborah, Gideon, Jephthah, and Samson. Gideon's son Abimelech also receives significant attention as a usurper of power in ch. 9. The minor judges are Shamgar, Tola, Jair, Ibzan, Elon, and Abdon. The judges seem to be ordered in such a way that their personal characteristics and response to God mirror the downward spiral of Israel as a whole. The first judge, Othniel, is a war hero who has no faults. The second judge, Ehud, has a minor handicap; he is left-handed (described in the Hebrew text as 'infirm in his right hand'). The third judge, Deborah, is a woman, a fact that would present many hindrances in the society of that time. Next came Gideon who was hesitant and even fearful. References to fearfulness occur seven times in chs. 6-8. Furthermore, the Gideon cycle ends with idolatry, with the Israelites worshiping Gideon's ephod. After Gideon died, his son Abimelech seizes power and proclaims himself to be king. Jephthah, the next judge, is an outcast, the son of a prostitute who makes a rash vow that results in the unlawful sacrifice of his daughter.[6] Samson is the final judge, and although he is called by God and set apart as a Nazirite from birth, he pursues prostitutes, gives free reign to his anger, fails to deliver Israel, and is the only judge who was captured by the enemy.

The third major section of Judges (17.1-21.25) consists of two narrative appendices that seem to parallel the two introductions. In chs. 17 and 18 the Danites steal a household idol from a man named Micah, and they establish an idolatrous worship center in Dan. Chapters 19 through 21 describe in gory detail the rape, murder, and dismemberment of a Levite's secondary wife. Because the Benjaminites where unwilling to punish the criminals, the other Israelites engage them in battle and nearly eradicate the tribe of Benjamin. The first of the concluding narratives is concerned with

---

[6] Not everyone, of course, believes that Jephthah really sacrificed his daughter. The issue, however, is not directly germane to the argument here.

idolatry, and the second results in civil war. Judges, therefore, begins with the Israelites' fighting against their enemies and concludes with their fighting each other. These two concluding narratives suggest that Israel had fallen to a state of chaos, violence, immorality, idolatry, and depravity.

Chapters 17 through 21 might be perceived as superfluous because their narratives do not include any judges. The primary focus of the book of Judges, however, is not the judges themselves; rather, the primary focus is on the relationship between Yahweh and Israel. The narratives of the judges form the matrix in which that relationship is explored. Neither the introduction nor the conclusion of Judges is superfluous. On the contrary, they confirm to the hearer essential elements of the plot that bring unity and coherence to the larger narrative.

Features of Chapter Ten

At the end of the lengthy Gideon/Abimelech episode (chs. 6-9), Abimelech is killed by a nameless woman, who drops a millstone[7] on his head as he and his army are attacking the tower of Thebez. The narrator adds a moral to the end of the story: 'God repaid the evil of Abimelech … and God returned all the evil of the Shechemites upon their own heads' (9.56-57).

Following the death of Abimelech, two of the minor judges are mentioned very briefly. The text says, 'After Abimelech, there arose to save Israel, Tola, son of Puah' (10.1). Tola judged Israel 23 years, but no details of his exploits are recorded. 'There arose after him, Jair the Gileadite, and he judged Israel 22 years' (10.3). His activities are not chronicled either.

After accounts of the two minor judges, a familiar refrain appears for the sixth time within the Book of Judges: The Israelites 'did what was evil in the sight of Yahweh' (10.6).[8] Every previous judge cycle has begun with this indictment, and the hearer would

---

[7] Recent archaeological discoveries show that individual households used small millstones weighing eight to ten pounds. See Denise Dick Herr and Mary Petrina Boyd, 'A Watermelon Named Abimelech', *BAR* 28.1 (2002), pp. 34-37, 62.

[8] This refrain appeared once in the introduction (2.11), then it serves as the beginning of every major judge cycle (3.7; 3.12; 4.1; 6.1).

likely expect that another standard cycle has commenced. In this fifth cycle, however, the idolatry of the Israelites seems to have increased: 'they served the Baals and the Ashtartes, the gods of Aram, the gods of Sidon, the gods of Moab, the gods of the Ammonites, and the gods of the Philistines. Thus, they forsook Yahweh and did not serve him' (10.6). Among the four previous cycles, only the first one had specifically named Israel's idols; they had worshiped the Baals and Asherahs (3.7).[9] Therefore, when compared to the earlier cycles, the appearance of such an array of foreign gods in ch. 10 raises the intensity level of this episode and makes Israel appear quite guilty.[10] The intensity is heightened further by the addition of a summarizing accusation: 'Thus they forsook Yahweh and did not serve him'.

The cycle returns to normal with v. 7: 'The anger of Yahweh was hot against Israel, and he sold them into the hand of the Philistines and into the hand of the Ammonites'. These enemies crushed and oppressed Israel for 18 years, and 'Israel was greatly distressed' (10.7-9). There is nothing unusual about this element of the cycle, unless it is the uniqueness of registering two enemies and the use of two quite intensive words for oppression (רעץ, *shatter* and רצץ, *crush*) that are not used elsewhere in Judges to describe Israel's oppression.[11] Previous cycles, however, have demonstrated considerable variety of expression and some intensity when disclosing the nature of the enemies' oppressions. For example, Jabin had 'squeezed (לחץ) the Israelites with force (בחזקה) for 20 years' (4.3). The most detailed account of oppression is found in the Gideon cycle, where five verses at the beginning of the story are devoted to the Midianites' actions, and other aspects of their activities are mentioned throughout the narrative.

---

[9] Cf. Tammi J. Schneider, *Judges* (Berit Olam; Collegeville, MN: Liturgical Press, 2000), p. 160.

[10] Cf. Barry G. Webb, *The Book of Judges: An Integrated Reading* (JSOTSup, 46; Sheffield: JSOT Press, 1987), p. 44; and Daniel I. Block, *Judges, Ruth* (NAC 6; Nashville, TN: Broadman & Holman Publishers, 1999), p. 344.

[11] Block, *Judges, Ruth*, p. 345.

Next, as usual, 'The Israelites cried unto Yahweh' (10.10).[12] Their cry, however, is followed by quite an unusual addition: the content of their cry is recorded. On this occasion, they not only cry out for help, but they blurt out a confession: 'We have sinned against you, in that we have forsaken our God and we have served the Baals' (10.10). Never before in Judges had the content of their cry been revealed, and never before had Israel confessed any sin. It would appear that Israel is expressing genuine repentance toward God.

At this point, the hearer would likely expect the appearance of the next element of the standard judge cycle, God's raising up a judge to bring salvation to Israel (3.9; 3.15; 4.4; and 6.11). God, however, does not respond as expected. He declares,

> Was it not from Egypt and from the Amorites and from the Amorites and from the Philistines – and when the Sidonians and Amalek and Maon oppressed you, you cried unto me, and I saved you from their power? But you have forsaken me and served other gods; therefore, I will not save you again. Go and call upon the gods that you have chosen. They will save you in the time of your distress (10.11-14).

Yahweh reminds Israel of his faithfulness, mercy, and salvation in the past. He points back all the way to Egypt and then lists six more enemies from which he had saved them.[13] This is the only time in Judges that Yahweh responds verbally to Israel's cries. In previous rebukes of Israel, God had employed an angel (2.1), and prophets (4.4 and 6.8). The immediacy of the dialogue is accentuated by the lack of a mediating angel or prophet. The tone of the rebuff is quite sarcastic, 'Go cry to the gods you have chosen'.[14] Yahweh seems to be completely unresponsive to Israel's cries and unconcerned about their suffering. Pressler reads this rebuff as 'the passionate, pained response of a lover whose love is betrayed one too

---

[12] The same Hebrew word (זעק) is used for 'cry' in 3.9; 3.15; 6.6,7; 10.10 and 10.14. In 4.3 the word is צעק, which is a variant spelling of the same root. Cf. BDB, p. 858.
[13] List of nations in Judg. 10.11-12 and previous deliverance: Amorites (Num. 21; Josh. 24.8); Ammonites (Judg. 3.13); Philistines (Judg. 3.31); Sidonians (Josh. 13.6; Judg. 3.3); Amalekites (Judg. 6.3, 33; 7.12) Maon (Josh. 15.55. The LXX has Midian instead of Maon, perhaps pointing to the Midianites in Judges 6).
[14] Cf. Webb, *Judges: An Integrated Reading*, p. 45.

many times'.¹⁵ God's response is unprecedented and completely unexpected. The basic plan of the book appears to have been established in Judges 3, but this divine intransigence was not included as part of the standard cycle.

As in previous cycles, the narrator informs the hearer that God is very angry at the Israelites, but in ch. 10, the anger of God is given further expression in his speech. He refuses to aid Israel again, and he sarcastically recommends they seek the help of the foreign gods. Additional evidence for the passionate tone of God's speech may be found in the Hebrew grammar of vv. 11 and 12. Yahweh's speech in verse 11 is an incomplete sentence that contains no verb.

ויאמר יהוה אל־בני ישראל
הלא ממצרים ומן־האמרי ומן־בני עמון ומן־פלשתים

> And Yahweh said unto the sons of Israel, 'Was it not from Egypt and from the Amorite and from the sons of Ammon and from the Philistines ... ?'

Verse 12 follows with,

וצידונים ועמלק ומעון לחצו אתכם ותצעקו אלי
ואושיעה אתכם מידם

> 'And the Sidonians and Amalek and Maon oppressed you, and you cried unto me, and I saved you from their hand.'

Verse 12, therefore, is a complete sentence and makes sense as it stands, but v. 11 is incomplete, and cannot be attached grammatically to v. 12. The critical apparatus of the *BHS* suggests that v. 11 is corrupt and recommends the addition of the verb הושעתי ('I saved') as an emendation, even though there is no manuscript support for such a move.¹⁶ Translations have smoothed out the verse by supplying the missing verb; for example, the King James Version reads: 'And the LORD said unto the children of Israel, *Did not I deliver you* from the Egyptians, and from the Amorites, from the children of Ammon, and from the Philistines?'¹⁷ Commentators insist

---

¹⁵ Carolyn Pressler, *Joshua, Judges, and Ruth* (Westminster Bible Companion; Louisville, KY: Westminster John Knox Press, 2002), p. 198.

¹⁶ Rudolf Kittel *et al.*, *Biblia Hebraica Stuttgartensia* (Stuttgart: Deutsche Bibelgesellschaft, 3rd emended edn, 1987), p. 421.

¹⁷ Italics original. The following translations offer similar solutions: JPS, NASB, RSV, NIV, NRSV, NAB, NJB, NKJV, and TNK. I was unable to find any

on emending v. 11, either by adding a verb, by removing the preposition מִן, or by doing both. Boling declares that 'the verses have clearly suffered in transmission'.[18] Gesenius allows for the legitimate existence of rhetorical anacoluthon, but he sees no reason for its use in Judges ten. Therefore, he also calls for emendation.[19]

Alberto Soggin argues that the corruption of v. 11 is made obvious by the abnormal attaching of the preposition מִן directly to the names of the nations ('from Egypt', etc.), when the usual terminology for salvation in Judges is 'saved from the hand of' (2.16, 18; 6.9, 14; 8.22; 9.17; 10.12; 13.5).[20] In regard to Judges, Soggin is correct; but מִן can be used with יָשַׁע, as it is in 2 Sam. 22.4 (אִוָּשֵׁעַ וּמֵאֹיְבַי, 'I will be saved from my enemies'). Furthermore, when Judges speaks of Egypt, the preposition מִן is often attached to מִצְרַיִם (2.1; 6.8; 6.13; 11.13; and 11.16). It seems, therefore, that the use of the preposition מִן may be conditioned by the placing of Egypt first in the list.

In spite of the universal calls for emendation, there is good reason to accept the text as it stands. In fact, any clarifying emendation

---

translation that allows v. 11 to stand without a verb. Some translations (including the Vulgate and Luther) join vv. 11 and 12 into one sentence, choosing to remove the preposition מִן from v. 11. Both A and B versions of the LXX remove the anacoluthon, but they do so in different ways.

[18] Robert G. Boling, *Judges: A New Translation with Introduction and Commentary* (AB; Garden City, NY: Doubleday, 1975), p. 192; George F. Moore, *A Critical and Exegetical Commentary on Judges* (ICC; New York: Charles Scribner's Sons, 1895), pp. 281-82; J. Alberto Soggin, *Judges: A Commentary* (OTL; Philadelphia: Westminster Press, 1981), p. 202; Block, *Judges, Ruth*, p. 346; Robert H. O'Connell, *The Rhetoric of the Book of Judges* (VTSup 63; Leiden: Brill, 1996), pp. 467-68. Other commentators do not mention the anacoluthon, but in their translations they emend v. 11; e.g. Schneider, *Judges*, p. 160; Pressler, *Joshua, Judges, and Ruth*, p. 197; Michael Wilcock, *The Message of Judges: Grace Abounding* (Downers Grove, IL: InterVarsity Press, 1992), p. 108; Martin, *Judges*, p. 135; Webb, *Judges: An Integrated Reading*, p. 43

[19] GKC, pp. 505-506. Gesenius' examples of anacoluthon are Gen. 23.13; 31.52; Exod. 34.10; Num. 14.21; 32.20; Deut. 17.2; 24.1; and 29.21. Other grammars do not mention anacoluthon; nor do they discuss Judg. 10.11-12. E.g. Paul Joüon and T. Muraoka, *A Grammar of Biblical Hebrew* (Subsidia Biblica 14; 2 vols.; Roma: Editrice Pontificio Instituto Biblico, 1991); Bruce K. Waltke and Michael Patrick O'Connor, *An Introduction to Biblical Hebrew Syntax* (Winona Lake, IN: Eisenbrauns, 1990); Christo H.J. Van der Merwe, J.A. Naudé, and Jan H. Kroeze, *Biblical Hebrew Reference Grammar* (Biblical Languages: Hebrew 3; Sheffield: Sheffield Academic Press, 1999).

[20] Soggin, *Judges*, p. 202.

would detract significantly from the mood of the text, which is expressed in the explosive tone of the anacoluthon. The extraordinary form of expression matches the extraordinary content of the expression. God is frustrated with Israel, and his frustration is evident in his strained response. The broken grammar manifests the passionate outburst of an offended God. Verse 11 is the fractional speech of a furious God. To remove the tension from Judg. 10.11-12 would be equivalent to removing the Song of Deborah from ch. 5 because we have the prose account of the same events in ch 4 Just as poetry creates a mood, so does direct speech; and the speech of ch. 10 creates a dense mood of complex emotion, which must not be easily dismissed.

After Yahweh threatened to abandon Israel to their own devices, they repeated their confession and supplemented it with the reiteration of their plea for help, saying 'We have sinned; do, yourself, to us whatever is good in your sight, only please deliver us this day' (10.15). The redundant use of the pronoun 'you' (אתה) with the imperative 'do' (עשה) shows that Israel wants to be delivered (נצל) from the enemy and placed under the discipline of God himself. Apparently, they preferred a punishment that proceeded directly from God (disease, crop failure, natural disasters, etc.) rather than one that came through the mediation of an enemy people.[21] Although Yahweh did not respond to their plea for deliverance, 'They put aside their foreign gods from among them and they served Yahweh' (10.16). They proceeded to discard their idols and to serve (עבד) the Lord, actions which function in the narrative as a counterpart or inclusio to the beginning of the episode in v. 6, which states, 'they forsook Yahweh and did not serve (עבד) him'. In v. 6 they *do not* serve Yahweh, but in v. 16 they *do* serve Yahweh.

The putting away of their idols and their serving of Yahweh would appear to be the consequence of genuine repentance. It would be natural for the hearer to expect God's mercy and forgiveness to accompany Israel's repentance. Yet, Yahweh does not answer, showing that 'deliverance does not mechanically follow confession'.[22] Furthermore, he does not speak again until Judges 13

---

[21] Cf. David, who also chose discipline from the hand of God rather than from the hand of the enemy (2 Sam. 24.14).
[22] Pressler, *Joshua, Judges, and Ruth*, p. 197.

when the angel of Yahweh announces the coming birth of Samson. Although Yahweh does not speak, the narrator furnishes a glimpse into the heart of God with these concluding words: 'And his soul was grieved by the misery of Israel' (10.16b). Yahweh does not answer, and he does not save Israel, but he is moved to grief by the misery of Israel. 'Israel's suffering is God's grief.'[23] At the beginning of this narrative, he was angry at Israel because of their unfaithfulness; but now he is suffering along with them. The hearer is left with quite an ambiguous situation. God has not answered; he has not saved; but he is sympathetic to Israel's plight.

In the first half of the book, Israel 'cried' out to Yahweh in their suffering and he saved them time and again. There is no indication that they ever confessed their sin or that they ever repented of their sin. Over and over Yahweh saved Israel on account of his compassion (as in the exodus). However, in Judges 10 the hearer is faced with a stunning countermove by Yahweh – he refuses to save the Israelites even though they confess their sins, rid themselves of idols, and return to the worship of Yahweh. To the exilic and postexilic traditionists who advocated the efficacy of repentance, ch. 10 must have been quite a theological challenge, and perhaps was a provocation to deep debate within the community.[24]

The above survey of Judges 10 discloses several striking features: 1) Verses 6-16 offer details of the longest dialogue between God and Israel within the book of Judges;[25] 2) The dialogue is unmediated. That is, the text does not report the presence of an angel, prophet, or any other messenger; 3) It records the longest list of idols in Judges; 4) It is the only time in Judges that Israel is said to have repented and laid aside their idols; 5) It is the only time in Judges that Yahweh refuses to come to the aid of his people when they call upon him; 6) The passage brings into focus the conflict between Yahweh's anger and his compassion, a conflict that is occasioned by the rebellion of his covenant people. In light of the

---

[23] Abraham Joshua Heschel, *The Prophets* (2 vols.; New York: Harper & Row, 1962), II, p. 151.
[24] Cf. K.L. Noll, 'Deuteronomistic History or Deuteronomic Debate? (A Thought Experiment)', *JSOT* 31 (2007), pp. 311-45.
[25] Cf. J. Gordon Harris, Cheryl Anne Brown, and Michael S. Moore, *Joshua, Judges, Ruth* (NIBC; Peabody, MA: Hendrickson Publishers, 2000), p. 221.

covenant, he is well within his rights to abandon Israel (cf. Deut. and Judges 2-3);[26] yet he cannot bear to see Israel suffer.

The Role of Chapter Ten within the Book Judges

After ch. 10, the whole texture of the narrative changes. The land never again has rest. Never again is deliverance (נצל) or salvation (ישע) attributed to God. For the most part, in the remainder of the book, God is silent, speaking only in two episodes. Furthermore, God's relative silence is accompanied by his relative inactivity. For the reasons stated above, the dialogue between God and Israel in 10.6-16 is the major turning point in the book, and its parallels to ch. 3 demonstrate that it serves as a 'theological introduction' to chs. 11-21.[27]

The Lord's shocking reply is just the beginning of several divergences from the standard judge cycle. The stories of the final two judges (Jephthah and Samson) depart significantly from the pattern of the first four episodes. For example, Jephthah was the only judge who was not chosen by Yahweh.[28] The reason for Yahweh's silence during the process of Jephthah's unique appointment is found in Judg. 10.6-16 – Yahweh declared his withdrawal from Israel. In the Samson cycle, it is made clear that Israel sinned again, but it is not said that God is angry; it is not recorded that the people cry out for salvation; it is not reported that God saved Israel; and it is not said that the land had rest.

It has been argued that ch. 10 is not the turning point in Judges but rather that the Abimelech episode signals the new direction in the narrative.[29] Without a doubt, Abimelech is a central character in the narrative, and his role is both vital and complex.[30] The

---

[26] Cf. Wilcock, *Message of Judges*, p. 105.
[27] Boling, *Judges*, p. 193.
[28] Block, *Judges, Ruth*, p. 337. The final judge, Samson, is different from all other judges in at least three ways. First, he is chosen from before his birth and is destined to be a judge and a nazirite all the days of his life. Second, he never raises an army to engage the enemy, the Philistines. Third, he fails to save Israel.
[29] Harris, Brown, and Moore, *Joshua, Judges, Ruth*, p. 218; Gooding, 'The Composition of the Book of Judges', pp. 70-79; Block, *Judges, Ruth*, p. 335.
[30] Since this chapter does not focus on Abimelech, his role in the overall narrative of Judges will not be detailed here. For more on Abimelech, see Thomas A. Boogaart, 'Stone for Stone: Retribution in the Story of Abimelech and

movement from Gideon (who refuses to be king) to Abimelech (who makes himself king) is a powerful introduction to the theme of monarchy, a theme that is revisited later in the book. The argument for Abimelech as the turning point in the book, however, appears to be based upon questionable assumptions. First, the argument assumes that speech of God (as found in Judges 10) is less significant than the actions of other characters.[31] Second, it assumes that the various source materials in Judges can be ranked in levels of importance based upon their relative age.[32] According to this view, Judges 10, being a Deuteronomic source, occupies the third and latest strata, and is, therefore, virtually disposable. Third, the argument for Abimelech's priority is partially based upon historical criticism's penchant for pursuing the perceived political agenda of the documents. That is, since the Abimelech story relates to the monarchical theme (a political agenda), it must carry more weight than ch. 10, which pursues a religious agenda.[33] Fourth, the argument for Abimelech as the turning point underestimates the narrative value of the minor judges who are chronicled in 10.1-5. The accounts of Tola and Jair function in the narrative as a temporal buffer between the story of Abimelech in ch. 9 and the speech of God that begins in 10.6. More than an entire generation (45 years) passes from the time of Abimelech's illegitimate rule to the time when God refuses to save Israel.

Shechem', *JSOT* 32 (1985), pp. 45-56; J.P. Fokkelman, 'Structural Remarks on Judges 9 and 19', in M. Fishbane, E. Tov, and W. Fields (eds.), *Sha'arei Talmon* (Winona Lake, IN: Eisenbrauns, 1992), pp. 33-45; and J. Gerald Janzen, 'A Certain Woman in the Rhetoric of Judges 9', *JSOT* 38 (1987), pp. 33-37. Most other articles on Abimelech are historical critical studies.

[31] Cheryl Brown offers the following point: 'The length and detail of this divine speech is significant; for in Hb. narrative convention, important points are often communicated in the form of direct speech, and how much more in the form of divine speech;' in Harris, Brown, and Moore, *Joshua, Judges, Ruth*, p. 221.

[32] Cf. for example: 'The story of Abimelech is one of the oldest in the book of Judges, and in various ways one of the most instructive,' Moore, *Judges*, p. 238.

[33] Historical critics tend to read the biblical documents as political propaganda packaged in the guise of religion, while I would view them the opposite way – they are religious documents with political implications. It should be noted that the theme of kingship is not accepted unanimously as the major theme of Abimelech's story. See Barry G. Webb, 'The Theme of the Jephthah Story (Judges 10.6-12.7)', *RTR* 45 (1986), pp. 34-43., who argues that retribution is the controlling theme.

The Passions of God

When the hearer of Judges reaches 10.6 and hears the words 'The Israelites again did what was evil in the sight of Yahweh', and 'the anger of Yahweh grew hot against Israel, and he sold them into the hand' of the enemy, and 'the Israelites cried out to Yahweh', s/he would expect to see the repetition of the whole judge cycle for the fifth time. The expectations of the hearer are shattered, however, by the unfolding of a unique scenario: Yahweh refuses to help Israel. 'I saved you time and again', the Lord says, 'but I will save you no more'. The hearer naturally expects the next event to be Yahweh's raising up of a savior, but no such action ensues. Instead of naming a judge/savior, the Lord responds to Israel's cries with a stinging rebuke, reminding them of all the times he has saved them in the past. Yahweh declares that this time he will not save them. His mercy has been used up. All hope is not lost, however, for in v. 16, he groans with compassion, 'he was deeply distressed by Israel's suffering'.

This episode highlights the two poles that represent God's relational passions. At one end is the anger of God, and at the other end is the compassion of God (cf. Exod. 34.6-7). The judge cycle of ch. 10 begins with the statement of God's anger: 'The anger of Yahweh was hot against Israel, and he sold them into the hand of the Philistines and into the hand of the Ammonites' (10.7). His anger is apparently justified, given the depths of idolatry into which the Israelites had fallen. By this time, the hearer of Judges would be familiar with the cycle that included Israel's idolatry and Yahweh's angry response. The theme of God's anger was introduced in ch. 2, and the cause of that anger was attributed to the actions of the Israelites who worshiped other gods and in doing so 'provoked/vexed Yahweh' (2.12). The idolatry of Israel is further described as a breach of the covenant and as disobedience.[34] The Lord said, 'This people have transgressed my covenant … and have not heard/obeyed my voice' (2.20). God had been faithful to the covenant (2.1), but Israel was unfaithful and disobedient.

Apparently, the Lord's anger intensified as the list of foreign gods grew longer and as Israel persisted in apostasy. In ch. 10, the

---

[34] Cf. Pressler, *Joshua, Judges, and Ruth*, p. 197.

Lord reminds Israel of his repeated salvation from enemy after enemy, while Israel continued to relapse into idolatry. It seems that Israel's chronic unfaithfulness and ingratitude provoked God to the point that he was forced to employ drastic measures in his dealings with his people.[35] If he did not vigorously confront Israel, the covenant would be in danger of irreparable mutilation. Since the Lord had declared earlier that he would never break his covenant (2.1), his refusal to save the Israelites must be interpreted as an emergency measure, calculated to discipline them severely. 'A personal relationship binds Him to Israel ... The divine commandments are not mere recommendations for man, but express divine concern, which, when, realized or repudiated, is of personal importance to him'.[36]

Compassion stands at the other end of the spectrum of God's passions, but ch. 10 shows little evidence of that compassion. It is only the second part of v. 16 that offers a small ray of hope, a glimmer of light, an indication that God's compassion had not failed. It declares that the Lord 'was grieved at the misery of Israel'. Apparently, Israel's suffering affected God in such a way that his compassion was aroused. Their misery caused him sorrow. This closing verse in the exchange between the Lord and Israel reveals a small opening in the door of hope that God had slammed shut.

The equivocal nature of God's response to Israel in 10.6-16 perhaps produces mixed expectations in the hearer. Will Yahweh again come to Israel's aid and deliver them as he did in the past? Or, will he resolutely refuse to respond to what may be once again a temporary and shallow rededication of a rebellious and recalcitrant people. This uncertainty regarding God's attitude is denied, however, by Avi Shiveka, who argues that v. 16 does not include any movement toward compassion on God's part. Shiveka makes this assertion by insisting that in this case the word עמל does not mean 'misery' as it has been translated; rather, but that it means 'deceit'. If עמל means 'deceit', then the latter part of the verse would read, 'and he was grieved by the deceit of Israel'. Therefore, Shiveka argues that the deceit of Israel would be their attempt to persuade God that they were repentant when in fact they were not. Their

---

[35] Cf. Moore, *Judges*, p. 278.
[36] Heschel, *The Prophets*, II, p. 24.

deceit would be their feigned repentance, their pretense, their hypocrisy.³⁷

Shiveka's concern for v. 16 is to be commended, when so many scholars have ignored the implications of God's passions. Furthermore, he appreciates the significance of ch. 10 for the interpretation of the second half of Judges. Shiveka is correct when he argues that ch. 10 presents a God who is angry with his people, frustrated by their continual backsliding, and disappointed in all their previous claims to repentance. He is also correct in his proposal that God's reticence to comfort and aid Israel will have repercussions in the Jephthah story. He is not correct, however, in his translation of עמל as 'deceit'. Shiveka's argument rests upon two grounds. First, he suggests that the translation 'he was grieved by the deceit of Israel' is more consistent with the context of ch. 10. With this translation, Yahweh's persistent refusal to aid Israel continues to the very end of the passage. Second, he points to texts where עמל is paired with words that mean 'deceit', and he argues that since the words are paired together, they must be synonyms.

Shiveka's linguistic argument is unconvincing, however, because the pairing of words by no means requires that the paired words be synonyms.³⁸ The usage of עמל does not vary in the Hebrew Bible, and the lexica consistently define עמל as a noun meaning 'toil', 'trouble', 'misery', 'labor', and they never define it as 'deceit'.³⁹

Although the meaning of עמל is consistent, there are two distinct ways that it can used. It can signify either the 'toil' or 'misery' that one suffers, or it may signify the 'toil' or 'misery' that one causes others to suffer. Many nouns that express a verbal quality are capable of similar dual usage, but the basic meaning of those terms remains the same. Whenever עמל is paired with 'deceit', the causative

---

³⁷ Avi Shiveka, '"Watiqzar Nafsho Ba'amal Yisrael": A New Understanding', *Beth Mikra* 172 (2002), pp. 77-86.

³⁸ Karl Bernhardt, 'און', *TDOT*, I, p. 142.

³⁹ *BDB*, p. 765; *HALOT*, p. 845; *KB*, p. 715; David Thompson 'עמל', *NIDOTTE*, III, pp. 435-37; Siegfried Schwertner, 'עמל', *TLOT*, II, p. 924; *CHALOT*, p. 276; Avraham Even-Shoshan, *A New Concordance of the Old Testament* (Jerusalem: Kiryat Sefer, Baker/Ridgefield edn, 1983), p. 897. A few representative verses are Job 3.20, 'Why is light given to him that is in misery (עמל), and life to the bitter in soul;' Job 11.16, 'Because you shall forget your trouble (עמל), and remember it as waters that pass away;' and Prov. 31.7, 'Let him drink, and forget his poverty, and remember his misery (עמל) no more.'

force of the noun comes into play. In those cases, the words 'misery' and 'deceit' are complementary, but they are not synonymous. Both words fit into the same semantic field and designate coexistent forms of oppression.[40] For example in Job 15.35, 'They conceive misery (עמל), and give birth to trouble (און),[41] and their womb prepares deceit (מרמה)'.[42] In addition, עמל can be followed by a functional genitive; and, as is the case with other verbal nouns, that genitive may be an objective genitive or it may be a subjective genitive. That is, the phrase 'the misery of Israel' can denote the misery suffered by Israel or it can mean the misery that Israel causes. In Judges ch. 10, Israel is obviously the sufferer, not the cause of suffering.[43]

In addition to the texts and the lexica, the translations are consistent in rendering עמל as 'misery', 'suffering', 'trouble'. Among the ancient versions, the Septuagint translates עמל with κόπος, ('a striking, beating ... toil, trouble').[44] Targum Jonathan uses עמל and expands the verse by adding צער (pain, sorrow); the Vulgate uses 'miseria' (misery). The following translations use some form of the word 'misery': Geneva Bible, Authorized King James Version, New King James Version, New International Version, New American Standard Version, New American Bible, Revised Standard Version, New Living Translation, the Jewish Publication Society TANAKH. The New Revised Standard Version reads 'suffer'; the New Jerusalem Bible says 'suffering', and the New English Bible employs 'plight'. The following non-English versions all utilize terms that are synonymous with 'misery' and 'suffering': Luther Bibel, *geplagt*; Elberfelder Bibel, *Elend*; Reina-Valera, *aflicción*; Bible in Français Courant, *accablement*; La Sacra Bibbia Nuova Riveduta, *afflizione*; Leidse Vertaling, *lijden*; Netherlands Bible Society Version, *ellende*; and the Ou Vertaling in Afrikaans, *moeite*. Thus, it seems clear that Bible translators have consistently understood עמל as a form of suffering.

---

[40] Schwertner, 'עמל', pp. 924, 926; Thompson, 'עמל', p. 436; R.B. Allen, 'עמל', *TWOT*, II, p. 675.

[41] Knierim, R., 'און', *TLOT*, I, p. 60; *DCH*, I, p. 141.

[42] Another example is Ps. 10.7, 'His mouth is full of cursing (אלה), deceit (מרמה), and fraud (תך); under his tongue is misery (עמל) and trouble (און)'.

[43] Cf. Webb, *Judges: An Integrated Reading*, pp. 46-48.

[44] *LSJ*, p. 978.

Shiveka's other argument, which is based upon contextual considerations, on the surface seems reasonable; it makes sense that God's frustration with Israel might continue until the end of the passage. The weight of linguistic evidence against Shiveka, however, requires another view of the context. Is it possible that wider contextual factors may contribute to the meaning of the text? Since ch. 10 functions as an introduction to the second half of Judges, it may be instructive to explore possible parallels in the introduction to the first half of the book. The pattern for the judge cycle in 2.11-19 does, in fact, show evidence of such a parallel.[45] God's anger is revealed in 2.14, and his compassion is expressed in 2.18. God becomes angry because of Israel's idolatry and he saves them because he is moved with compassion. The Lord 'saved them from the hand of their enemies ... because the Lord was sorry (נחם) on account of those who tyrannized and oppressed them' (2.18b). The verb נחם is used frequently in the Hebrew Bible to signify God's change of mind or actions. It can be translated 'repent', 'regret', or 'be sorry'.[46] Regardless of the precise meaning that is assigned to נחם, one thing is clear; God's sympathy for the suffering of Israel was a major factor in his decision to save them. The same sympathy is expressed in the words of 10.16, 'his soul was grieved by the misery of Israel'.

The Vulnerability of God

Chapter 10 of Judges brings into focus the apparent conflict between Yahweh's anger and his compassion, a conflict that derives from the covenant relationship between God and his people. The angel of the Lord had said in ch. 2:

> I brought you up from Egypt, and I brought you to the land that I had sworn to your ancestors. And I said, 'I will not break my covenant with you forever. And you, do not make a covenant with the inhabitants of this land; tear down their altars.' But you have not heard/obeyed my voice (2.1-2).

---

[45] Pressler, *Joshua, Judges, and Ruth*, p. 198.
[46] *HALOT*, p. 688; *KB*, p. 608; H.J. Stoebe, 'נחם', *TLOT*, II, p. 738; *DCH*, V, p. 663.

In light of the Lord's initial rebuke of Israel, one could suggest that the underlying theo-logic of Judges is based upon the covenant relationship between God and Israel.[47] God has chosen to enter into a genuine relationship with his people, and that relationship causes God himself to be vulnerable to abuse, neglect, and personal injury. As soon as the Lord chose to enter into the covenant, he submitted himself to a position of personal risk.[48] The covenant relationship 'reveals a divine vulnerability, as God takes on all the risks that authentic relatedness entails. Because of what happens to that relationship with those whom God loves, God suffers.'[49]

Yahweh's negative response to Israel's cries in ch. 10 marks a clear departure from the expected cycle and begs for an explanation. Apparently, God's change of response shows that he is not mechanical in his response to sin and/or repentance; rather, his response is truly relational.[50] In ch. 10, the cry of the Israelites is more sincere than ever; they repent, confessing twice, 'we have sinned'. They demonstrate their authentic repentance by casting aside their idols and serving Yahweh. Yet in spite of their apparent change of heart and action, the Lord refuses to come to their aid.

The interaction between Yahweh and Israel in Judges 10 suggests that by entering into a covenant relationship with Israel, the God of Judges has put himself at risk or made himself vulnerable in at least three ways. First, the God of Judges is vulnerable to repeated rejection – God is faithful, but Israel is not faithful. God has kept his covenant obligations, but Israel has broken the covenant over and over. God has repeatedly rescued Israel, but their gratitude has been short-lived. Israel's relationship to God is one of freedom, based upon intergenerational covenant renewal. That freedom may be illustrated in the challenge of Joshua, who said to Israel, 'Choose today whom you will serve' (Josh. 24.15). In the Book of Judges, the Israelites chose over and over again to serve the gods of the Canaanites; and when they served the gods of the Canaanites, they

---

[47] Cf. Harris, Brown, and Moore, *Joshua, Judges, Ruth*, p. 132.
[48] Jürgen Moltmann, *The Crucified God: The Cross of Christ as the Foundation and Criticism of Christian Theology* (Minneapolis: Fortress Press, 1993), pp. 271-75.
[49] Fretheim, *Suffering of God*, p. 78; see also pp. 36-37 and 76-77; and Boling, *Judges*, p. 193.
[50] For a theological argument for the relationality of God, cf. Pinnock, 'Divine Relationality', pp. 3-26.

were forced to serve the Canaanites as well. Freedom does have its limits.

Second, the God of Judges is vulnerable to attempted manipulation. The Israelites' recurring cycle of rebellion and their repentance in ch. 10 may epitomize their attempts to use God, to abuse their relationship with God. Over and over they had committed what was evil in the sight of God, but God had forgiven them each time. It is only natural that they would anticipate forgiveness once again, if they repented. Their repeated rebellion may indicate to the hearer that the Israelites were attempting to manipulate God to their own ends, presuming upon his mercy, and taking advantage of his compassion.[51] Further, the hearer may sense that their efforts to manipulate and exploit God were successful for a time. But in ch. 10 it becomes clear that the Lord is refusing to allow that manipulation to continue.

Third, the God of Judges is vulnerable to internal conflict. In ch. 10 of Judges, God is angry; he is so angry that he refuses to save his covenant people from oppression. An angry God is a terrible presence, but even more terrible would be an absent God, a detached God, an apathetic God, an indifferent God. As Moltmann stated, 'The opposite of love is not wrath, but indifference. Indifference towards justice and injustice would be a retreat on the part of God from the covenant. But his wrath is an expression of his abiding interest.'[52] Yes, God is angry; he is so angry that he speaks with broken grammar (10.11). He is so angry that he becomes sarcastic: 'Go and cry out to the gods that you have chosen. They will save you' (10.14).[53] He is angry with Israel; nevertheless, 'his soul is grieved by the misery of Israel' (Judg. 1.16). On the one hand, he is so angry that when Israel repents for the second time, he remains silent. On the other hand, he is moved with intense compassion; he is grieved by their suffering; he suffers with them. The words of v. 16 indicate a draining, depleting, diminishing, exhausting compassion.[54] According to Nosson Scherman, 'The verse likens God to a

---

[51] Cf. Block, *Judges, Ruth*, p. 347.

[52] Moltmann, *The Crucified God*, p. 272.

[53] God's words here express an 'angry tone'; Webb, *Judges: An Integrated Reading*, p. 45.

[54] Similar words are used to describe Samson's exhaustion from Delilah's constant inquiries.

sensitive human being, who cannot bear to see the suffering of a beloved friend. Even though the friend has wronged him and does not deserve mercy, the person feels compelled to try and relieve the friend's agony'.[55] Abraham Heschel asks, 'What hidden bond exists between the word of wrath and the word of compassion, between "consuming fire" and "everlasting love"?'[56] The Lord appears to be torn in two directions.[57] According to Fiddes, this inner conflict is 'the torment of God's desire for his people, a longing which is suffused by a sense of failure and disappointment. "Struggle" within God' is an expression of his pain.[58] He will not be manipulated and exploited, but he cannot bear to remain idle while his people suffer. It is a tension that remains unresolved in Judges.

Conclusion

God is often portrayed by theologians as impassable, unemotional. Biblical statements of his emotions have been identified as anthropopathisms, figures of speech that do not represent the true nature of God.[59] In the same way that anthropomorphisms represent God's character and actions in a symbolic way (e.g. his eyes represent his omniscience), anthropopathisms represent his will and his decrees. Thus, the impassable God does not really become angry because anger is a mere human emotion. The anger of God is no more than an ancient metaphor for God's impassionate sense of justice.[60] The God of Judges, however, is presented in the narrative as a passionate character.

Although the character of God in Judges is only one of many sources for theological inquiry, I would suggest that the voice of

---

[55] Nosson Scherman, *The Prophets: Joshua/Judges. The Early Prophets with a Commentary Anthologized from the Rabbinic Writings* (Artscroll; Brooklyn, NY: Mesorah Publications, 1st Rubin edn, 2000), p. 182.
[56] Heschel, *The Prophets*, II, p. 23.
[57] Pressler, *Joshua, Judges, and Ruth*, p. 198.
[58] Paul S. Fiddes, *The Creative Suffering of God* (New York: Clarendon Press, 1988), pp. 23-24.
[59] Fretheim, *Suffering of God*, p. 6.
[60] A detailed introduction to the doctrine of impassibility may be found in Fiddes, *The Creative Suffering of God*. From a biblical perspective, cf. Fretheim, *Suffering of God*; and Heschel, *The Prophets*, II, pp. 27-47, 79-86. For a theological reflection on God's suffering in the cross, cf. Moltmann, *The Crucified God*.

this text should not be silenced. The question of God's passibility/impassibility has serious implications for theology, anthropology, Christology, soteriology, ecclesiology, and pastoral theology. If God is impassible, then he did not suffer in Christ; and the incarnation is partially emptied of its significance. According to Moltmann, 'To speak here of a God who could not suffer would make God a demon. To speak here of an absolute God would make God an annihilating nothingness.'[61] If God is impassible then human affections must be a result of the fall, and salvation must include deliverance from the affections. Humanity, however, was created in the image of God; and, like God, humanity has the capacity for relating, loving, hating, hurting, grieving, hoping, and caring. These capacities are not the result of the fall, for when the human was first created, it was God's own judgment that 'it is not good for the human to be alone' (Gen. 2.18). As a perfect human, created in God's image, the human needed companionship, relationship; therefore, God created a companion.[62]

If God himself is impassionate and incapable of genuine relationships, then where is our model for the church, for community? Where is our model for intimacy? Why should the church concern itself with relationships, family, and care? Community and intimacy are difficult enough as it is, but with an impassible God they become impossible. 'An apathetic God makes apathetic believers.'[63] Steven J. Land has pointed forward theologically by insisting on the value of orthodoxy, orthopraxy, and orthopathy. His important work shows that orthodoxy is dead without right relationship (Jas 2.19, 'even the demons believe'); orthopraxy is empty without right motives (cf. 1 Corinthians 13); and orthopathy is attained not through renouncing pathos (*à la* Augustine),[64] but through embracing the pathos of God. Moltmann writes,

> God in Auschwitz and Auschwitz in the crucified God – that is the basis for a real hope which both embraces and overcomes

---

[61] Moltmann, *The Crucified God*, p. 274; Cf. also Fiddes, *The Creative Suffering of God*, p. 145.
[62] The term 'human' is used here because gender was irrelevant before Eve's creation.
[63] Fiddes, *The Creative Suffering of God*, p. 48.
[64] Fiddes, *The Creative Suffering of God*, p. 17; and Heschel, *The Prophets*, p. 83.

the world, and the ground for a love which is stronger than death and can sustain death. It is the ground for living with the terror of history and the end of history, and nevertheless remaining in love and meeting what comes in openness for God's future. It is the ground for living and bearing guilt and sorrow for the future of man in God.[65]

The possibility of embracing God's pathos is explored by Samuel Solivan, who declares that the incarnation, death, and resurrection of Jesus 'serves as a tangible paradigm of correspondence between God's orthopathos and the possibility of our own'.[66] The doctrine of passibility/impassibility has serious consequences for pastoral theology. What kind of God should be preached and imitated, the impassionate God or the compassionate God who grieves over the suffering of Israel?[67]

It is true that the affections of God are not equivalent to the affections of humans.[68] Human affections, although not sinful, are influenced by sin. Unlike humans, God's emotions and actions are always appropriate to the situation. Unlike humans, God does not internalize his anger. God is healthy and whole while humans are often unhealthy and dysfunctional.[69] Furthermore, it is true that a tension exists between the immutability of God and the passibility of God; but surely it is a tension that can be accommodated within a theological tradition that affirms the tension-filled mysteries of the trinity, and the incarnation. Reason and logic cannot always decide questions of biblical interpretation. Moreover, 'What truly is logic? Who decides reason?'[70]

Finally, the doctrine of passibility/impassibility has serious consequences for pastoral theology. What kind of God should be preached and imitated, the dispassionate God or the God who grieves over the suffering of Israel?[71] The God of Judges is not a

---

[65] Moltmann, *The Crucified God*, p. 278.
[66] Samuel Solivan, *The Spirit, Pathos and Liberation: Toward an Hispanic Pentecostal Theology* (JPTSup 14; Sheffield: Sheffield Academic Press, 1998), p. 38.
[67] Cf. Fretheim, *Suffering of God*, p. 24.
[68] Cf. Fretheim, *Suffering of God*, p. 8; Heschel, *The Prophets*, II, p. 55.
[69] Cf. Moltmann, *The Crucified God*, p. 271.
[70] From John Nash's Nobel Prize acceptance speech in Ron Howard, *A Beautiful Mind*, Universal Studios, 2002.
[71] Cf. Fretheim, *Suffering of God*, p. 24.

cold and calculating God. He is not a distant and detached God. He is not a God whose essence is pure reason and unaffected logic. He is not the *movens immobile*. He is the God who is 'an ever present help' (Ps. 46.1). He is the God who is 'full of compassion' (Ps. 78.38). He is the God who is touched 'with the feelings of our infirmities' (Heb. 4.15). He is the God who knows every hair on our head and who sees every sparrow that falls (Luke 12). He is the God who invites us to cast all of our 'care upon him' (1 Pet. 5.7). He is the God who 'grieved in his heart' over the sins of Noah's generation (Gen. 6.6). He is the God who came down to Egypt to save the Israelites because he 'heard their cries' and he knew (ידע) 'their sorrows' (Exod. 3.7). He is the God who was afflicted when Israel was afflicted (Isa. 63.9). He is the God who roared through Amos and wept through Jeremiah. He is the God who 'was moved with compassion' toward the multitude (Mt. 9.36). He is the God who suffers with those who suffer (Heb. 2.18), the God who weeps with those who weep (Jn 11.35), the God who shares the feelings of alienation with those who are alienated, the God who endures hatred with those who are hated (Jn 15.18-19), the God who suffers persecution with those who are persecuted (Acts 9.4, Rev. 12.5-6), the God who is abused along with those who suffer abuse (Zech. 2.12), the God who feels the needs of the orphan and the widow, the God who experiences oppression with those who are oppressed (Mt. 25.45). He is rejected; he is cursed; he is blamed; he is questioned; he is misunderstood; and his heart is broken by it all. God in Christ suffered (Lk. 24.26); he suffered unto death (Philippians 2). God has suffered and he has the scars to prove it (Jn 20.27).

Some would have an unscarred God, a God who does not suffer. They want the God of philosophy, the God of ethics, the broad-minded God, the reasonable God, the tolerant God, the God who never struggles – not a God with scars. But the scars are there, reach out and touch them. Put your hand in his side. This God with scars is able to sympathize with us. In the dark hour of our hopelessness, when the earth is soaked in blood, when billions of people are broken, alone, helpless, persecuted, forgotten, hated, and oppressed, we cannot be saved by a soft, safe, secluded God. We need the God with scars. The impassible God cannot give courage to the persecuted. He cannot speak to those who hurt. The impassible God has no answer for the wounded, the sick, the dying, the unpitied, the lonely, the poverty stricken, who ask the questions: 'Does God know what it is to suffer? Did he ever go without bread? Was he ever betrayed? Was he ever abandoned? Was his body ever racked with pain?' The impassible God has no answer, but the God of Judges, the God of the Bible, the God of the Cross has suffered pain; he has been betrayed, abandoned, and forsaken. He says to us, 'Do not fear suffering (Rev. 2.10), because I suffer with you.' There is pain in the heart of God; there are tears in his eyes. Yet in the end, he will gather his people unto himself, and he will dwell with them; they will be his people, and he will be their God. At that time he will weep no more, and neither will they, for he will 'wipe every tear from their eyes' (Rev. 21.3-4).

3

TONGUES OF ANGELS, WORDS OF PROPHETS: DIVINE COMMUNICATION IN THE BOOK OF JUDGES

Introduction

The mention of the book of Judges calls forth images of battle between Israel and the Canaanites, tales of murder and intrigue, and stories of extraordinary characters. The topic of divine speech, however, rarely surfaces in discussions of Judges. Although the voice of God is a topic that should resonate with Pentecostals, whose distinctive theology includes the charismatic revelatory gifts, when approaching Judges, they give most of their attention to the Spirit passages. Pentecostals take note of the empowering activity of the Spirit of Yahweh,[1] and they observe the questionable moral character of the judges upon whom the Spirit descends.[2] Like

---

[1] Pentecostal-Charismatic studies of the Spirit of Yahweh in Judges include: Stanley M. Horton, *What the Bible Says About the Holy Spirit* (Springfield, MO: Gospel Pub. House, 1976), pp. 33-42; George T. Montague, *The Holy Spirit: Growth of a Biblical Tradition* (An Exploration Book; New York: Paulist Press, 1976), pp. 17-18; John Rea, *The Holy Spirit in the Bible: All the Major Passages About the Spirit: A Commentary* (Lake Mary, FL: Creation House, 1990), pp. 48-55; Wilf Hildebrandt, *An Old Testament Theology of the Spirit of God* (Peabody, MA: Hendrickson Publishers, 1995), pp. 112-18.

[2] E.g. Horton, *Holy Spirit*, p. 35, reveals an awareness of the tension between purity and power when he acknowledges that sometimes God worked 'in spite of' the judges. See also Chapters 5 and 7 of this work.

everyone else, however, Pentecostals hardly reflect on the voice of God in Judges.

Notwithstanding its apparent obscurity, the speech of God figures prominently in nine episodes of Judges, episodes that are crucial to the development of the narrative.³ In these episodes, God speaks in response to the priestly inquiry; he speaks through the angel of Yahweh; he speaks through prophets; he speaks through a dream; and he speaks directly, with the means of communication unstated.⁴ It is the purpose of this chapter to survey the divine communication in Judges by briefly examining each of the nine episodes in which God's speech is reported. I will conclude with a summary of the significance and implications of those divine interventions.

The Voice of God

'Judah shall go up' (Judges 1.2)

Divine communication is a significant element in the opening episode of the book of Judges, for as soon as the narrative gets underway, God is invited to speak. After the death of Joshua, the Israelites seek Yahweh's direction for leadership by means of the first recorded priestly inquiry. They ask, 'Who shall go up first for us against the Canaanites, to fight against them?' (Judg. 1.1). In the books of Exodus through Deuteronomy, there is no need for such an inquiry, because Yahweh speaks face to face with Moses. After the death of Moses, Yahweh again takes the initiative to speak to Joshua quite directly.⁵ After Joshua's death, however, the Israelites begin to inquire of Yahweh by means of the High Priest.⁶

In response to Israel's inquiry, Yahweh names Judah as the tribe of leadership,⁷ saying, 'Judah shall go up. I hereby give the land into

---

³ See Martin, *The Unheard Voice of God*.
⁴ According to my count, the Hebrew roots אמר (to say) and דבר (to speak) are used 49 times in Judges with God (or one of his agents) as the subject. Also, in reference to the speech of God, the root צוה (to command) is used 4 times and the word קול (voice) is used 3 times. Taken together, we find in Judges 56 references to the speech of God.
⁵ It is recorded 14 times that Yahweh spoke to Joshua (Josh. 1.1; 3.7; 4.1, 8, 15; 5.2, 9; 6.2; 7.10; 8.1, 18; 10.8; 11.6; 20.1)
⁶ Scherman, *The Prophets: Joshua/Judges*, p. 118.
⁷ Although Judges 1 does not mention the tabernacle or the priests, the verb שאל (to ask) followed by the preposition ב (in, with, by), signifies the cultic ritual

his hand' (Judg. 1.2), thus introducing a new structure of leadership for Israel. For the first time in the canonical story, the narrative lacks a central character. After the death of Joshua, Yahweh does not choose a single person as national leader. When the Israelites ask Yahweh, 'Who shall go up for us first?', Yahweh names the tribe of Judah as preeminent. The absence of a replacement for Joshua might suggest a 'sense of uncertainty'[8] about Israel's future paradigm of leadership, but the personal guidance of Yahweh appears to be continuing.[9]

This first episode of Judges supplies important narrative indicators, including the temporal setting and the main characters of the story. According to these first two verses: (1) the story of Judges occurs just after the death of Joshua; (2) the main characters are the Israelites and Yahweh; and (3) the story involves the Israelites' continuing struggle to gain control of the land from the Canaanites. Furthermore, the opening verses of Judges suggest that the Israelites were operating purposefully in a unified fashion and were acting faithfully toward God. It is clear, however, that the conquest of the land is not complete, a fact that foreshadows the conflict that escalates throughout the book.

'You have not heard my voice' (Judges 2.2)

After Yahweh names Judah as the tribe of leadership (Judg. 1.2), the succeeding verses are devoted to Judah's battles, in which he defeats numerous enemies and claims new cities. Verse 19 records Judah's first defeat, which is followed by a long register of failures that lists the tribes and their lack of success.

Yahweh responds to the failure of the Israelites by sending the angel of Yahweh, who brings a passionate message of rebuke from Yahweh (2.1-5). He begins with a reference to the exodus tradition,

---

of 'inquiring, consulting'; *BDB*, p. 982. Inquiring of Yahweh would involve the priest and would occur in the communal setting of the tabernacle. Soggin admits as much, but still wants to see an explicit reference to the tabernacle. Cf. Soggin, *Judges*, p. 20. This may have been the first use of the *Urim* and the *Thummim* (Exod. 28.30; Num. 27.21); cf. Scherman, *Joshua/Judges*, p. 118.

[8] Pressler, *Joshua, Judges, and Ruth*, p. 130.
[9] The lack of a national leader does not imply an absence of leadership on the tribal level. The hearer of Judges would be aware of earlier texts (such as Josh. 23.2) that indicate the existence of leadership categories that include 'elders' (זקנים), 'heads' (ראשים), 'judges' (שפטים), and 'officers' (שטרים).

declaring, 'I brought you up from Egypt and I brought you into the land that I swore to your ancestors' (2.1). The reference to the exodus characterizes Yahweh as their savior and suggests that their future prospects in Canaan are based not upon their commitment to Yahweh but on his commitment to them. The mention of the ancestors affirms God's continuing faithfulness in his relationship with the people of Israel. This is not a new God who speaks; he is the God of Abraham, the God of Isaac, and the God of Jacob.

Yahweh continues his speech with a reaffirmation of his faithfulness: 'I will not break my covenant with you forever' (2.1). Yahweh insists that he is a God who can be trusted, a God of covenant faithfulness – forever. The hearer of Judges 2 would understand that Yahweh is the Israelites' great king who has freely chosen to know them as his unique liberated covenant people and who has unconditionally pledged himself to be faithful to them even in the face of their disobedience to the stipulations to which they had agreed.

After insisting upon his own fidelity, Yahweh addresses the Israelites with this accusation: '[I said] you shall make no covenant with the inhabitants of this land; you shall throw down their altars: but ye have not heard (שמע) my voice. What is this you have done?' (2.2). Yahweh's indictment of the Israelites suggests the following implications: (1) Unlike the gods of Canaan, Yahweh is the God who speaks. (2) Yahweh's reference to the hearing of his 'voice' rather than to the keeping of his 'commands' suggests a personal relationship, a relational context. (3) The Israelites' failure to hear the voice of Yahweh is their fundamental and underlying error. Israel had vowed eagerly to listen to Yahweh (Josh. 24.24), but now their vows are broken. The crucial point of Judg. 2.1-5 is that while Yahweh has been faithful to his covenant with the Israelites, they have been unfaithful.[10] (4) Yahweh's question to Israel, 'What is this you have done?', is an expression of personal injury and emotional vulnerability to human offense. This question, coupled with the terse and laconic style of delivery, indicates that Judg. 2.1-5 is a passionate speech from a God who is invested in his covenant people.

---

[10] Israel's unfaithfulness reaches its consummation at the end of Judges, where it is said, 'they all did what was right in their own eyes' (17.6; 21.25).

Although Yahweh promises that he will never break his covenant, a covenant that includes his giving of the land, he concludes his speech by declaring that he will discipline Israel by allowing the Canaanites to remain as thorns and snares. Yahweh, however, will not entirely abandon Israel. Yahweh's response to the infidelity of the Israelites is not legalistic and not mechanistic; moreover, his response is not altogether predictable; for although the Israelites show signs of repentance by weeping and offering sacrifices, he does not relent in his decision to allow the Canaanites to remain.

Yahweh's speech serves as a dramatic conclusion to the first half of the prologue (Judg. 1.1-2.5). In terms of dramatic structure, Judg. 1.1-31 can be understood as the introduction to the drama ('*Einleitung*') and Yahweh's speech (Judg. 2.1-5) is the causal moment ('*das erregende Moment*'), which signals the beginning of rising action in the drama.[11] In fact, it is Yahweh's professed commitment not to break the covenant forever that, together with Israel's recurring violations of the covenant, accounts for the dialectical forces that generate the long-acknowledged cyclical motion of the rest of the book. Thus, Yahweh's speech sets the agenda for the narrative that follows.

'They transgressed my covenant' (Judges 2.20)
A second introduction (Judg. 2.6-3.6) retells the death of Joshua and then describes the subsequent apostasy of the Israelites. Like the first introduction, the second introduction concludes with a divine speech. Yahweh's speech (Judg. 2.20-22) restates elements of his earlier speech; but, rather than speaking directly to the Israelites as in Judg. 2.1-5, Yahweh speaks about Israel in the third person. The two speeches may refer to the same event, with the second speech coming in the form of a report that is directed to the hearers of Judges.

In this second rebuke Yahweh comes right to the point by stating the cause of his dissatisfaction with the Israelites. He says, 'Because

---

[11] Gustav Freytag, *Die Technik des Dramas* (Leipzig: S. Hirzel, 1897), p. 107. *Das erregende Moment* is given the name 'initiating action' by Lewis Turco, *The Book of Literary Terms: The Genres of Fiction, Drama, Nonfiction, Literary Criticism, and Scholarship* (Hanover, NH: University Press of New England, 1999), p. 41; and 'inciting moment' by Robert E. Longacre, *An Anatomy of Speech Notions* (Lisse: Peter de Ridder Press, 1976), pp. 199-217.

this nation has transgressed my covenant that I commanded their ancestors, and they have not heard my voice …' (2.20). Earlier in the chapter, the narrator describes the sin of Israel as idolatry, that is, the forsaking of Yahweh and the worshiping of the Baals (Judg. 2.11-13). In his speech, however, Yahweh characterizes the sin of the Israelites in terms of his covenant relationship with them. The hearer of Yahweh's speech may be reminded of Yahweh's earlier word to Moses:

> Behold, you will sleep with your ancestors; and this people will rise up and play the harlot after the gods of the foreigners of the land, where they go to be among them, and they will forsake me, and violate my covenant that I have made with them (Deut. 31.16).

The reference to the Israelites as 'this people' in Deut. 31.16, parallels 'this nation' in Judg. 2.20, and the charges that the Israelites will 'play the harlot' (זנה) after foreign gods and will 'forsake' (עזב) Yahweh find their counterparts in Judg. 2.17 and 13 respectively. Furthermore, the breaking of the 'covenant' is the focus of both Deut. 31.16 and Judg. 2.20.

God's covenant with the Israelites demands their absolute allegiance, and their disloyalty offends God, moving him to act in judgment. In response to Israel's unfaithfulness, Yahweh declares, 'I also will no longer drive out before them any of the nations that Joshua left before he died' (2.21). In spite of the apparent severity of his judgment, Yahweh names a salvific or disciplinary purpose for allowing the Canaanites to remain in the land. The Canaanites will be allowed to remain in the land in order to provide the new generation with the opportunity to prove themselves faithful in the face of severe temptation (2.22) and in the conduct of war (3.1-6).

The dual introduction to Judges (1.1-2.5 and 2.6-3.6) prepares the hearer for the stories that follow and offers, through the construction of a theological paradigm for the period, a rationale for the cycle of judges. The Israelites fail to vanquish the Canaanites completely and subsequently engage in idolatrous syncretism. According to the introduction, therefore, the Israelites' root problem is their refusal to hear and obey God's word: 'You have not heard (שמע) my voice' (2.2). The charge is repeated three more times in

Judges: 'They would not hear the judges' (2.17a); 'They have not heard my voice' (2.20); 'You have not heard my voice' (6.10).

'Go … I have given Sisera into your hand' (Judges 4.6-7)

The first and paradigmatic[12] judge is Othniel, who is hailed earlier as a heroic warrior (Judg. 1.13), and the second judge is left-handed Ehud (3.12-30), who defeats King Eglon of Moab.[13] Then, after the brief mention of Shamgar, who saves the Israelites from the Philistines (3.31), Deborah is introduced as a prophet who is 'judging Israel' (4.4-5) in Ephraim. As a judge, the people come to her for justice, and as a prophet, she speaks for Yahweh.[14] The strength of her personality may be reflected in her description as a 'woman of torches' or 'woman of lightning bolts' (4.4), which could suggest a fiery or assertive disposition.[15]

It is not insignificant that a woman fills these roles that are traditionally assigned to men. I find it ironic that after the words of Deut. 18.15, 'The Lord will raise up for you a prophet like me from among your brothers', the first person who is called a prophet is not a 'brother' but a 'sister'.[16] Mieke Bal, in reflecting on the role of Deborah, observes that 'the only judge who combines all forms of leadership possible – religious, military, juridical, and poetical – is a

---

[12] Cf. Block, *Judges, Ruth*, p. 149; and Lawson Grant Stone, 'From Tribal Confederation to Monarchic State: The Editorial Perspective of the Book of Judges' (PhD Diss., Yale University, 1988), pp. 260-89, where Stone provides an extended discussion of Othniel's paradigmatic role in Judges.

[13] Ehud, as he approaches King Eglon, declares that he brings to the king דבר־אלהים ('a secret message' or 'the word of God'). Ehud's statement suggests a claim of divine endorsement and guidance. Perhaps we could infer that God had spoken to him and provided the strategy for his victory.

[14] I use the term 'prophet' rather than 'prophetess' because the gendered terminology is a manifestation of Hebrew grammatical categories and is not an expression of different roles. In the contemporary Church we would not refer to a woman priest as 'priestess', and neither should we refer to a woman prophet as a 'prophetess'.

[15] The Hebrew phrase אשת לפידות is normally translated as 'wife of Lappidoth', but the noun לפיד ('torch' or 'lightning bolt'), which occurs 13 times in the Hebrew Bible (4 times in Judges: 7.16, 20; 15.4, 5) is always masculine '*lappidim*', not '*lappidoth*'. I would argue that the change to feminine form is due to its use as a modifier of the word 'woman' (אשת). Is there any narrative significance to the fact that Deborah is called 'Woman of Torches'; and, later, both Gideon and Samson used torches?

[16] Her prophetic role is ignored by John Gray, *Joshua, Judges, and Ruth* (NCBC; Greenwood, SC: Attic Press, rev. edn, 1977), who names the prophet of Judg. 6.7 as the 'first emergence of the prophet in Israel' (p. 171).

woman and calls herself and/or is addressed as "a mother in Israel"'.[17] Bal and other interpreters such as Elie Assis are correct to point out the uniqueness of Deborah's judgeship, but in so doing they fail to recognize that each of the judges is unique.[18]

Deborah is clearly a judge (4.4-5) who rises up to bring deliverance (5.7-8), and who embodies the programmatic statement in the prologue, which says that Yahweh 'raised up judges, who saved them out of the hand of those who plundered them' (2.16). As a judge, Deborah stands within the tradition of Moses and the leadership structure attributed to Moses (Exod. 18.13-26). The biblical narrative prior to the book of Judges establishes a system of tribal leadership that includes judges, but the exact structure of leadership is not fully discernable. Like the texts that describe the office of prophet, these texts about judges assume that men will fill the position, but women are not explicitly forbidden from doing so.

---

[17] Mieke Bal, *Death & Dissymmetry: The Politics of Coherence in the Book of Judges* (Chicago Studies in the History of Judaism; Chicago: University of Chicago Press, 1988), pp. 209-10.

[18] Elie Assis, 'Man, Woman, and God in Judg 4', *SJOT* 20.1 (2006), pp. 110-24 (p. 111). Block, *Judges, Ruth*, pp. 193-97, has expended considerable effort to classify Deborah as different from the other judges. Cf. Daniel I. Block, 'Deborah among the Judges: The Perspective of the Hebrew Historian', in A. Millard, J. Hoffmeier, and D. Baker (eds.), *Faith, Tradition, and History* (Winona Lake, IN: Eisenbrauns, 1994), pp. 229-53; and Daniel I. Block, 'Why Deborah's Different', *BR* 17.3 (2001), pp. 34-40, 49-52. Devotion to a male leadership model is expressed as well by Herbert Wolf, 'Judges', in F.E. Gaebelein (ed.), *The Expositor's Bible Commentary* (Grand Rapids: Zondervan, 1992), III, pp. 375-508, who, incredibly and without any biblical warrant, insists that Deborah's 'prominence implies a lack of qualified and willing men' (p. 404). If God prefers male leaders, then why does he not dispense with Deborah entirely and call Barak directly, as he calls Gideon later? Or why does he not raise up a leader from birth, as he raises up Samson and Samuel? It is not from necessity that God uses Deborah but from his divine choice. It has been argued as well that the ministry of women is an exception that God allows only in times of extreme spiritual chaos. If that were true, we would expect Deborah to be one of the final judges, since the Israelites grow more unfaithful as the book progresses. I would argue that male domination is the aberration, caused by human sinfulness, and that in God's redeemed kingdom there is no domination or subjugation (cf. Gal. 3.28). For a recent Pentecostal presentation regarding the leadership role of women, see Kimberly Ervin Alexander and R. Hollis Gause, *Women in Leadership: A Pentecostal Perspective* (Cleveland, TN: Center for Pentecostal Leadership & Care, 2006). I contend that women should be welcomed at all levels of leadership, both civil and ecclesiastical.

As a prophet, Deborah speaks three prophetic words and she utters a song of praise. Her first act is to summon Barak, and by the word of the Lord she commissions him to attack King Jabin of Canaan, who had oppressed the Israelites for 20 years. Her words are not lacking in detail, as she specifies the location where Barak is to encamp, the number of soldiers that he is to recruit, the names of the tribes who will be involved, the name of the enemy general, and the exact location of the battle (4.6-7).

Speaking as the messenger of Yahweh,[19] she assures Barak of victory, declaring, 'I will give him into your hand' (4.7). There is no indication in the text that Barak questions Deborah's credentials or that he is disturbed by her gender; nevertheless, his response is less than enthusiastic. He requires that Deborah accompany him to the battle, and because of his demand that she be physically present, he is deprived of the glory.[20] Consequently, Deborah proclaims that the glory of victory will go to a woman,[21] and at this point in the narrative that woman appears to be Deborah herself.

Deborah escorts Barak to the place of battle, and when the armies have assembled she commands Barak, 'Rise up; for this is the day in which Yahweh has given Sisera into your hand; has not Yahweh gone out before you?' (4.14).[22] In addition to Deborah's first prophetic word that served as the initial command to Barak, she now delivers a second word that specifies the exact timing for Barak's attack on the enemy. Deborah's words sound much like those of Moses, who promises the Israelites, 'It is Yahweh who goes before you; he will be with you; he will not fail you' (Deut. 31.8).[23] Like before, she speaks with no hint of uncertainty, providing Barak with the assurance that he needs to initiate the battle.

---

[19] The phrase 'Has not Yahweh, the God of Israel, commanded' is used to introduce the words of Yahweh, and takes the place of the messenger formula 'Thus says Yahweh'.

[20] It might be inferred that Barak's response arises out of doubt and disobedience, but cf. the words of Moses to God in Exod. 33.15. See Assis, 'Man, Woman, and God in Judg 4', pp. 120-23, who sorts out the implications of Barak's demand that Deborah accompany him.

[21] Some scholars conclude that in the poetic version of the battle (Judges 5) Deborah is portrayed as the leader of the army. Cf. Susan Ackerman, *Warrior, Dancer, Seductress, Queen: Women in Judges and Biblical Israel* (AB Reference Library; New York: Doubleday, 1998), p. 31.

[22] Cf. the words of Yahweh to Gideon (Judg. 7.9) and David (1 Sam. 23.4).

[23] Cf. Exod. 23.23; 32.34.

Why Deborah does not lead the army is left unstated, but I would suggest that it has something to do with her role as prophet.[24] Deborah's activity seems to parallel that of Moses when the Amalekites attacked Israel in the wilderness (Exod. 17.8-13). Just as Deborah directs Barak to engage in battle, Moses directs Joshua, who serves as commander of the army in the wilderness. Similarly to Deborah, Moses issues the initial command (Exod. 17.9), and he accompanies Joshua to the battle zone, but he does not participate in the battle nor issue orders regarding the conduct of battle. Finally, Moses' recording of the battle story in a scroll (Exod. 17.14) may be compared to Deborah's recounting of her story in song.[25] Assis writes that Deborah's 'act' of deliverance is 'in the act of delivering prophecy'.[26]

The prophecies of Deborah are fulfilled when the Israelites win the battle, and the glory of killing Sisera goes to Jael, a woman who drives a tent peg through the head of the unsuspecting general. The war is followed by a victory song that glorifies Yahweh, Deborah, Barak, and Jael and makes a mockery of Sisera and his defeat.

In light of the connections between prophecy and song (Exod. 15.20, 1 Sam. 10.5; 18.10, 1 Chron. 25), we might classify Deborah's song as prophetic praise; however, the song includes no messenger formula and no direct speech from Yahweh. Nevertheless, the song includes at least one word of divine communication: 'Curse Meroz, says the angel of Yahweh, curse severely its inhabitants, because they did not come to the help of Yahweh, to the help of Yahweh

---

[24] Often it is assumed that it is Deborah's gender that prevents her participation in the battle; cf. Assis, 'Man, Woman, and God in Judg 4', p. 119. The relationship between prophecy and warfare is explored, along with its attendant scholarship by Rick Dale Moore, *God Saves: Lessons from the Elisha Stories* (JSOTSup 95; Sheffield: JSOT Press, 1990), pp. 128-47, who observes that it is 'Israel's prophet, not its conventional military resources, that represents the true strength and salvation of the nation in its confrontation with foreign military aggression' (pp. 128-29).

[25] Cf. Bruce Herzberg, 'Deborah and Moses', *JSOT* 38.1 (2013), pp. 15-33, who also observes these connections between Deborah and Moses. It should be noted that my observations were published prior to Herzberg. See Lee Roy Martin, 'Tongues of Angels, Words of Prophets: Means of Divine Communication in the Book of Judges', in S.J. Land, R.D. Moore, and J.C. Thomas (eds.), *Passover, Pentecost, and Parousia: Studies in Celebration of the Life and Ministry of R. Hollis Gause* (JPTSup,36; Blandford Forum, UK: Deo Publishers, 2010), pp. 33-53.

[26] Assis, 'Man, Woman, and God in Judg 4', p. 119.

against the mighty ones' (Judg. 5.23).[27] In Judges, the angel of Yahweh brings a word of rebuke to the Israelites (2.1-5), a word of commission to Gideon (6.11-24) and a word of annunciation to Samson's mother (13.2-23). Here, in Deborah's song, the angel appears, as if singing along with Deborah and Barak, and then he breaks in with a solo part. The angel's pronouncement is the concluding word to the section of the song that praises those who fought for Yahweh and condemns those who did not fight (5.9-23). The town of Meroz is singled out for special judgment because it lies within the vicinity of the battlefield,[28] and its inhabitants[29] would have heard and ignored Barak's call to arms.

The song of victory is longer than the prose narrative, and its placement at the end of the Deborah cycle leaves the hearer quite hopeful concerning Israel's future. The song concludes with these words: 'Thus all your enemies will perish, O Lord; but those who love you are like the rising of the sun in its strength' (5.31).[30]

'Do not fear the gods of the Amorites' (Judges 6.10)

The mood of hope and optimism created by the song of Deborah is replaced immediately by a mood of extreme desperation[31] when the Israelites rebel yet again (6.1), and Yahweh gives them into the hand of the Midianites and Amalekites,[32] who for seven years rob the Israelites of their crops and livestock, leaving the land impoverished and the people helpless. The narrative portrays Israel's suffering as more severe than in earlier cycles, a fact that builds the tension to a higher level, indicating that 'things may be getting

---

[27] The phrase 'against the mighty ones' (בגבורים) might be translated instead, 'with the mighty ones', thus signifying the army of Barak.

[28] Cf. Wolf, 'Judges', p. 414.

[29] It has been argued that in this context the Hebrew יֹשְׁבִים (inhabitants) means 'rulers'. See Norman K. Gottwald, *The Tribes of Yahweh: A Sociology of the Religion of Liberated Israel, 1250-1050 B.C.E.* (Maryknoll, NY: Orbis Books, 1979), pp. 512-34.

[30] This mention of Yahweh worshipers as 'those who love' him is a rare early acknowledgement of the emotional aspect of Israelite religion according to Eichrodt, *Theology of the Old Testament*, I, p. 251.

[31] Cf. Scherman, *Joshua/Judges*, p. 151; and Webb, *Judges: An Integrated Reading*, p. 144.

[32] Midianites and Amalekites are 'echoes from the past' according to Wilcock, *The Message of Judges*, p. 76, who points out that Moses' wife was Midianite (Exod. 2.15-22) and that early in the Israelites' wilderness journey they were attacked by the Amalekites (Exod. 17.8). See also Num. 31.1-12 and Deut. 25.17-19.

worse'.³³ The Midianites are not content to rule or to rob the Israelites; they seem to be intent upon rendering the land uninhabitable for the Israelites, thus displacing them from the land that Yahweh had given them.³⁴

As before, the Israelites cry out to Yahweh for help, but the usual cyclical pattern is interrupted when, before he raises up a deliverer, Yahweh sends to them an unnamed prophet.³⁵ This makes two consecutive cycles in which a prophet has entered the story at precisely the same point, and the hearer might anticipate that this prophet would function as a judge, in much the same fashion as Deborah functioned in the previous cycle.³⁶ This prophet, however, functions differently from Deborah in at least three ways: (1) the nameless prophet addresses the whole people of Israel, whereas Deborah addresses only Barak, an individual; (2) Deborah arises with an encouraging word of victory, but the anonymous prophet brings a stinging word of reprimand;³⁷ and (3) the prophet of ch. 6 interrupts the cyclical pattern while Deborah functions within the pattern, fulfilling the role of judge.³⁸

The verb forms in the prophet's message indicate that Yahweh is the primary character within the speech itself. The first six verbs have Yahweh as their subject: (1) 'I myself (אנכי) brought you up (העליתי) from Egypt'; (2) 'I brought you out (ואציא) from the house

---

³³ J. Clinton McCann, *Judges* (Interpretation: A Bible Commentary for Teaching and Preaching; Louisville, KY: John Knox Press, 2002), p. 63.

³⁴ Cf. David Lieberman, *The Eternal Torah: A New Commentary Utilizing Ancient and Modern Sources in a Grammatical, Historical, and Traditional Explanation of the Text* (River Vale, NJ: Twin Pines Press, 1979), II, p. 116. This is contra Bernon Lee, 'Fragmentation of Reader Focus in the Preamble to Battle in Judges 6:1-7:14', *JSOT* 25 (2002), pp. 65-86 (71-72), who limits his description of the Midianite threat as a 'series of raids'. Gaining control of the trade route may be the Midianite objective, which requires the removal of the Israelites. Cf. Gottwald, *The Tribes of Yahweh*, p. 432.

³⁵ Cf. L. Juliana M. Claassens, 'The Character of God in Judges 6-8: The Gideon Narrative as Theological and Moral Resource', *HBT* 23.1 (2001), pp. 51-71 (p. 56). Cf. Dennis Olson, 'Judges', in *The New Interpreter's Bible: Numbers-Samuel* (12 vols.; Nashville, TN: Abingdon Press, 1994), II, pp. 721-888 (p. 792).

³⁶ See Lillian R. Klein, *The Triumph of Irony in the Book of Judges* (Bible and Literature 14; Sheffield: Almond, 1988), p. 50, who suggests that the reader may expect this prophet to be even more effective than Deborah, but he is not effective at all.

³⁷ Cf. Pressler, *Joshua, Judges, and Ruth*, p. 169.

³⁸ Cf. Olson, 'Judges', pp. 795-96.

of bondage'; (3) 'I delivered you (ואצל) from the hand of Egypt'; (4) 'I dispossessed them (ואגרש) from before you'; (5) I gave to you (ואתנה) their land'; and (6) 'I said to you, "You shall not fear (תיראו) the gods of the Amorites"'. By this unbroken series of assertions, Yahweh claims to be Israel's God, Israel's savior, Israel's victor, and Israel's provider. The emphasis upon the person of Yahweh is strengthened further by the emphatic pronoun that precedes the first verb. This combination of pronoun and verb produces a phrase that occurs here for the first time in the Old Testament: 'I myself brought you up (אנכי העליתי) from Egypt'.[39] Yahweh alone is Israel's savior.

Yahweh completes his self-testimony with one more word. He declares, 'I said to you, "I am Yahweh your God; you shall not fear the gods of the Amorite"' (6.10).[40] Yahweh's exclusive claim for the loyalty of Israel stands at the core of the Torah, and when Yahweh says 'you shall not fear the gods of the Amorites' (6.10), his use of the verb 'to fear' is meant to prohibit the 'worship', 'reverence' and 'service' of other gods.[41] On several occasions Yahweh forbids the worship of other gods (Deut. 11.16), the service of other gods (Deut. 13.6) or the pursuit of other gods (Deut. 6.14), and the Decalogue begins with this word: 'I am Yahweh your God, who brought you out of the land of Egypt, out of the house of bondage. You shall have no other gods before me' (Exod. 20.2-3).[42]

When compared to Yahweh's earlier rebuke of the Israelites (2.1-5), this speech suggests that the Israelites have regressed in their covenant relationship to Yahweh although they have not

---

[39] This combination of pronoun and verb, אנכי העליתי ('I, even I brought up'), is found only in two other Old Testament texts: 1 Sam. 10.18 and Amos 2.10.

[40] The Amorites are well-known in the biblical narrative, being mentioned 60 times in Exodus through Joshua, but the phrase 'the gods of the Amorites' appears in only one other text, in which Joshua challenges the Israelites, 'choose for yourselves today whom you will serve: whether the gods which your fathers served which were beyond the River, or the gods of the Amorites in whose land you are living' (Josh. 24.15).

[41] Cf. *DCH*, IV, p. 278, who includes the definition 'revere, be in awe of'. See also, *HALOT*, I, p. 433.

[42] The use of the word 'fear' in Judg. 6.10 foreshadows the Gideon narrative. See Barnabas Lindars, 'Gideon and Kingship', *JTS* 16 (1965), p. 317, n. 1, who writes that the prophet's speech is 'incorporated by the narrator to prepare for the dialogue in the call story'.

abandoned him altogether. In the earlier speech, Yahweh scolds the Israelites for their passive failure to tear down the Canaanite altars, but now he scolds them for a more active role in illicit worship.[43] As in his earlier speech (2.1-5), Yahweh here summarizes Israel's entire rebellion in one concise judgment: 'But you did not hear my voice' (6.10). The impact of this singular verdict is made all the more striking by its rude appearance following the long series of verbs that declare Yahweh's faithful deeds. Unlike Yahweh's earlier speech (Judg. 2.1-5), this speech comes abruptly to an end with no pronouncement of penalty, no statement of consequences for the unfaithfulness of the Israelites, and no response from the Israelites. Their lack of response leaves the impression that they are continuing to disregard Yahweh's voice. They have cried out to Yahweh for his aid, but they do not hear when he answers.[44]

The placement of Yahweh's speech in the midst of the cyclical pattern, rather than outside the pattern, makes it an integral part of the Gideon cycle, and themes of the speech are continued later in the Gideon narrative. I conclude that Yahweh's speech foreshadows the Gideon narrative in at least four ways: (1) it highlights the Egypt/exodus tradition;[45] (2) it portrays the Israelites as syncretistic worshipers; (3) it introduces the theme of fear; and (4) it calls attention to the continuing theme of hearing the voice of Yahweh.

Olson argues that this speech marks a transitional point in the narrative of Judges and begins the second major section of the book.[46] In light of the Israelites' repeated idolatry and in light of their unwillingness to hear the voice of Yahweh, Olson suggests further that the prophet's speech may cause the hearer to question

---

[43] Historical, archaeological, and social research on early Israel suggests that the worship of multiple gods was the rule rather than the exception, and that the term 'syncretism' itself must be reconsidered. See Erhard Gerstenberger, *Theologies in the Old Testament* (trans. John Bowden; Minneapolis: Fortress Press, Fortress Press edn, 2002), pp. 274-81; Goldingay, *Israel's Faith*, pp. 38-40; and David Penchansky, *Twilight of the Gods: Polytheism in the Hebrew Bible* (Louisville, KY: Westminster John Knox Press, 2005), p. 33.

[44] Is it possible that, in a similar fashion, we cry out for the biblical text to speak to us, but we hear what we want to hear and turn a deaf ear to the rest?

[45] Egypt is mentioned in nine verses of Judges: 2.1, 12; 6.8, 9, 13; 10.11; 11.13, 16 and 19.30; and the exodus seems to be in the background of Judg. 5.5 and 21. Cf. the language of Ps. 77.14-20, which is similar to Judges 5.

[46] Olson, 'Judges', pp. 795-96. The third major section of Judges commences with Yahweh's speech in Judg. 10.11-16.

whether God has reached the limits of his patience.⁴⁷ Surprisingly, Yahweh once again demonstrates his mercy; and, in spite of the Israelites' obstinacy, he does not abandon them.

'Yahweh is with you, mighty warrior' (Judges 6.12)

After the prophet's stinging rebuke, the scene shifts suddenly to a man named Gideon, who is threshing his grain in the wine press so that he will not be discovered by the Midianites. He is approached by the angel of Yahweh, who commissions him as the next deliverer, and before the story comes to an end, Gideon has received 13 distinct communications from God in four different episodes.

God's first communication with Gideon comes in the form of a call narrative in which the angel of Yahweh confronts Gideon with a surprising declaration – 'Yahweh is with you, mighty warrior' (6.12). The angel's statement is surprising to the hearer, since Gideon has been revealed in the previous verse not as a mighty warrior but as a farmer who is hiding from the Midianites. The angel's statement is surprising to Gideon as well, given his context of constant oppression, which indicates to him that Yahweh is *not* with the Israelites. Gideon, unaware that the messenger is Yahweh, gives voice to his frustration, by recounting Israel's deliverance from Egypt and then lamenting, 'but now Yahweh has forsaken us and given us into the hands of the Midianites' (6.13).⁴⁸ Apparently, Gideon's theology does not allow for the possibility that Yahweh might be *with him* even in the midst of suffering.

The angel of Yahweh does not answer Gideon's complaint that Yahweh has not saved them; instead, he points to Gideon himself as Yahweh's instrument of salvation. The angel says, 'Go in this your might, and you shall save Israel from the hand of the Midianites; have I not sent you?' (6.14). Thus Gideon, who charges God with failing to save Israel, is himself charged with the task of salvation. Notwithstanding Gideon's objections, Yahweh promises to 'be

---

⁴⁷ Olson, 'Judges', pp. 795-96.
⁴⁸ Gideon had heard of the exodus and Yahweh's faithfulness in the past, but he had not experienced Yahweh's 'wonders' (נִפְלְאֹת); cf. the use of the same term in Exod. 3.20; 15.11 and Josh. 3.5. The failure to appreciate Yahweh's former saving acts is reflected as well in Judg. 2.10, 'And there arose a new generation after them who did not know Yahweh nor the works that he had done for Israel'.

with' Gideon, enabling him to defeat the enemy (Judg. 6.16; cf. Exod. 3.12).

This first dialogue between God and Gideon concludes with Gideon's request for a sign and God's gracious performance of that sign. When Gideon brings an offering of meat and bread and places it upon a rock, the angel touches the offering with his staff, and flames burst forth from the rock and consume the sacrifice. The angel vanishes, causing Gideon to fear for his life, because he realizes that he has 'seen the angel of Yahweh face to face' (6.22). Yahweh then speaks a final word of assurance to Gideon: 'Peace be to you; fear not; you will not die' (6.23).

Gideon's first encounter with God exhibits numerous similarities to the call narrative of Moses[49] and casts Gideon as a new Moses,[50] invested with divine authority, who will deliver the Israelites from oppression. Gideon's call narrative also provides a setting for his own consecration through his presentation of a sacrifice.

That same night, Yahweh speaks the second time to Gideon, commanding him to destroy his father's altar to Baal and the Asherah beside the altar (cf. Judg. 2.2). Gideon is to build an altar to Yahweh on the site of the razed altar and offer up a whole burnt offering to Yahweh (6.25-26). Gideon obeys, but he works surreptitiously by night because he is 'afraid' (6.27). This is the first and only time in Judges when a judge acts in direct opposition to the Canaanite gods, and the angry response of Gideon's neighbors highlights their thoroughgoing idolatry.

After the Spirit of Yahweh empowers Gideon to muster an army who will resist the Midianites,[51] God graciously answers Gideon's repeated requests for a sign (using the fleece). Yahweh then speaks to Gideon a third time, informing him that the Israelite army is so large that they might be tempted to attribute the victory to their

---

[49] Mark S. Smith, 'Remembering God: Collective Memory in Israelite Religion', *CBQ* 64.4 (2002), pp. 634-38. For a list of these similarities, see Chapter 6 of Martin, *The Unheard Voice of God*.

[50] Lindars, 'Gideon and Kingship', p. 317. Lindars summarizes the work of Walter Beyerlin, 'Geschichte und heilsgeschichtliche Traditionsbildung im alten Testament: Ein Beitrag zur Traditionsgeschichte von Richter 6-8', *VT* 13 (1963), pp. 1-25.

[51] Just as the speech of God is an important element in the overall pattern of divine activity in Judges, so is the coming of the Spirit upon the Judges. This aspect of God's activity is explored in Chapter 5 below.

own strength rather than to God's help. In order to reduce the size of the army, Yahweh allows all those who are fearful to return to their homes (7.3). With ten thousand soldiers remaining, Yahweh sifts Gideon's army the second time and chooses only the three hundred who lap water like a dog.[52] The fact that the testing occurs at the Fearful Spring (7.1) leads Lindars to conclude that the test ensures that only the bravest men will be retained in the army.[53]

Before Gideon engages the Midianites in battle, Yahweh speaks to him the fourth and final time, telling Gideon to go down to the Midianite camp where he will 'hear what they say' (7.11). At the camp Gideon overhears a Midianite soldier recounting a dream in which a loaf of bread rolled into the camp and flattened a tent. The soldier interprets the dream as a prediction of Gideon's victory by the power of Yahweh. As soon as Gideon hears the dream, 'he worshiped' (7.15), and he returned full of confidence to his awaiting army.

The fact that it is Yahweh who directs Gideon to go down into the camp of Midian suggests that Yahweh himself is the source of the prophetic dream. Yahweh's words to Gideon, 'you will hear (שמע) what they say', may convey both the literal sense of Gideon's overhearing the Midianite soldier and the theological sense of Gideon's finally perceiving the authenticity of God's word. Ironically, although Gideon has difficulty hearing the word of the angel of Yahweh and the word of Yahweh himself, he finally hears the voice of Yahweh speaking through an enemy soldier (Judg. 7.9-11).

'I will not save you again' (Judges 10.13)
Upon Gideon's death, his son Abimelech[54] claims the kingship of Shechem and rules until he falls to the retribution of Yahweh.

---

[52] The use of the word 'dog' (כלב) suggests to me an allusion to Caleb (also כלב), the only person besides Joshua who was unafraid of the Canaanites and who has already been featured prominently in Judges (1.12, 13, 14, 15, 20; and 3.9). Earlier allusions to Caleb include Othniel, the first judge, who is the nephew of Caleb; the husband of Jael, hero of Judges 4-5, who is a relative of Caleb (1 Chron. 2.55); and the name of the site where Jael kills Sisera (קדש, 'Qadesh', cf. Num. 13.26, the location where Caleb speaks to Israelites and enjoins them not to fear the inhabitants of the land).

[53] Lindars, 'Gideon and Kingship', p. 319.

[54] Abimelech means in Hebrew 'my father is king'. We are not told whether the name is suggestive of Yahweh's rule or of Abimelech's (or Gideon's?) ambitions.

Abimelech is followed by two minor judges: Tola and Jair. The Israelites sin once again, and Yahweh gives them into the hands of the Philistines and the Ammonites who oppress them for 18 years. The Israelites cry out to Yahweh for his aid, but in light of the idolatry of Gideon, the dictatorship of Abimelech, and two more implied cycles of sin and deliverance, Yahweh speaks directly to the Israelites and angrily declares that he is finished with them (10.11-16). Yahweh says,

> Was it not from the Egyptians and from the Amorites and from the Ammonites and from the Philistines – and when the Sidonians and Amalek and Maon oppressed you, you cried unto me, and I saved you from their power? But you have forsaken me and served other gods; therefore, I will not save you again. Go and call upon the gods that you have chosen. They will save you in the time of your distress (Judg. 10.11-13).

Yahweh reminds the Israelites of the numerous times that he has saved them, yet they continue to forsake him and serve foreign gods. He furiously rebukes them and announces that he will save them no more. The tone of Yahweh's rebuff is quite sarcastic,[55] 'Go and call upon the gods you have chosen', perhaps alluding ironically to Joshua's covenant renewal ceremony where the Israelites 'chose' to serve Yahweh (Josh. 24.22). In response to Yahweh's reprimand, the Israelites, for the first time in Judges, confess their sin, put away the foreign gods, and renew their worship of Yahweh.

In light of the apparent repentance of the Israelites and the previous mercies of Yahweh, the hearer of Judges would likely expect Yahweh to respond by changing his mind (cf. Judg. 2.18) and by raising up a judge who would bring salvation to the Israelites (cf. 3.9; 3.15; 4.4; and 6.11). God, however, does not respond as expected. Yahweh's refusal to rescue his people is all the more unexpected given his earlier declaration: 'I will never break my covenant' (2.1). The cycle of sin and salvation that is repeated four times earlier in the book of Judges (3.7-11; 12-30; 4.1-5.31; 6.1-8.28) will not be repeated quite the same again.

This speech suggests that the relationship between Yahweh and Israel is fractured and is in danger of irreparable breakage. Since we

---

[55] Cf. Webb, *Judges: An Integrated Reading*, p. 45.

are familiar with the subsequent biblical narratives of Samuel and Kings, we know that the fracture will be repaired; consequently, it is difficult for us to recognize the significance of Yahweh's impassioned speech and to take seriously his dejection. The voice of Yahweh in Judg. 10.6-16 is angry, injured, frustrated and weary; but it is a voice that must be heard.

'He will begin to save Israel' (Judges 13.5)
In the first half of the book of Judges, the role of God is clear – when the Israelites sin, he hands them over to an enemy for discipline; and, when they cry out to him, he raises up a judge who delivers them. However, the second half of Judges – following Yahweh's withdrawal in Judg. 10.13 – forces us to linger in the midst of ambiguity, as the tension surrounding the role of God continues unabated and as the narrative refuses to bend to our wishes for an easy resolution.[56]

As a result of Yahweh's refusal to offer further aid to the Israelites, the elders of Gilead, by their own initiative, seek out Jephthah to be their leader; and the narrative continues to display the tension between Yahweh's faithfulness and his frustration. The tension is evident in that, although the Spirit of Yahweh comes upon Jephthah, Yahweh does not prevent the sacrifice of Jephthah's daughter, and he does not prevent the intertribal battles that follow Jephthah's victory. Throughout the Jephthah story, Yahweh remains silent.

The tension between Yahweh's anger and his compassion persists and even grows stronger in the Samson cycle. In contrast to earlier cycles, the Israelites do not cry out for God's help, but still he reveals his compassion by appointing Samson from before birth. The angel of Yahweh appears to Samson's mother with a word of promise:

> Although you are barren, having borne no children, you shall conceive and bear a son. Now be careful not to drink wine or strong drink, or to eat anything unclean, for you shall conceive and bear a son. No razor is to come on his head, for the boy

---

[56] For an excellent survey of the increasingly ambiguous role of Yahweh in the narrative, see J. Cheryl Exum, 'The Centre Cannot Hold: Thematic and Textual Instabilities in Judges', *CBQ* 52 (1990), pp. 410-31. While I have focused my attention on the speech of Yahweh, Exum devotes the bulk of her study to Yahweh's actions.

shall be a nazirite to God from birth. And he will begin to save Israel from the hand of the Philistines (Judg. 13.3-5).

The angel's revelation to Samson's mother is noteworthy for several reasons. First, Yahweh's breaking of his silence indicates that he may be returning to full engagement with his people. Second, in light of his mother's barrenness, Samson's birth can be understood as a miracle, a fact that might anticipate divine blessings upon Samson's life. Third, the calling of Samson to be a nazirite adds to the sense of purpose and devotion attached to his life. Fourth, the annunciation narrative includes elements that bring to mind the call of Gideon, who was successful in delivering the Israelites from their oppressor; therefore, the angel's visitation to Samson's mother might suggest that he also is destined for victory. Fifth, the ambiguous declaration that Samson will 'begin' to save Israel, might be the single possible portent of Samson's lack of effectiveness.

Although Yahweh speaks to Samson's mother, he never speaks to Samson himself. Throughout the Samson narrative, Yahweh repeatedly gives his Spirit to Samson; and the narrative states that Yahweh is working behind the scenes, directing Samson's actions (14.4) and answering his prayers (15.18-19; 16.28).[57] Although Samson never admits his errors and never utters words of repentance, Yahweh restores his strength for his last act of vengeance upon the Philistines. The role of God in the affairs of Israel continues to be unclear to the hearer of the Samson story.

'Judah is first' (Judges 20.18)

In the epilogue to Judges, Yahweh disappears almost entirely. The characters invoke the name of Yahweh (17.2, 3, 13), but Yahweh himself is silent. The final chapters of Judges recount unspeakable atrocities that are enacted while Yahweh remains intentionally uninvolved, allowing the Israelites to 'do what is right' in their own eyes (17.6; 21.25).

When the Israelites decide to go to battle against the Benjaminites, one of their own tribes, they turn to Yahweh for his direction. In an episode that recalls Judg. 1.1-2, the Israelites inquire of Yahweh, 'Who shall go up first to fight the Benjaminites?', and

---

[57] The silence of Yahweh is continued from Judges into 1 Samuel, where we are told 'the word of Yahweh was rare in those days' (1 Sam. 3.1).

Yahweh replies, 'Judah is first' (20.18). The Hebrew text says only 'Judah is the first' (יהודה בתחלה); it does not repeat Judg. 1.2, 'Judah shall go up' (יהודה יעלה). Thus, at this point, Yahweh refrains from authorizing the battle explicitly. The Israelites proceed to battle, but are defeated, and after weeping before Yahweh they inquire of him again, this time asking, 'Shall we go up again to fight the Benjaminites?', and Yahweh replies in the affirmative (20.22). They fight for a second day, and again they are defeated. They weep, fast, offer sacrifices and inquire again. This time, Yahweh not only instructs them to continue the battle, but he insures the Israelites of victory (20.28). The Israelites who once fought together against the Canaanites are now warring against one of their own tribes.

Yahweh's role in the battle is ambiguous, in that, even though he responds to the inquiries of the Israelites, he causes the war to be prolonged. Perhaps Yahweh's drawing out of the Israelite conflict is a reflection of his own prolonged inner conflict that he experiences as he is forced repeatedly to choose his response to the chronic infidelity of the Israelites.

Conclusions

The foregoing discussion of divine communication suggests that the voice of God functions as an important narrative element within the book of Judges. Both the frequency of divine speech and its strategic location within the narrative point to its importance as a crucial piece of the interpretive puzzle of Judges.

The placement and the content of the divine word in Judges are consistent with other thematic indicators in the book that manifest the spiraling decline of Israel's devotion to Yahweh, the gradual disintegration of the covenant relationship between Yahweh and Israel, and the escalating tension within the passions of Yahweh himself. The first episode of the book of Judges begins with an assuring, guiding word from Yahweh, but that episode concludes with a judging, disciplining word in which Yahweh declares his displeasure with the Israelites. That word of discipline is repeated at the end of the introduction, and Yahweh does not speak again until the beginning of the third cycle of evil, oppression, and salvation, when Deborah arises as a prophet. Deborah's ministry is the culmination, or high point among the stories of the effective judges. Her story is followed immediately by a nameless prophet who introduces the beginning of the transitional period of Gideon and Abimelech. Yahweh's frequent communications with Gideon lend divine authority and expectation to his leadership, and we are quite disappointed when, after his miraculous victory, his foolhardy actions plunge the Israelites anew into the abyss of idolatry. In Yahweh's final speech to the Israelites, his words pour forth a surge of frustration, and he refuses to save them again. He is mostly silent for the second half of the book of Judges, venturing forth only to announce the birth of Samson and to answer the Israelites' final inquiry concerning their intertribal conflict.

Taken together, Yahweh's speeches show that, although the actions of the Israelites are essential to the story, it is Yahweh who decides the course of the narrative. Repeatedly, Yahweh speaks of himself as the God who brought the Israelites out of Egypt. His numerous allusions to the exodus, along with the fact that he saves the Israelites even when they show no sign of repentance, suggest that all of Yahweh's acts of salvation in Judges flow from the paradigm of the exodus.

In my hearing of the voice of Yahweh in Judges, I did not always hear what I expected to hear, and I did not always hear what I wanted to hear. I heard of Yahweh's oath, his covenant, his mighty acts, and his faithfulness. However, I did not hear a solution to every conflict nor the erasing of every troubling tension. I did not hear the comforting words of closure, for in Judges, the anger of Yahweh seems to be longer than a 'moment' (Ps. 30.5). Even in the epilogue (chs. 17-21), there was no closure, no resolution. Thus, Lillian Klein, can remark that 'the book of Judges does not resolve; it devolves in disorder'.[58] In the voice of Yahweh, I heard disappointment – 'What is this you have done?' (Judg. 2.2). I heard threat – 'I will not save you again' (10.13). I heard chiding frustration – 'Call on the gods you have chosen; they will save you' (10.14). Finally, I heard nothing but deathly, alienating, disturbing silence – enough to make one ache for another word 'just once more' (16.28).

---

[58] Klein, *The Triumph of Irony in the Book of Judges*, p. 190.

4

YAHWEH CONFLICTED: UNRESOLVED THEOLOGICAL TENSION IN THE CYCLE OF JUDGES

Introduction

The cyclical framework of the book of Judges has been analyzed from a number of perspectives. For the most part, these different perspectives have supplemented one another and have led to a continuing refinement of the scholarly consensus regarding the cycle of Judges. Martin Noth argued that the framework was a secondary deuteronomistic addition to the original stories of the judges,[1] and Walter Beyerlin further divided the added material into two redactional layers. Beyerlin argued as well that the cycle could be reduced to two separate components – sin/punishment and cry/deliverance.[2] Walter Brueggemann, building on Beyerlin, identified the streams of theological tradition that produced the two components and the social interests that were served by them.[3] Frederick Greenspahn focused on the theology of the framework, and although he went too far by seeking to unify the cycle into a single movement

---

[1] Martin Noth, *Überlieferungsgeschichtliche Studien* (Halle: M. Niemeyer, 1943), pp. 3-4.

[2] Walter Beyerlin, 'Gattung und Herkunft des Rahmens im Richterbuch', in Ernst Würthwein and Otto Kaiser (eds.), *Tradition und Situation: Studien zur alttestamentlichen Prophetie. Artur Weiser zum 70 Geburtstag* (Göttingen: Vandenhoeck & Ruprecht, 1963), pp. 1-29.

[3] Brueggemann, 'Social Criticism', pp. 73-90.

of oppression and deliverance, he argued convincingly that Yahweh's acts of deliverance were based upon the theology of the exodus and the covenant rather than on a theology of repentance.[4] Taking Robert Polzin's literary study[5] as a point of departure, J. Cheryl Exum explored the role of the cycle within the narrative of Judges. She noted especially the correspondence between the breakdown of the cycle in the latter part of the book and the increasingly ambiguous role of Yahweh in the narrative.[6]

The combined work of the aforementioned scholars serves as the foundation upon which I intend to build further as I probe the theological content of the cyclical pattern in Judges. I argue here that the cycle in its two primary movements (sin/punishment and cry/salvation) registers a deep theological tension within the character of Yahweh himself, an ongoing tension between his anger and his compassion. I propose further that the breakdown of the cycle in the latter part of Judges is a result of Yahweh's exasperation and his unwillingness to make a final choice between justice or mercy for Israel. I conclude that the tension between Yahweh's anger and his compassion belongs to his disposition as a relational being; therefore, it is a tension that must not be mitigated in our exegesis or in our theology.

The Cycle of Judges

The prologue of Judges offers a programmatic summary of the book of Judges that previews the recurring cyclical pattern. The pattern consists of the following elements: (1) the Israelites do what was evil in the sight of Yahweh, forsaking Yahweh and serving other gods (2.11); (2) Yahweh becomes very angry with Israel (2.14); (3) he gives the Israelites over to the power of the enemy who oppresses them (2.14-15); (4) The Lord raises up judges, but the Israelites do not obey the judges (2.16-17); (5) The Lord has compassion on the Israelites on account of their suffering, and he delivers

---

[4] Greenspahn, 'Framework of Judges', pp. 385-96. On the significance of the exodus motif throughout the entire book of Judges, see Chapter 6 below.
[5] Robert Polzin, *Moses and the Deuteronomist: A Literary Study of the Deuteronomic History* (New York: Seabury Press, 1980), pp. 146-204.
[6] Exum, 'The Centre Cannot Hold', pp. 410-31.

them through the leadership of the judge (2.18);⁷ (6) After the judge dies, the cycle repeats, with each generation growing worse than the one that precedes it (2.19).

The repetitions of the cycle in Judges 3-16 follow the basic pattern that is detailed in the prologue.⁸ These narratives, however, utilize a variety of expressions when manifesting the elements of the pattern, and sometimes they include additional elements in the cycle. For example, in five of the cycles, the suffering of the Israelites results in their crying out to God for his help (3.9; 3.15; 4.3; 6.7; 10.10); and the first four narratives conclude with the words 'and the land had rest' (3.11; 3.30; 5.31; 8.28). Also, in the case of Othniel, Gideon, Jephthah, and Samson, it is said that the 'Spirit of Yahweh' came upon them (3.10; 6.34; 11.29; 13.25; 14.6; 14.19; 15.14). Thus, the pattern is generally the same, but each narrative includes unique details and variations on the scheme.⁹

Although each appearance of the cycle incorporates a unique combination of elements, the cycle can be reduced to two basic movements. The first movement of the cycle is the Israelites' sin and subsequent punishment and the second movement is the Israelites' cry and subsequent deliverance. Each of the two movements is rooted in the covenantal relationship between Israel and Yahweh, and each movement is generated by Yahweh's passionate response to Israel's actions.

Part One of the Cycle (Sin/Punishment)

The first movement in the cycle is consistent throughout Judges: 'the Israelites did that which was evil (הרע) in the sight of Yahweh' (Judg. 2.11; 3.7, 12; 4.1; 6.1; 10.6; 13.1). The nature of Israel's sin is

---

⁷ In light of 2.20-23, which describes the role of the remaining Canaanites to be that of a test for the Israelites, any deliverance can only be partial unless the Israelites genuinely repent. I understand 2.20-23 as a different formulation of 2.1-5. Although the nations *in the land* serve to test the Israelites' covenant faithfulness, it is nations from *outside the land* who serve as Yahweh's instruments to punish the Israelites when they prove unfaithful.

⁸ Serge Frolov, 'Rethinking Judges', *CBQ* 71 (2009), pp. 24-41, argues that the final cycle of Judges continues into 1 Samuel, but his conclusions do not affect my proposal here.

⁹ The variations in the elements of the cycle are charted in detail by O'Connell, *The Rhetoric of the Book of Judges*, pp. 22-25. O'Connell lists a total of 20 elements, 12 of which he considers 'essential' (p. 26). Regarding the Spirit of Yahweh in Judges, see Chapter 5 below.

defined further as idolatry. It is said that the Israelites 'served the Baalim. And they forsook Yahweh, the God of their fathers, who brought them out of the land of Egypt, and they followed other gods, of the gods of the people that were round about them, and they worshiped them, and they vexed Yahweh' (2.11b-12); they 'lusted (זנה) after other gods and worshiped them' (2.17); they 'forgot Yahweh their God, and served the Baalim and the Asheroth' (3.7b); they worshiped the gods of the Amorites (6.10); and they 'served the Baalim, and the Ashtaroth, and the gods of Aram, and the gods of Zidon, and the gods of Moab, and the gods of the Ammonites, and the gods of the Philistines; and they forsook Yahweh, and did not serve him' (10.6b).

Greenspahn argues that the sin of idolatry, which is prominent in the prologue, is absent in the cyclical framework of chs. 3-16. He insists that 'the evil' referred to in the stories of the judges is undefined and does not include idolatry.[10] Although my proposal does not require a specific identification of 'the evil', I would question Greenspahn's conclusion for two reasons. First, the practice of idolatry is included in the fabric of the Gideon story both at its beginning and at its end. Gideon's first act was to destroy the altar of Baal (6.25-32), and his final act was to construct a golden ephod that became an object of illicit worship (8.27). Moreover, it is stated that 'as soon as Gideon died, the Israelites returned and lusted (זנה) after the Baals, making Baal-berith their god' (8.33). Besides the Gideon narrative, there are indications of idolatry in the Ehud story's use of הפסילים (3.19, 26), which both the NIV and the NASB translate as 'the idols'. Furthermore, the Song of Deborah may be calling attention to idolatry when it speaks of 'new gods' being chosen

---

[10] Greenspahn, 'Framework of Judges', pp. 394-95. Following Beyerlin, 'Gattung und Herkunft', pp. 4-5, Greenspahn argues that the idolatry texts (2.11-13; 3.7; 10.6, 10-14) are deuteronomistic but the framework of chs. 3-16 is not ('Framework of Judges', p. 391). Cf. Philippe Guillaume, *Waiting for Josiah: The Judges* (JSOTSup 385; New York: T & T Clark, 2004), pp. 16-27. In her recent commentary, Susan Niditch sees both the framework and the idolatry texts as originating from 'Deuteronomically oriented writers' (*Judges: A Commentary* [OTL; Louisville, KY: Westminster John Knox Press, 2008], p. 49) and holds them together as the 'voice of the theologian' (pp. 10-11). Gregory T.K. Wong, *Compositional Strategy of the Book of Judges: An Inductive, Rhetorical Study* (VTSup 111; Leiden: Brill, 2006), pp. 181-90, proposes an even greater unity, arguing that the prologue is paradigmatic for the entire book of Judges.

(5.8),[11] and Samson's pursuit of foreign women may represent Israel's pursuit of foreign gods.[12] Second, it seems likely that the intended hearer of Judges would understand the phrase 'that which is evil in the eyes of Yahweh' as a reference to idolatry, given the canonical precedent. The book of Deuteronomy names 'the evil' as idolatry (4.23-26; 9.18-21; 17.2-3; 31.29), which will provoke Yahweh's 'anger' (4.25; 9.18; 31.20, 29), and which will result in severe divine punishment (4.26).

Whether or not 'the evil' is to be identified as idolatry, it is clear that Israel is repeatedly indicted for some form of grave disobedience to which Yahweh reacts.[13] Without exception, Yahweh's response to the sin of the Israelites is to deliver them over to their enemies for punishment (Judg. 2.14; 3.8; 3.12; 4.2; 6.1, 13; 10.7; 13.1). We are told that Yahweh's disciplinary actions are motivated by his anger toward Israel – 'His anger burned against Israel' (2.14, 20; 3.8. 10.7). Yahweh's anger is revealed further in the tone and content of his speeches to Israel. In his first speech (2.1-5) he angrily rebukes Israel for her unfaithfulness, and he then exclaims, 'What is this that you have done?' (2.2), a rhetorical question that is loaded with passion. His second speech (6.7-10) briskly employs a

---

[11] The translation of Judg. 5.8 is disputed, though every version that I consulted (LXX, NASB, NIV, JPS, NJB, NRSV) supports the rendering, 'They chose new gods'. For an opposing view, see Block, *Judges, Ruth*, pp. 226-27.

[12] So Edward L. Greenstein, 'The Riddle of Samson', *Prooftexts* 1.3 (1981), pp. 237-60.

[13] A number of interpreters argue that the sin of the Israelites is unbroken and grows worse throughout Judges. Greenspahn writes, 'the term *wayyosipu*, which precedes all but the first assertion that Israel did evil, should not be translated 'they again ...' but 'they continued ...', for the Bible makes no claim that their transgression ever stopped ('Framework of Judges', p. 394). Cf. Polzin, *Moses and the Deuteronomist*, p. 177. Two factors suggest that the case for unbroken sin is not as clear as Polzin and Greenspahn infer. First, the Hebrew ויספו, 'they added', i.e. 'again', nowhere in the Hebrew Bible means 'continued'. The term always refers to a series of repeated actions, not the continuity of one action. Second, there are other indications in the text that Israel's sin was not entirely continuous. E.g. the prologue declares that after the judges died the Israelites would return (ישבו) to their idolatry and do worse than the previous generation (Judg. 2.19). Also, if the Israelites continued to sin during the lifetime of the judges, the statement that they did evil 'after Ehud died' (Judg. 4.1 NRSV) would not make sense. Moreover, we are told that 'as soon as Gideon died, the Israelites relapsed (ישובו) and prostituted themselves with the Baals' (Judg. 8.33 NRSV). I would not argue that 'the evil' was completely eradicated, only that its severity was diminished for a time in the wake of Yahweh's saving actions.

series of five verbs to recount his gracious actions on behalf of Israel – 'I brought you out ... I freed you ... I rescued you ... I drove out ... I gave you.' He concludes with a sixth verb that serves as a fervent rebuke, 'I said to you, "You shall not worship the gods of the Amorites, but you have not obeyed my voice".' Yahweh's third speech (10.10-16) is extraordinarily harsh throughout. Yahweh reminds Israel that he had saved them from seven enemies, yet Israel continues to sin. He is so angry that he speaks with broken grammar: 'Was it not from Egypt and from the Ammonite and from the sons of Ammon and from the Philistines ... ? And the Sidonians and Amalek and Maon oppressed you, and you cried unto me, and I saved you from their hand' (10.11-12).[14] He then declares furiously and sarcastically, 'I will not save you again; cry to the gods you have chosen; they will deliver you' (10.13-14). The anger of Yahweh is his passionate response to personal affront, to covenant infidelity, to relational dysfunction created by Israel.[15] Thus, the first movement of the cycle (sin/punishment) is initiated by Israel's disobedience, which inflames Yahweh's intense anger, and he acts decisively to punish Israel.

Part Two of the Cycle (Cry/Salvation)

The second movement of the cycle begins when the oppressed Israelites cry out to Yahweh (3.9, 14; 4.3; 6.6, 7; 10.10).[16] Interpreters have often assumed that the cries of Israel are cries of repentance. Wellhausen, for example, characterized Israel's cry as evidence of '*Bekehrung*' ('conversion'),[17] and Burney declared that one of the lessons of Judges is that 'true repentance is followed by a renewal of the Divine favour.'[18] George F. Moore, however, observed correctly that Israel repents only on one occasion (10.10-16).[19] Recent

---

[14] On the anacoluthon in 10.11 see Martin, *The Unheard Voice of God*, pp. 204-206.

[15] I am not suggesting that anger is an 'attribute' of God in the theological sense, rather it is Yahweh's passionate response to human sin.

[16] As we will discuss below, the cycle begins to break down in ch. 10, and the Israelites do not cry out to Yahweh in the Samson cycle.

[17] Julius Wellhausen, *Prolegomena zur Geschichte Israels* (Berlin: Georg Reimer, 1883), p. 240. For Wellhausen, the four stages of the cycle were '*Abfall Drangsal Bekehrung Ruhe*' (pp. 240-41).

[18] C.F. Burney, *The Book of Judges, with Introduction and Notes* (London: Rivingtons, 1918), p. cxxi.

[19] Moore, *Judges*, pp. xv-xvi, footnote.

interpreters have confirmed Moore's observation,[20] but the occasional writer continues to use the terminology of repentance.[21] Michael Welker goes so far as to claim that in Judges the Israelites experience 'the forgiveness of sins';[22] but forgiveness language is entirely absent from Judges.

Rather than being a cry of repentance, Israel's cry in Judges (צעק/זעק) is reminiscent of the exodus (Exod. 2.23), where the cry is 'a plea to be delivered from oppression'.[23] Just as in the case of the exodus, the cry in Judges is sometimes no more than a groan (נאקה, Judg. 2.18; Exod. 2.24).[24] Israel's suffering under the Egyptian regime is paradigmatic for its later suffering at the hands of the tyrannical Canaanite rulers. 'The framework', writes Greenspahn, 'thus perceives the period of the judges as continuing the process initiated by the exodus in which Israel's suffering is dealt with by divine salvation'.[25]

These desperate cries of Israel awaken Yahweh to action, and he raises up a judge who saves Israel from their oppressor. The

---

[20] E.g. Brueggemann, 'Social Criticism', p. 83; Greenspahn, 'Framework of Judges', pp. 394-95; Polzin, *Moses and the Deuteronomist*, p. 155; Exum, 'The Centre Cannot Hold', p. 421; Wong, *Compositional Strategy of Judges*, p. 181, n. 11.

[21] E.g. Serge Frolov, *The Turn of the Cycle: 1 Samuel 1-8 in Synchronic and Diachronic Perspectives* (New York: Walter de Gruyter, 2004), pp. 47, 48; O'Connell, *The Rhetoric of the Book of Judges*, pp. 40-42; Robert B. Hughes and J. Carl Laney, *Tyndale Concise Bible Commentary* (The Tyndale Reference Library; Wheaton, IL: Tyndale House Publishers, 2001), p. 99; Walter C. Kaiser, *Toward an Exegetical Theology: Biblical Exegesis for Preaching and Teaching* (Grand Rapids, MI: Baker, 1981), p. 136; Richard L. Pratt, *He Gave Us Stories: The Bible Student's Guide to Interpreting Old Testament Narratives* (Brentwood, TN: Wolgemuth & Hyatt, 1990), p. 135; Israel Finkelstein and Neil Asher Silberman, *The Bible Unearthed: Archaeology's New Vision of Ancient Israel and the Origin of Its Sacred Texts* (New York: Free Press, 2001), p. 120; Victor H. Matthews, *Judges and Ruth* (New Cambridge Bible Commentary; Cambridge: Cambridge University Press, 2004), p. 53.

[22] Michael Welker, *God the Spirit* (trans. John F. Hoffmeyer; Minneapolis, MN: Fortress Press, 1994), p. 65.

[23] Brueggemann, 'Social Criticism', p. 83.

[24] Philippe Guillaume contends that the Israelite's 'groaning' in the prologue reflects an activity different from their 'crying' in the framework (*Waiting for Josiah*, p. 21). To my mind, the parallels in Exod. 2.23-24 and the semantic similarity of the two Hebrew terms suggest that 'groan' and 'cry' describe the same activity spoken of in two different ways. Cf. O'Connell, *The Rhetoric of the Book of Judges*, p. 40; and Wong, *Compositional Strategy of Judges*, p. 181, n. 13.

[25] Greenspahn, 'Framework of Judges', p. 395. It should be noted, however, that Israel's suffering in Judges is characterized as a punishment from Yahweh while the suffering in Egypt is not.

terminology employed in the calling of the judge may vary, and the description of the leader as a 'judge' or as a 'savior' may also vary. Nevertheless, in every cycle save one, Yahweh recruits a person who works on behalf of Israel to bring justice and safety. The one exception is the Jephthah cycle, in which Yahweh refuses to save Israel (10.13) and Jephthah is chosen by the elders of Gilead. Even then, however, Yahweh partially relents and puts his spirit upon Jephthah, who is subsequently empowered to defeat the invading Ammonites.

Therefore, the second movement (cry/salvation) is initiated by the actions of Israel, who 'cry' to Yahweh. Yahweh then responds decisively to change Israel's circumstances. Just as in the first movement, Yahweh's actions are grounded in his passions. We noted in the first movement that before Yahweh acted he was provoked to anger. In the second movement Yahweh is moved to compassion. Over and over it is Israel's suffering, not their repentance, that motivates Yahweh to save; therefore, every act of deliverance registers Yahweh's compassion. Moreover, the text explicitly confirms the empathy of Yahweh as the motivating force behind his actions when it declares that Yahweh 'saved them from the hand of their enemies ... because Yahweh was sorry (נחם) on account of those who tyrannized and oppressed them' (2.18b). The verb נחם is used frequently in the Hebrew Bible to signify God's change of mind or actions. It can be translated 'repent', 'regret', or 'be sorry'.[26] The use of נחם indicates that God's sympathy for the suffering of the Israelites is the major factor in his decision to save them. A similar but even deeper compassion is expressed in the words of 10.16, 'he was wearied by the suffering of Israel'.[27]

It seems clear, therefore, that the second movement of the cycle (cry/salvation) is initiated by the groans or cries of oppressed Israel. These cries arouse Yahweh's empathy, and he acts decisively to save Israel.

---

[26] HALOT, I, p. 688; KB, p. 608; Stoebe, 'נחם', p. 738; DCH, V, p. 663.

[27] By the time we reach ch. 10, the cycle is disintegrating and Yahweh refuses to save Israel, thus the compassion described in 10.16 does not extend so far as to include the change of mind that is expressed by נחם in 2.18b. For my argument (contra Polzin and others) that Judg. 10.16 registers Yahweh's suffering compassion, see Martin, *The Unheard Voice of God*, pp. 207-13.

Theological Tension Manifested in the Cycle

Walter Brueggemann argues that the two basic movements of the cycle arise from different social contexts and express competing and conflicting theological traditions.[28] According to Brueggemann, the first part of the cycle (sin/punishment) is a 'highly theologized version of retribution' based upon the 'correspondence of deed and consequence', and it justifies a dependable, orderly social structure.[29] The sin/punishment scheme can be used maintain discipline within the ranks of a movement such as that of the Mosaic community, or it can function to legitimate an existing establishment of ruling elite. In either case it serves to maintain an established order.

In contrast, the second part of the cycle (cry/salvation) stands in opposition to entrenched powers, structures, and institutions, and 'speaks of Yahweh as a source of political power who will liberate from another, lesser political power that oppresses'.[30] This second part of the formula reflects the radical graciousness of Yahweh as enacted in the exodus. Yahweh acts as deliverer to intervene and overthrow tyranny and oppression. The Israelites who were saved from the brutality of Pharaoh soon found themselves in need of deliverance from the pitiless Canaanite rulers who had ensnared and subjugated them.

Greenspahn agrees that the second part of the cycle is analogous to the theology of the exodus, reflecting 'a theology of election and grace, that is to say God's free and unconditioned commitment to Israel, a commitment which is not ultimately bound to Israel's own actions'.[31] The Israelites are reminded in Judg. 2.1-5 that Yahweh saved them from the slavery of Egypt not because they deserved salvation, but because he chose them to be his people. Yahweh's responsiveness is attributed to his commitment to his covenant with Israel and to his other previously uttered words (2.1-5, 20; 6.7-10; 10.10-16). Greenspahn states,

---

[28] Brueggemann, 'Social Criticism', pp. 73-90.
[29] Brueggemann, 'Social Criticism', p. 79.
[30] Brueggemann, 'Social Criticism', p. 84.
[31] Greenspahn, 'Framework of Judges', pp. 394-95. Interpreters continue to misconstrue the Judges framework as a single movement. Cf., e.g. Noll, 'Deuteronomistic History or Deuteronomic Debate?', p. 340.

God's response is occasioned not by Israel's religious fidelity, but rather by her need, just as it was at the time of the exodus. This is far removed from a concept of reward and punishment, reflecting instead a theology of election and grace, that is to say God's free and unconditioned commitment to Israel, a commitment which is not ultimately bound to Israel's own actions.[32]

The first movement, therefore, is based upon a dependable and predictable theology of justice, while the second movement is based upon a more open and surprising theology of mercy. The two-part nature of the cycle gives rise to the different interpretations of the cycle, which usually focus either on the causality that is found in part one of the cycle or on the grace that is evident within part two of the cycle. I find it significant that although the two parts of the cycle reflect two different theological approaches to the covenant relationship, the book of Judges holds them together within the one recurring cycle. Under the covenant, Yahweh consistently punishes evil deeds (he will 'by no means clear the guilty' [Exod. 34.7]), but he also responds with compassion toward those who suffer (he is 'merciful and gracious' [Exod. 34.6]). The uniting of these two movements into one recurring cycle manifests Yahweh's inner conflict, the theological tension between his justice and his mercy (i.e. between his anger and his compassion). As Pressler writes when reflecting on Judges 2, 'divine judgment and divine mercy are held in tension in the very heart of God'.[33]

Yahweh's Inner Conflict and the Breakdown of the Cycle

Yahweh's inner conflict is first displayed in his reprimand of Israel in Judg. 2.1-5. In this speech to Israel, he reaffirms his commitment to his gracious covenant relationship with Israel, but he is angered by Israel's disregard for that relationship. Thus Yahweh's professed commitment not to break the covenant forever (2.1) coupled with

---

[32] Greenspahn, 'Framework of Judges', pp. 394-95. The cycle of Judges 'minimizes the necessity of repentance' as a prerequisite to deliverance Robert Polzin, *Samuel and the Deuteronomist: A Literary Study of the Deuteronomic History: Part Two: 1 Samuel* (San Francisco: Harper & Row, 1989), p. 74.
[33] Pressler, *Joshua, Judges, and Ruth*, p. 135.

Israel's violation of the covenant (2.2) accounts for the dialectical forces that generate the cyclical motion of the rest of the book. Yahweh's sense of justice requires him to discipline Israel, but his compassion will not allow him to abandon his people.

The Breakdown of the Cycle
Yahweh's response to Israel alternates between anger and compassion as the cycle continues with the Othniel and Ehud narratives. In the Deborah narrative the completion of the cycle is threatened when Barak hesitates, and Yahweh chooses to withhold the glory from Barak (4.6-8). A more serious threat to the cyclical pattern comes in the Gideon cycle when Gideon requires repeated signs and assurances from Yahweh; but, in the end, the cycle runs its course with the components intact.

The tension between justice and mercy intensifies throughout Judges 3-9 on account of Israel's repeated offenses, and the cycle begins to break down in Judg. 10.6-16. At this point Yahweh becomes so frustrated that he refuses to allow the cycle to continue.[34] Here at the beginning of the Jephthah cycle when the Israelites cry out for help, Yahweh recounts the numerous times that he has delivered them, and he declares angrily, 'I will not save you again' (10.13). As a consequence of Yahweh's withdrawal, the Jephthah cycle lacks two important components that are found in all the previous cycles. First, Yahweh does not choose a judge. Because of his disengagement from the Israelites, Yahweh refuses to participate in the choosing of a deliverer. Consequently, Jephthah is chosen not by Yahweh but by the elders of Gilead. Second, at the end of the Jephthah narrative it is not said that the land had rest (perhaps because Jephthah defeated only one of the two oppressors named in 10.6).

The cyclical pattern is again incomplete in the Samson cycle, the only cycle in which the Israelites do not cry out to Yahweh for his help.[35] In fact they seem content to live under the domination of the Philistines rather than to join Samson in his fight against

---

[34] J.P.U. Lilley, 'A Literary Appreciation of the Book of Judges', *Tyndale Bulletin* 18 (1967), pp. 98-102, and Wong, *Compositional Strategy of the Book of Judges*, pp. 181-90, argue that deterioration is the major theme of the book of Judges, but neither Lilly nor Wong links the deterioration to the inner conflict of Yahweh.
[35] Block, *Judges, Ruth*, p. 337.

Philistine oppression (Judg. 15.11). In addition to the missing cry for help, the Samson cycle fails to include both salvation from the enemy and rest for the land. Samson's failure to effect salvation is important enough to the story that it is mentioned in his birth narrative when the angel of Yahweh says not that Samson will deliver Israel but that he will only 'begin' to deliver Israel (13.5). The cyclical pattern, therefore, is complete in the Othniel and Ehud narratives, is threatened in the Deborah and Gideon narratives, and finally collapses in the Jephthah and Samson cycles. The human participants in the narratives, as important as their roles are, are not responsible ultimately for the collapse of the cyclical framework. The cycle collapses in ch. 10 because of Yahweh's refusal to be manipulated further by Israel's unfaithful behavior pattern.

In the epilogue to Judges, Yahweh disappears almost entirely. Throughout the Micah story, the characters invoke the name of Yahweh (17.2, 3, 13), but Yahweh himself is silent. Micah's illicit activities prompt the first occurrence of the refrain, 'In those days there was no king in Israel' (17.6; 18.1; 19.1; 21.25). Since the covenant assumes that Yahweh is Israel's great king, and since Gideon, in his refusal of the monarchy, declares Yahweh to be Israel's only ruler (8.22-23), the refrain that there is no king in Israel may mean not only that Israel has no human king but also that God has withdrawn from manifesting his sovereign authority. The story of Micah and his idol merges into the story of the Danites and their search for a land to inhabit. They settle in Laish and use Micah's idol and priest to establish there a cultic center (18.27-30). The Danites give credit to God for their victory; but, as before, Yahweh himself neither speaks nor acts in the narrative.

The final chapters of Judges recount the unspeakable atrocities that are inflicted upon a Levite's secondary wife (19.25-30), who is raped, murdered and dismembered, and upon the women of Jabesh-gilead and Shiloh, who are kidnapped and forced to become wives to the Benjaminite remnant (21.12, 20-23). It is quite disturbing to the hearer of Judges that Yahweh does nothing to prevent the savagery of the Levite, the men of Gibeah, or the Benjaminites. Apparently, Yahweh is intentionally uninvolved, allowing the Israelites to 'do what is right' in their own eyes (17.6; 21.25). However, when the Israelites decide to punish the Gibeonite offenders by engaging in battle with Benjamin, who is one of their own tribes, they turn to Yahweh for his direction. In an episode that recalls Judg. 1.1-2, the Israelites inquire of Yahweh, 'Who shall go up first to fight the Benjaminites?', and Yahweh replies, 'Judah is first' (20.18). Unlike his response in Judg. 1.2, Yahweh's answer here is incomplete, since he does not include in his response the words 'go up' (יעלה), and he does not promise victory. By answering the inquiry, but not answering completely, Yahweh allows the Israelites to go into battle without his complete authorization. The Israelites are defeated, and after weeping before Yahweh they inquire of him again, and Yahweh replies in the affirmative (20.22), but again he does not promise victory. They fight for a second day, and again the Israelites are defeated. After a third inquiry, Yahweh not only instructs them to continue the battle, but he insures the Israelites of victory (20.28). The Benjaminites are decimated, and the other tribes mourn the aftermath of the civil war (21.1-7).

Yahweh's role in the narrative is ambiguous, in that, even though he responds to the inquiries of the Israelites, he causes the war to be prolonged. Perhaps Yahweh's drawing out of the Israelite conflict is a reflection of his own prolonged inner conflict. Could it be possible that Yahweh is turning the tables on Israel and forcing them to experience the same kind of conflicted situation which he is suffering? Like Yahweh, the Israelites are forced to choose between justice and mercy. They must decide just how severely to punish the Benjaminites and how to prevent the complete extermination of the tribe of Benjamin. Israel's choices are not easy ones, but they mirror the vexing choices that present themselves to Yahweh – justice or mercy.

Yahweh's Inner Conflict

A number of scholars have recognized the breakdown of the cycle, and Exum has noted the 'increasingly ambiguous role of the deity.'[36] I contend that the breakdown of the cycle is a result of Yahweh's inner conflict, which is registered in his speech of 10.7-16. In ch. 10, Yahweh is furious and does not save the Israelites, but he is wearied by their suffering. 'Israel's suffering is God's grief'.[37]

---

[36] Exum, 'The Centre Cannot Hold', p. 411.
[37] Heschel, *The Prophets*, II, p. 151.

Yahweh's resistance to saving Israel again (10.13), coupled with his suffering compassion (10.16), signals a major shift toward ambiguity in God's role. Although Exum attributes to Yahweh partial responsibility for the collapse of the cyclical pattern, she does not give sufficient weight to Yahweh's speech in Judg. 10.7-16, and she does not recognize, as I suggest here, that Yahweh's inner struggle is the source of his ambiguous actions in Judges 17-21. In ch. 10, Yahweh refuses to respond to Israel's cries. He refuses to act. Israel's ingratitude and continued forsaking of Yahweh have exhausted his patience so that he no longer responds to their cry for help. Yahweh's inner conflict is registered in his two apparently incompatible declarations: (1) 'I will never break my covenant' (2.1); and (2) 'I will not save you again' (10.13). Yahweh's refusal to save Israel stands in tension with his earlier declarations of faithfulness and his earlier acts of salvation. Although he does not bring complete salvation again, neither does he allow Israel to be completely destroyed by their enemies (chs. 11-16). Yahweh is unwilling to make a final choice between justice and mercy for Israel, but his withdrawal means that he leaves the Israelites to their own devices. His refusal to aid Israel explains why he does not intervene to save Jephthah's daughter, why his role in the Samson cycle is so ambiguous, and why he allows the civil war that almost destroys the Benjaminites.

Yahweh's resistance to manipulation in ch. 10 suggests that his compassionate deliverance is not a mechanical, automatic response. I suggest, therefore, that the breakdown of the cycle in the latter part of Judges is a result of Yahweh's frustration and his unwillingness to make a final choice between justice or mercy for Israel. I contend further that an important theological claim of Judges is that the tension between God's justice and his mercy is never dissolved.

Yahweh's Relational Nature

In Judges, both the anger and the compassion of Yahweh are grounded in his covenant relationship to Israel. He repeatedly hands the Israelites over to their oppressors because they have violated the covenant. Again and again he saves them from their enemies because they cry out in agony to him. In Judges 3-9 Yahweh's responses to Israel appear to be quite predictable, but in ch. 10, when for the first time Israel confesses and puts away its idols, Yahweh does not save, thus demonstrating that his actions are not at all mechanical. Instead, he shows that he relates genuinely to Israel as a covenant partner. Yahweh is so frustrated with his people that he will not respond even to their repentance. It is Yahweh's nature to respond both with promise and with judgment, with anger and with compassion, but those manifestations of his passions are not predetermined; they are not guaranteed.

I conclude, therefore, that the tension between Yahweh's anger and his compassion belongs to his disposition as a relational being; therefore, it is a tension that must not be mitigated in our theology. On the one hand, Western theology has emphasized justice, repentance, and obedience to God's commands. On the other hand, liberationist approaches have stressed God's compassion in the face of human suffering. Oppressed peoples, therefore, do not think of their need for God first in terms of forgiveness but in terms of deliverance from oppressive human structures.[38] Early in their history, religious movements tend to emphasize a more dynamic and open view of God. He is the God who intervenes to create a new order and a new way of being.[39] Entrenched religious institutions, however, stress a more stable and closed theology of God. He is the God who stands behind the present order and who authorizes the present structures. It is not necessary, however, to choose between the God of justice and the God of mercy, between the God who gives stability to the world and the God who intervenes. The two theologies of God are both present within the one cycle of Judges. Gerhard von Rad writes,

> every generation was confronted by Jahweh's whole historical revelation both in judgment and in salvation. It was not the case that one generation was subjected only to his wrath while the

---

[38] Cf., e.g. Terence E. Fretheim, 'Salvation in the Bible vs Salvation in the Church', *WW* 13 (1993), pp. 363-72; Solivan, *The Spirit, Pathos and Liberation*; and Richard Shaull and Waldo A. Cesar, *Pentecostalism and the Future of the Christian Churches: Promises, Limitations, Challenges* (Grand Rapids, MI: Eerdmans, 2000).

[39] Cf., e.g. Walter J. Hollenweger, *The Pentecostals* (trans. R.A. Wilson; Minneapolis, MN: Augsburg Pub. House, 1st U.S. edn, 1972), pp. 353-496.

next was solely subjected to his will to save. It was rather that each generation experienced the whole Jahweh.[40]

The book of Judges does not allow us to choose between these two Gods – the God of justice and the God of mercy. In Judges the two are one and the same.

Conclusion

The narrative of Judges displays a deep tension within the character of Yahweh, a tension between his anger and his compassion. By the end of the book, we might expect that either his anger or his compassion will gain the upper hand and win out over the other, but in fact, what proves to be Yahweh's strongest character trait is his ability to postpone decisive action. For him to abandon Israel completely is unthinkable in light of his earlier declaration: 'I will not break my covenant with you forever' (Judg. 2.2); but to prosper Israel in its disobedience is an equally unbearable affront to his sense of justice. Yahweh, therefore, chooses neither to forsake Israel nor to bless Israel. Yahweh is able to bear the tension indefinitely, to continue in ambiguity, to suffer in silence. He does not enjoy the tension, but he endures.

Yahweh's first speech (2.1-5) registers the source of the conflict between Yahweh and the Israelites, which grounds and generates the two-fold cyclical pattern. The tension between his justice and his mercy intensifies throughout chs. 3-9, and ch. 10 marks the turning point of the narrative and the collapse of the cyclical pattern. I have shown how the tension between Yahweh's anger and his compassion continues unresolved from the third speech through the ensuing narratives to the end of the book. I have demonstrated that the inner tension between Yahweh's anger and his compassion is the cause of the ambiguity regarding Yahweh's role in the second half of Judges. While this ambiguity has been acknowledged in recent scholarship, I have shown that the source of the ambiguity rests in the tension expressed in Yahweh's conflicted passions.[41]

---

[40] Rad, *Old Testament Theology*, I, p. 332.

[41] I do not go so far as to suggest that the theme or focus of Judges is the passions of Yahweh, nor that the primary message of the book is the conflict in

Thus the tension between Yahweh's anger and compassion is a tension that generates the cycle in the first place, a tension that causes the eventual breakdown of the cycle, and a tension that is not resolved at the end of the book of Judges. Amazingly, the book of Judges refuses to soften Yahweh's inner struggle as he responds to the behavior of Israel, his covenant partner.

Yahweh's passions. The themes of Judges are numerous and complex; see Martin, *The Unheard Voice of God*, pp. 91-95.

5

POWER TO SAVE!?: THE ROLE OF THE SPIRIT IN THE BOOK OF JUDGES

Introduction

The Spirit of Yahweh (רוח יהוה) appears seven times in the book of Judges,[1] and these seven texts have enjoyed more than a little attention, having been included in a number of studies on the Holy Spirit.[2] The studies, however, are brief and have not given sufficient attention to the place of the Spirit of Yahweh within the overall narrative of Judges. My goal is to bring a fresh perspective to bear upon the Spirit in Judges by utilizing a literary-theological approach that appreciates the references to the Spirit as a part of the larger narrative context.

I argue that the Spirit of Yahweh in Judges functions primarily as the dynamic presence of Yahweh that compels and empowers the judges to effectuate Yahweh's salvation of his covenant people. Other scholars have proposed similar interpretations,[3] but have

---

[1] Judges 3.10 records the first canonical appearance of the phrase רוח יהוה. The other six appearances in Judges are 6.34; 11.29; 13.25; 14.6; 14.19; and 15.14.

[2] E.g. Dale Moody, *Spirit of the Living God: The Biblical Concepts Interpreted in Context* (Philadelphia: Westminster Press, 1968), pp. 14-15; Montague, *The Holy Spirit*, pp. 17-18; Horton, *Holy Spirit*, pp. 33-42; Rea, *Holy Spirit*, pp. 53-55; Welker, *God the Spirit*, pp. 50-74; and Hildebrandt, *An Old Testament Theology of the Spirit of God*, pp. 112-18.

[3] See John Goldingay, *Old Testament Theology: Israel's Gospel* (Downers Grove, IL: InterVarsity Press, 2003), p. 541, who writes that the Spirit comes on a leader and 'he or she is inspired to undertake extraordinary ventures for the sake of the people's freedom and well-being'. Cf. Welker, *God the Spirit*, who describes the

omitted consideration of important features of the narrative. I argue further that each of the stories of the judges presents a unique perspective on the role of the Spirit. Samson, for example, is a paradoxical character who is repeatedly empowered by the Spirit to perform feats that have no apparent relation to the salvation of Israel. Even though he is the most powerful judge in Judges, he is unable to save Israel from the Philistines.

The Prologue of Judges

The book of Judges begins with a prologue (1.1-3.6) that sets the stage for the stories of the judges (3.7-16.31). The first part of the prologue (1.1-2.5) recounts the warfare that continues between the Israelites and the Canaanites following the death of Joshua. The tribes of Israel undertake the task of securing their individual territories by driving out the remaining Canaanites, but many of the tribes are unsuccessful. Yahweh censures the Israelites, declaring that their failure is a result of their violation of the covenant (2.1-5) and that, consequently, Yahweh will allow the Canaanites to continue as 'adversaries' and 'their gods will be a snare' (2.3).

The second part of the prologue (2.6-3.6) offers a programmatic summary of the book of Judges that previews the book in terms of a recurring cyclical pattern. The cycle begins when the Israelites forget Yahweh and engage in idolatry. The behavior of the Israelites provokes Yahweh to anger and he disciplines them by handing them over to an oppressive enemy. The Israelites then cry out to Yahweh for deliverance, and Yahweh is moved with compassion because of their suffering. Finally, Yahweh raises up a judge who saves the Israelites from their enemy, and the land enjoys a time of peace. Although each appearance of the cycle incorporates a unique combination of elements,[4] the cycle can be reduced to two basic

---

Spirit's work in 'early' (p. 51) texts under the heading: 'In deliverance out of collective distress and sin: Restoration of solidarity and of the community's capacity for action – Spirit and process of emergence' (p. 52). Unfortunately, Welker's synthetic theological approach does not treat the Judges texts separately from similar texts in 1 Samuel.

[4] The variations are charted in detail by O'Connell, *The Rhetoric of the Book of Judges*, pp. 22-25. Julius Wellhausen, *Prolegomena to the History of Israel* (trans. J. Sutherland Black and Allan Menzies; Edinburgh: Adam & Charles Black, 1885), p. 231, lists the elements of the cycle as 'rebellion, affliction, conversion, peace'.

movements. First, the Israelites rebel and God punishes them. Second, the Israelites cry to God and he saves them.[5] The uniting of these two movements into one recurring cycle registers the theological tension between the justice of God and the mercy of God (cf. Exod. 34.6-7).[6] Finally, the prologue predicts that the idolatry of the Israelites will grow more egregious with each repetition of the cycle and that the relationship between Israel and Yahweh will deteriorate (2.17, 19).

Othniel: Paradigmatic Deliverer

Once the prologue has established the pattern for the book, the stories of the judges get under way, beginning with a short, concise narrative that features Othniel as the first of the judges. A mere five verses, the story reads:

> The Israelites did evil in the sight of Yahweh; they forgot Yahweh their God, and they worshiped the Baals and the Asherahs. And the anger of Yahweh burned against Israel, and he sold them into the hand of King Cushan-rishathaim of Aram-naharaim; and the Israelites served Cushan-rishathaim eight years. The Israelites cried out to Yahweh, and Yahweh raised up a savior for the Israelites, and he saved them, Othniel son of Kenaz, Caleb's younger brother. The Spirit of Yahweh came upon him, and he judged Israel, and he went out to war, and Yahweh gave King Cushan-rishathaim of Aram into his hand; and his hand

---

Instead of the impersonal taxonomy of Wellhausen (and other scholars), I would prefer to use the more relational language of the biblical text, which presents the cycle in the form of concrete verbal clauses: Israel did evil; Yahweh sold them; Israel cried out; Yahweh raised up a judge; etc.

[5] Cf. Beyerlin, 'Gattung und Herkunft', pp. 1-29; and Brueggemann, 'Social Criticism', pp. 101-14.

[6] Most interpreters, unwilling to retain the theological tension, have chosen to describe the cycle as one of justice, in which the deliverance of the Israelites is conditioned upon their repentance, or one of mercy, in which the anger of God is eclipsed by his compassion. I contend, however, that an important theological claim of Judges is that the tension between God's justice and his mercy is never dissolved. See Chapters 1, 2, and 4 above. Welker claims that these deliverances are 'experiences of the forgiveness of sins' (*God the Spirit*, p. 65), but forgiveness language is entirely absent from Judges.

prevailed over Cushan-rishathaim. And the land had rest 40 years. And Othniel son of Kenaz died (Judg. 3.7-11).

The completeness of the elements in the cyclical pattern, the brevity of the story, and the flawless performance of Othniel suggest that he is the paradigmatic deliverer in the book of Judges.[7]

As predicted in the prologue, the Othniel story begins with the idolatry of the Israelites and Yahweh's judgment of their sin. 'On the basis of sin', writes Welker, 'Israel loses its internal unity, its coherence. Inasmuch as Israel forgets God and turns to the idols of peoples of other lands, it loses its internal coherence. It loses the power to defend itself against outside aggression and oppression'.[8] Then, after the Israelites serve Cushan-rishathaim for eight years, they cry out to Yahweh. The Hebrew word עבד, used here to describe the servitude of the Israelites, is the same word that represents their bondage in Egypt (Exod. 1.13-14), and the word זעק expresses their cries in both situations (Exod. 2.23). In Judges, just as in Exodus, the Israelites cry out in the midst of their suffering and Yahweh responds with compassion, raising up a savior who saves them (ישע). The Spirit of Yahweh (רוח יהוה) comes upon Othniel and he judges Israel, and he goes to war, and he accomplishes salvation. Yahweh, the God who saves them from the servitude of Egypt, now hears their cries and saves them from the servitude of Cushan-rishathaim.[9] The Spirit of Yahweh, therefore, strengthens Othniel for the task of breaking the community-threatening power of oppression.[10] With the coming of the Spirit, a 'process of emergence sets in, a process that in an unforeseen manner constitutes a new beginning, new relations, a new reality'.[11]

---

[7] See Stone, 'From Tribal Confederation to Monarchic State', pp. 260-89, who argues for the paradigmatic role of Othniel. Cf. Yairah Amit, *The Book of Judges: The Art of Editing* (trans. Jonathan Chipman; Biblical Interpretation 38; Leiden: Brill, 1999), p. 54.

[8] Welker, *God the Spirit*, p. 63.

[9] Cf. Brueggemann, *Theology of the Old Testament*, who shows the significance of the exodus tradition and how it is carried forward (pp. 173-81). See also Chapter 6 of this work below.

[10] Although the Spirit enables the judges to lead Israel into battle, Welker argues that the Spirit is not a 'spirit of war' (*God the Spirit*, pp. 52-58).

[11] Welker, *God the Spirit*, pp. 64-65.

The text seems to assume that the hearer[12] will know the meaning of the phrase רוח יהוה. It is well established that the Hebrew רוח has a broad semantic range that includes 'wind', 'breath', 'air', 'disposition', 'vigor', and 'spirit'.[13] In some cases, it is difficult to choose which of these meanings of רוח best fits the context;[14] but in most cases, an examination of biblical patterns of usage clarifies the meaning. Although there is some value in establishing an original core meaning such as 'air in motion' or the like,[15] such a broad definition is of little use in determining the meaning of רוח in a specific text. The context and collocations of רוח must take precedence over any diachronic or etymological reconstructions when determining the meaning of רוח in each context.[16]

The meaning of רוח as 'wind', while not bearing directly upon the book of Judges, is part of the conceptual fabric of the book's theology of salvation. Israel's primal salvation narrative is the exodus, which is effected by Yahweh's direct intervention, an intervention that sometimes comes through the agency of the mysterious and powerful רוח. Yahweh uses an east wind (רוח) to bring the locust plague against the Egyptians and a west wind (רוח) to drive them into the sea (Exod. 10.13, 19). It is the east wind (רוח) that Yahweh uses to divide the waters, allowing the Israelites to pass over on dry ground (Exod. 14.21). Dale Moody contends that 'the

---

[12] I prefer the term 'hearer' over 'reader', because 'hearing' expresses more precisely the goal of a Pentecostal approach to Scripture. See Chapter 3 of Martin, *The Unheard Voice of God*.

[13] *BDB*, pp. 924-25; *HALOT*, II, pp. 1198-2000.

[14] Furthermore, in some texts the meanings may interchange and merge into dynamic word play. E.g. Ezekiel 37 and Isaiah 40-42. On the nuances of רוח in the latter text, see John Goldingay, 'The Breath of Yahweh Scorching, Confounding, Anointing: The Message of Isaiah 40-42', *JPT* 11 (1997), pp. 3-34.

[15] Ludwig Köhler, *Old Testament Theology* (trans. A.S. Todd; Philadelphia: Westminster Press, 1957), p. 140; cf. J. Barton Payne, 'רוח', *TWOT*, II, p. 836. See also Walter C. Wright, 'The Use of *Pneuma* in the Pauline Corpus with Special Attention to the Relationship between *Pneuma* and the Risen Christ' (PhD Diss., Fuller Theological Seminary, 1977), pp. 10-16, who argues that the original meaning of רוח is probably 'breath'; and Harold D. Hunter, *Spirit-Baptism: A Pentecostal Alternative* (Lanham, MD: University Press of America, 1983), p. 23, who prefers 'wind' as the most fundamental meaning. Hunter's work was updated and reprinted as *Spirit Baptism: A Pentecostal Alternative* (Eugene, OR: Wipf & Stock, 2009).

[16] Cf. Alphonsus Benson, 'The Spirit of God in the Didactic Books of the Old Testament' (STD Diss., Catholic University of America, 1949), p. 71.

primacy of the exodus in Israel's faith promoted *ruach* as the metaphor for God's direct action in nature and history'.[17] This powerful רוח appears in the exodus story as the invading presence of God, of which Michael Green writes, 'the Beyond has come into our midst, and we can neither organize nor domesticate him'.[18]

More directly related to the book of Judges is the meaning of רוח as 'Spirit'. The intended audience of Judges would be aware of the Hebrew traditions regarding רוח as the Spirit of Yahweh and would import those traditions to this text. Furthermore, a hearer of the biblical narrative from Genesis to Judges would have some awareness of the nature and functions of the Spirit in relation to humanity, to the community and to leadership. For example, a hearer of the Torah would know that the abiding presence of Yahweh's Spirit sustains human life (Gen. 6.3); the Spirit gives Joseph the ability to interpret dreams (Gen. 42.38), thus saving Israel (Gen. 50.20); the Spirit enables artisans to construct the priestly garments (Exod. 28.3) and the tabernacle (Exod. 31.3; 35.31);[19] Yahweh's Spirit is upon Moses and is given to 70 elders who prophesy and who then serve as assistants to Moses (Num. 11.17-29); the Spirit of God inspires the prophecy of Balaam (Num. 24.2); Joshua is chosen to be Moses' successor because the Spirit is 'in' him (Num. 27.18); and when Moses lays his hands upon Joshua he is 'filled' with the Spirit (Deut. 34.9).[20] These texts seem to suggest that in the Torah the Spirit of God relates to humans as the *untamable gift of the energizing presence of Yahweh*.[21]

---

[17] Moody, *Spirit of the Living God*, pp. 13-14.
[18] Michael Green, *I Believe in the Holy Spirit* (I Believe 1; Grand Rapids, MI: Eerdmans, 1975), pp. 19-20.
[19] In the texts that I cite here, the Spirit of wisdom is clearly a gift of divine empowerment.
[20] Apparently, Joshua is chosen partly because the Spirit is already in him, yet the Spirit comes into him in even greater measure when Moses lays his hands upon him.
[21] Cf. Gordon D. Fee, *God's Empowering Presence: The Holy Spirit in the Letters of Paul* (Peabody, MA: Hendrickson Publishers, 1994), who concludes that the Spirit functions in the Old Testament as the 'empowering presence' of God (p. 8). While the trinitarian nature of the Spirit is not a concern of these texts, it has been noted that Yahweh is the only ancient Near Eastern deity who has a spirit. Other gods may control the *ruach* (wind), but they have no *ruach* (spirit): Lloyd R. Neve, *The Spirit of God in the Old Testament* (Centre for Pentecostal Theology Classics Series; Cleveland, TN: CPT Press, 2011), p. 1; and Hildebrandt, *An Old Testament Theology of the Spirit of God*, p. 5. Cf. Goldingay, *Israel's Gospel*, p. 541 who

Not only do these texts from the Torah clarify the nature and function of the Spirit of Yahweh, but they also prepare the hearer of Judges for the appearance of the Spirit in the story of Othniel. The coming of the Spirit upon Othniel is the only element of the cyclical pattern that is not explicitly named in the prologue; therefore, the hearer might be surprised by this first biblical appearance of the phrase רוח יהוה.[22] An examination of the Spirit's role in Israel's Torah, however, places Othniel within the trajectory of earlier leaders. That is, in light of the Spirit's empowerment of previous leaders (Joseph, Moses, the 70, and Joshua), the hearer of Judges might assume that Spirit empowerment is a necessary qualifier for leadership in Israel and that the 'personal encounter is not for its own sake – it is for the sake of the community'.[23] Thus, the importance of Othniel's reception of the Spirit becomes clearer as the 'mark of God's chosen' leader,[24] and the Spirit's authorization of Othniel positions him in the company of the past heroes of Israel.

The commissioning of leaders by Yahweh often includes the promise that his presence will be *with* the leader. It might be argued that the phrase רוח יהוה is a way of speaking about this personal *presence* of Yahweh. Therefore, we hear Yahweh say to Moses, 'I will be with you' (Exod. 3.12), and later we hear that Yahweh's Spirit is upon Moses (Num. 11.17-29). In the same fashion, we hear the narrator of Judges say that Yahweh will be 'with' the judges that he raises up (Judg. 2.18.), and later we hear that the Spirit of Yahweh comes upon Othniel (3.10).[25] Further into Judges, we hear Yahweh say to Gideon, 'I will be with you', then we hear that the Spirit of

---

contends that the *ruach* of Yahweh indicates that he is present 'in part, but not in whole'.

[22] The phrase רוח יהוה occurs 27 times in the Hebrew Bible. Although the phrase is not found in the canon prior to Judges, there are two texts in which the Spirit is suffixed by a possessive pronoun whose antecedent is Yahweh. Yahweh speaks of 'my Spirit' (Gen. 6.3), and Moses remarks, 'would that all of the people of Yahweh were prophets and that Yahweh would put his Spirit upon them' (Num. 11.29).

[23] Brueggemann, *Theology of the Old Testament*, p. 571. Cf. Welker, *God the Spirit*, who insists, 'in no instance is the descent of the Spirit merely a private affair' (p. 75); and Benson, 'Spirit of God', p. 72.

[24] Wolf, 'Judges', p. 398.

[25] See Amit, *Judges: Art of Editing*, p. 161, who apparently recognizes the correlation between 2.18 and 3.10, since she places the two verses opposite each other in a chart.

Yahweh 'clothed' Gideon (6.34). The coming of the Spirit, therefore, corresponds to the promise that God will be 'with' his chosen leader[26] and is a manifestation of the presence of Yahweh.[27]

As the presence of Yahweh, the Spirit that comes upon Gideon and the other judges is designated as the Spirit of 'Yahweh' (יהוה) rather than the Spirit of 'God' (אלהים). This consistent use of 'Yahweh' over 'God' adds a personal quality to the narrative, since Yahweh is the distinctive personal name of Israel's covenant God.[28] The book of Judges prefers the name 'Yahweh', which appears 175 times, over the broader name 'God', which is used only 15 times;[29] and up to this point in Judges, the name 'Yahweh' is used in every reference to the God of Israel except in the speech of Adoni-bezek (1.7). Therefore, it is Yahweh who swears to give the land to the Israelites (2.1); it is Yahweh who brings them up out of Egypt (2.1); it is Yahweh who promises to keep covenant forever (2.1); it is Yahweh who directs the tribes in the conquest (1.1-2); it is Yahweh who gives the Canaanites and Perizzites into the hand of Israel (1.4); it is Yahweh who gives victories to Judah and Joseph (1.19-22); it is Yahweh who sends his angel (2.1); it is Yahweh to whom the Israelites make sacrifice (2.5); it is Yahweh who is angered by Israel's idolatry (2.14); and it is Yahweh who promises to raise up judges (2.16). Consequently, it is the Spirit of Yahweh which comes upon Othniel in order to assure the realization of Yahweh's commitments.[30]

I would argue that the personal name 'Yahweh' claims priority in Judges because it is Yahweh who is the creator of Israel as an alternative egalitarian community that stands over against the oppressive regimes of Egypt and Canaan.[31] The Spirit of Yahweh, therefore,

---

[26] Webb, *Judges: An Integrated Reading*, p. 127.

[27] Cf. Moody, *Spirit of the Living God*, p. 12.

[28] Cf. Stanley M. Horton, 'The Holy Spirit in the Book of Judges', *Paraclete* 3 (1969), pp. 9-14 (14).

[29] The number 15 does not include the 10 places where the phrase 'Yahweh God' (יהוה אלהים) occurs, because in those cases the more general name (אלהים) is subordinate to the personal name (יהוה).

[30] The phrase *ruach Yahweh* demonstrates that 'it is Yahweh himself who came to the rescue by raising up the judge/deliverer'. Barnabas Lindars, *Judges 1-5: A New Translation and Commentary* (Edinburgh: T&T Clark, 1995), p. 134.

[31] Cf. George E. Mendenhall, 'Hebrew Conquest of Palestine', *BA* 25 (1962), pp. 66-87 (73-86).

comes upon Othniel in resistance to Cushan-rishathaim, who represents the Canaanite system of tyrannical city-states. Yahweh is the God who stands outside every human system of power, control, and oppression and who critiques those systems and who, as divine warrior, delivers his people from the domination of those evil systems.[32] Yahweh is Israel's king, her suzerain, who guarantees freedom from the human structures of authority that seek to dominate and enslave. The Spirit of Yahweh, therefore, is the Spirit of the Mosaic covenant, the Spirit that is 'at work giving new order and new orientation',[33] the Spirit of a new kind of God who is not beholden to human centers of power. The Spirit of Yahweh is the Spirit of the God who is free to bestow his saving power upon whomsoever he will, who is faithful to his covenant people, who passionately embraces those who suffer, and who suffers with them.[34] Consequently, the Spirit functions in the Othniel cycle to authorize and enable Othniel as a warrior judge who accomplishes Yahweh's salvation of Israel (3.9).

This first judge is a person who knows the struggle against the Canaanites and who is known as a victor (Judg. 1.11-15); in fact, he is the only victor in the first chapter of Judges who is mentioned by name. Othniel, the nephew of Caleb, defeats the town of Kiriath-sepher and achieves notoriety as a local leader.[35] However, once Yahweh determines to save Israel from Cushan-rishathaim, he chooses Othniel as the first of the judges, and Othniel is propelled beyond the level of clan leader to the status of national savior. Although historical evidence indicates that the judges ruled as tribal chieftains over small regions, the narrative of Judges portrays them

---

[32] Cf. Bruce C. Birch *et al.*, *A Theological Introduction to the Old Testament* (Nashville: Abingdon Press, 1999), pp. 113-14. See also, Georges Auzou, *La Force de l'Esprit, Étude du 'Livre des Juges'* (Paris: Éditions de l'Orante, 1966), p. 75, who insists that the power of the Spirit is always for the liberation of the land. Auzou writes, 'Il est manifeste, d'autre part, que ce don d'une énergie supérieure est en relation avec la libération du territoire sauf dans le texte de 14, 6, il s'agit toujours d'ennemis à vaincre, à exterminer ou à expulser'.

[33] Welker, *God the Spirit*, p. 51.

[34] Solivan, *The Spirit, Pathos and Liberation*, highlights the biblical witness to God's redeeming compassion (pp. 72-77) and maintains that the Spirit-filled church will imitate the compassion of God in formation of redemptive community (pp. 103-112).

[35] I find no evidence for Welker's contention that the Spirit uses leaders who do 'not really fit into any community' (*God the Spirit*, p. 51).

as national leaders.[36] Therefore, in the account of Othniel's rule, his tribal affiliation is not mentioned, but he is identified as one who 'judged Israel' (3.10).[37] The narrative, by repeatedly utilizing the terms 'Israel' (ישראל) and 'sons of Israel' (בני ישראל), frames the story in terms of national participation and significance. The first judge, therefore, is a person who is recognized as a local leader but who is subsequently authorized and empowered by the Spirit of Yahweh to enter a larger arena of influence. In this regard, Othniel stands in continuity with the 70 elders, who before the Spirit 'rested' (נוח) upon them (Num. 11.25) were known (ידע) to be leaders (Num. 11.16) and with Joshua, who before the Spirit 'filled' (מלא) him (Deut. 34.9) had the Spirit 'in' (ב) him (Num. 27.18) and served as Moses' assistant.

The text declares that 'the Spirit of Yahweh came upon Othniel', and the Hebrew phrase 'came upon him' (ותהי עליו) is suggestive of several points: 1. As mentioned above, it is the Spirit who is the active subject of the verb, and Othniel is a recipient of the action; 2. The Spirit is not a part of Othniel either physically or psychologically, but comes to him from outside; 3. The Spirit's action registers Yahweh's movement from perceived absence to perceived presence;[38] and 4. The phrase 'came upon' is a vivid figure of speech that signifies a theological concept in phenomenological terms.

The theological concept is that the Spirit of Yahweh empowers, energizes, and equips Othniel for the task of saving the Israelites. It has been asserted almost universally that the work of the Spirit in Judges is temporary and external rather than lasting and inward.[39] Although the text is nearly silent regarding the exact nature of the Spirit's work in the Old Testament, the judges show evidence of courage, wisdom, and faith, traits which are produced by the coming of the Spirit and which might easily be understood as manifesting an inward work. I am not arguing that an inward transforming

---

[36] Cf. Wellhausen, *Prolegomena to the History of Israel*, p. 234.

[37] For a more thorough discussion of the nationalistic agenda of Judges, see Chapter 5 of Martin, *The Unheard Voice of God*.

[38] Cf. Horton, 'The Holy Spirit in the Book of Judges', p. 14, who writes that the Spirit is not 'a mere influence coming from a God who is far away'.

[39] It should not be surprising that scholars differ in their interpretations of the Old Testament data regarding the Spirit, given the persistent diversity of interpretations of the more abundant New Testament data.

work of the Spirit is a primary concern of the texts in Judges; I insist only that the possibility of an inward work of the Spirit should not be discounted before the evidence is examined. The external language of 'coming upon' presents no difficulty, since even the New Testament also uses terminology that seems to represent an outward presence of the Spirit when the theological interpretation requires an inward transformation. Jesus promises his disciples that after he goes away, he will send another paraclete, who will remain 'with' (μετά) them forever (Jn 14.16). In the book of Acts, in a time when theologians expect the Spirit to be 'inside' the Christian, we read that the Spirit 'fell upon' (ἐπέπεσεν ... ἐπὶ) the believers at Cornelius' house (Acts 10.44). I would contend that, in both the Old and New Testaments, the Spirit originates from without the believer but produces effects within the believer.[40] Gideon, who appears later in Judges, experiences the transformative effect of the coming of the Spirit. J. Paul Tanner argues that the Gideon narrative is structured to highlight Gideon's fear and to show the change that transpired in Gideon as God crafted the circumstances in such a way that Gideon moves from fear to faith.[41] Earlier in the canon, the spirit is 'upon' Moses, but his journey of faith bears the marks of genuine spiritual formation under the continuing influence of the Holy Spirit. The narratives of Joseph and Joshua record a similar depth of spiritual growth.

In regard to the duration of the Spirit's presence with the judges, it should be noted that episodic charismatic endowments can be found as well in the New Testament book of Acts. The ability of the Apostles to perform signs and wonders is not continuous and neither is it within their control (Acts 5.3-11; 13.9-11; 16.16-18). These temporary endowments, however, do not negate the ongoing, inward working of the Spirit in the same persons. Similarly, the judges experienced temporary charismatic endowments, but the

---

[40] For a discussion of the inward work of the Spirit in the Old Testament, particularly in the life of David, see Leonard P. Maré, 'Some Remarks on the Spirit of God in the Life of David', *EP* 88 (2006), pp. 30-41 (35-40). See also, Gary Fredricks, 'Rethinking the Role of the Holy Spirit in the Lives of Old Testament Believers', *TJ* 9.1 (1988), pp. 81-104; and E. John Hamlin, *At Risk in the Promised Land: A Commentary on the Book of Judges* (ITC; Grand Rapids, MI: Eerdmans, 1990), p. 95.

[41] J. Paul Tanner, 'The Gideon Narrative as the Focal Point of Judges', *BSac* 149 (1992), pp. 146-61 (160).

text gives some indication that the Spirit continued to be with them. Yahweh, for example, is said to be 'with' the judge, and Yahweh saves Israel 'all the days of the judge' (2.18). Once the judges were chosen by Yahweh and endowed with the Spirit, those judges continued to serve for a number of years (8.28; 10.2, 3; 12.7, 9, 11, 14; 15.20; 16.31). Furthermore, it is said of Samson that 'Yahweh departed from upon him' (16.20), a statement that might suggest the Spirit's ongoing presence until that point in time.[42]

Even though the nature of the Spirit's work may continue to be disputed, the emphasis of the text seems clear enough – Yahweh chooses to impart his energizing presence to Othniel, making him a human participant in Yahweh's salvific plan.[43] On the one hand, Yahweh is free to work independently of human agents, sometimes arranging events, routing the enemy, and employing natural forces to bring about Israel's salvation. In fact, he sometimes works *against* Israel in this fashion, giving the unfaithful Israelites into the power of their enemies, and in the process, he 'strengthens' the enemy (Judg. 3.12). His strengthening of the enemy, however, is impersonal and from a distance, since at no time do we hear that the Spirit of Yahweh comes upon one of the enemy leaders.[44] On the other hand, when Yahweh decides to move on behalf of Israel, he recruits a human partner who serves in an active role of leadership, a human partner who 'succeeds in restoring loyalty, solidarity, and the capacity for communal action among the people'.[45] The story of Othniel, therefore, witnesses to the 'important role of human agency in partnership with the redeeming activity of God'.[46]

These human agents, raised up by Yahweh, are not members of a hereditary line of leaders; their authority derives from the charismatic endowment of the Spirit.[47] Moreover, there is no indication

---

[42] In a similar fashion, I would argue that the Spirit was present with Moses throughout his time of leadership (Num. 11.17-29) and the Spirit continued to be upon Joshua as well (Deut. 34.9; Num. 27.18). Later in the canon, the Spirit was with Saul until 'Yahweh departed from him' (1 Sam. 16.14). Cf. the prayer that is attributed to David, 'take not thy Holy Spirit from me' (Ps. 51.11).

[43] Cf. Horton, *Holy Spirit*, p. 35.

[44] The Spirit, however, comes upon a non-Israelite, Balaam, for the purposes of saving Israel. Cf. the naming of Cyrus as the Lord's 'anointed' (Isa. 45.1).

[45] Welker, *God the Spirit*, p. 53; cf. p. 56.

[46] Birch *et al.*, *A Theological Introduction to the Old Testament*, p. 122.

[47] Rea, *Holy Spirit*, p. 49.

in the text that Othniel seeks the position of judge or that he in any way controls the working of the Spirit. It is Yahweh who takes the initiative to choose Othniel and who functions as the active subject in the phrase, 'Yahweh raised up a savior' (3.9). Then it is the Spirit of Yahweh who is subject in the phrase, 'the Spirit of Yahweh came upon him' (3.10). The Spirit of Yahweh is not under human control and cannot be domesticated for human purposes. Only after Yahweh takes action in choosing Othniel and the Spirit of Yahweh takes action in coming upon him does Othniel take action to judge Israel and go to war. Othniel is moved by the Spirit to participate with Yahweh in the divine liberating mission. Yahweh, therefore, is moved by the cries of Israel, and Othniel is moved by the coming of the Spirit.

Gideon: Timorous Warrior

Only four of the judges are said to be empowered by the Spirit of Yahweh, yet it might be inferred from the paradigmatic nature of the Othniel story that the Spirit of Yahweh comes upon all of the judges. Moreover, the Hebrew Bible's apparent valuing of Spirit empowerment as enablement for leadership could point to the same conclusion – that every judge is empowered by the Spirit. However, since the biblical text does not directly ascribe the Spirit of Yahweh to Ehud or Deborah, I will not attend to their stories, except to say that the expected cyclical pattern of sin, punishment, cry, and deliverance provides the narrative framework for the stories.

The fourth appearance of the cyclical framework identifies Gideon as the second of the judges to be explicitly empowered by the Spirit of Yahweh. The Midianites, the oppressors in the Gideon story, are more destructive than Israel's previous subjugators (Judg. 6.1-6). The Midianites have so terrified Gideon that he fearfully threshes his grain in his wine press so that he will not be discovered and plundered (6.11). There at the wine press, the angel of Yahweh confronts Gideon with a surprising declaration – 'Yahweh is with you, mighty warrior' (6.12). The truth of the angel's statement is denied by Gideon, who gives voice to his frustration by recounting Israel's deliverance from Egypt and then lamenting, 'but now

Yahweh has forsaken us and given us into the hands of the Midianites' (6.13).

Unlike Othniel, Gideon has no previous experience as a warrior or as a leader, and the hearer of the story might wonder why Gideon is chosen as a judge. Although the text does not specify the reason for Yahweh's recruitment of Gideon, I would point to two suggestive elements in the text. First, Gideon displays knowledge of Israel's salvation from the bondage of Egypt, and he questions why Yahweh's saving power has not been exercised to deliver Israel from the oppression of the Midianites. Gideon's reference to the 'wonders' (נפלאת) of the past could indicate that his family ('ancestors', v. 13) had sung the Song of Moses, which speaks of the 'wonders' of Yahweh's salvation (Exod. 15.11; see also Josh. 3.5). At the least, Gideon is clearly aware of the traditions of the exodus, and he has yearned for divine deliverance in his own time. Second, it is revealed later in the story that Gideon's own father is guilty of syncretism and harbors an altar to Baal (6.25). Gideon, therefore, is an appropriate choice for the role of judge, since he is intimately aware of the idolatry of the Israelites, and he has contemplated the traditions of Yahweh's saving power. The angel of Yahweh proceeds to commission Gideon himself as Yahweh's instrument of salvation (ישע). Thus Gideon, who charges God with failing to save Israel, is himself charged with the task of salvation, and Yahweh promises to 'be with' him (6.16).

Gideon's first encounter with God exhibits numerous similarities to the call narrative of Moses[48] and casts Gideon as a new Moses,[49] invested with divine authority, who will deliver the Israelites from oppression. A comparison of the stories reveals the following points of contact, most of which involve the call narrative: 1. Gideon is working for his father while hiding from the Midianites (Judg. 6.11), and Moses is in hiding while working for his father-in-law, a Midianite (Exod. 3.1); 2. The angel of Yahweh acts as initial agent of encounter (Judg. 6.11; Exod. 3.2); 3. The deliverance from Egypt is central to both encounters (Judg. 6.13; Exod. 3.10); 4. The speaker changes from the angel to Yahweh (Judg. 6.14; Exod. 3.4); 5. Both are called to save Israel (Judg. 6.14; Exod. 3.10); 6. Both are

---

[48] Smith, 'Remembering God', pp. 634-38.
[49] Lindars, 'Gideon and Kingship', p. 317.

sent (שלח) by Yahweh (Judg. 6.14; Exod. 3.10); 7. Both offer objections to the call (Judg. 6.15; Exod. 3.11); 8. Both are given signs (Judg. 6.17; Exod. 4.2-8); 9. Yahweh says to both, 'I will be with you' (Judg. 6.16; Exod. 3.12); 10. Yahweh produces miraculous fire (Judg. 6.21; Exod. 3.2); 11. A staff is used to produce a miraculous sign (Judg. 6.21; Exod. 4.2-3); 12. The initial acts of both Gideon and Moses create controversy (Judg. 6.25-32; Exod. 5.21); 13. Both narratives involve the collection of gold to make an idol (Judg. 8.24-27; Exod. 32.2-4);[50] 14. Gideon names his firstborn 'Jether', the name of the father-in-law of Moses (Judg. 8.20; Exod. 4.18);[51] 15. The stories of both Gideon and Moses include episodes of failure near the end (Judg. 8.27; Num. 20.11-12). The references to the exodus and the similarities between Gideon and Moses combine to place the 'Gideon saga in the framework of the Yahweh covenant'.[52]

Since Gideon seems destined to imitate Moses' salvation of Israel, the hearer is not surprised when the Spirit of Yahweh comes upon Gideon. Gideon's first act of obedience, however, is performed before the Spirit enters the narrative (6.25-32). The Spirit of Yahweh comes upon Gideon only after we learn of the impending attack of the enemy. The Midianites assemble their army, cross the Jordan River and encamp in the Valley of Jezreel. Then, 'the Spirit of Yahweh clothed Gideon, and he sounded the *shofar*' (6.34).[53] The effect of the Spirit is immediate, as Gideon assembles the Abiezrites and the tribes of Manasseh, Asher, Zebulun, and Naphtali, and they go up to engage the Midianites in battle (6.35). The Spirit of Yahweh, working through Gideon, creates a 'renewal of the people's unanimity and capacity for action, a renewal of the people's power of resistance in the midst of universal despair'.[54]

---

[50] A. Graeme Auld, 'Gideon: Hacking at the Heart of the Old Testament', *VT* 39 (1989), pp. 257-67 (257).
[51] Klein, *The Triumph of Irony in the Book of Judges*, p. 62.
[52] Lindars, 'Gideon and Kingship', p. 317
[53] The grammar indicates a compound sentence with the first clause providing circumstance to the second clause. Consequently, the coming of the Spirit and Gideon's sounding of the trumpet are united into a single event. Oddly enough, this grammar places the Spirit's action in the background while the blowing of the trumpet is in the foreground. See Alviero Niccacci, *The Syntax of the Verb in Classical Hebrew Prose* (trans. Wilfred G.E. Watson; JSOTSup 86; Sheffield: JSOT Press, 1990), pp. 64-66.
[54] Welker, *God the Spirit*, p. 53.

Gideon's first work had been a private project, achieved under the cover of darkness, but after the Spirit comes upon him, he positions himself as a public leader who emerges from the shadows into the light of day. Before the Spirit strengthens Gideon, he stands by in silence while his father defends his actions (6.28-32); but after the Spirit comes upon him, Gideon speaks for himself.

Although interpreters agree that the Spirit empowers Gideon in some fashion, they do not agree on the correct translation of לבשה, the Hebrew verb that is used to describe the coming of the Spirit of Yahweh upon Gideon.[55] The most common use of the *qal* verb לבש is 'put on',[56] which would produce the translation, 'The Spirit of Yahweh put on Gideon'. In this translation, therefore, Gideon is the garment that clothes the Spirit, and the Spirit is on the inside of Gideon. Most Bible versions, however, translate the verb לבש as 'clothe', or something similar, a translation that designates the Spirit as the clothing that covers Gideon. Some of these translations render לבש in a more literal sense, for example: 'came upon' (KJV, NASB, NIV), 'covered' (CJB), 'enveloped' (CSB, NAB, TNK), 'clothed around' (NJB), 'clothed' (ESV), and ἐνέδυσεν ('clothed', Codex Alexandrinus), and *induit* ('clothed', Vulgate). Other versions, however, choose to translate לבש according to its effect upon Gideon, for example: 'took possession of' (RSV, NRSV), 'took control of' (NET), and ἐνεδυνάμωσεν ('strengthened', Codex Vaticanus). The narrative seems to indicate, however, that terminology of possession and control is probably too strong, since there is no indication in the text that Gideon loses control of his own volition.

Notwithstanding the more common sense of לבש as 'put on', I contend (in agreement with most translations) that in this case there are good reasons to translate לבש as 'clothe'. First, other terminology would serve better if the writer wishes to locate the Spirit 'inside' Gideon. Other texts, for example, state that the Spirit 'enters' Ezekiel (Ezek. 2.2); the Spirit 'fills' Joshua, the artisans, and Micah (Deut. 34.9; Exod. 28.3; 31.3; 35.31; Mic. 3.8); and the Spirit is 'in' Joseph, Joshua, and Daniel (Gen. 41.38; Num. 27.18; Dan. 4.8, 9, 18; 5.11). Second, the meaning and significance of the 'clothing'

---

[55] The verb is *qal* perf. 3rd fem. sing. The fem. gender agrees with רוח (Spirit).
[56] *HALOT*, I, p. 519; *CHALOT*, p. 173. Cf. *BDB*, p. 527, which calls the Spirit's action an 'incarnation'.

metaphor is appropriate only if it is the Spirit who is the clothing. The functions of clothing are to give protection, beautification, identification, or covering; and if Gideon is the clothing of the Spirit, it would imply that Gideon provides the Spirit with these benefits. Third, although the argument is correct that a less ambiguous construction, 'Gideon was clothed (*pual*) by the Spirit',[57] could have been used, such a construction would make Gideon, rather than רוח, the subject of the verb.[58] It is important that Spirit is the subject (as in every case in Judges), since it is the Spirit, not Gideon, that initiates the encounter and confers power. Fourth, the *qal* passive form of לבש means 'clothed', not 'was put on', suggesting that the active form (which we have here) can mean 'clothe' rather than 'put on'.[59] Finally, the ambiguity of the Judg. 6.34 is mitigated by Job 29.14 where, like here, the object of clothing serves as the subject of the verb. The verse reads, 'I put on righteousness, and it clothed me (לבש); my just cause was like a robe and turban'. Job's statement that righteousness 'clothed' him is parallel to the final part of the verse, in which his 'just cause' (משפט) is like a robe and turban, both of which are objects of clothing. When the article of clothing serves as the subject, the verb does not mean 'put on', rather it means 'clothe' or 'cover'.[60] I agree, therefore, with Klein, who concludes that Gideon is 'surrounded by the spirit of Yahweh, as with a mantle; he "wears" the divine spirit'.[61]

If, as I have argued, the Spirit clothes Gideon, what is the significance of the imagery of clothing? The basic functions of clothing are to conceal (Gen. 3.21), to protect (Hag. 1.6), to adorn (2 Sam. 1.24), and to categorize the wearer within a social situation (Gen.

---

[57] Cf. 1 Kgs 22.10, where the *pual* ptc., 'clothed with garments', is found. Also, the *qal* passive ptc. is found in a number of texts. The expected passive form of לבש, the *nifal*, does not occur in the Hebrew Bible.

[58] See Nahum M. Waldman, 'The Imagery of Clothing, Covering and Overpowering', *JANES* 19 (1989), pp. 161-70, who argues that the wording of Judg. 6.34 may be a result of syntactic restructuring or grammatical transformation that results in the meaning 'clothe' for לבש (pp. 166-69). Waldman presents copious examples from the ANE and Rabbinical sources.

[59] 1 Samuel 17.5; Prov. 31.21; Ezek. 9.2, 11; 10.2, 6; 23.6, 12; 38.4; Dan. 10.5; 12.6; Zech. 3.3.

[60] *HALOT*, I, p. 519. Cf. J. Gamberoni, 'לבש', in *TDOT*, VII, p. 463; and Waldman, 'Imagery of Clothing', pp. 166-67. Waldman cites a parallel to Judg. 6.34, in which a G-form of *labasu* in Nuzi is used in the sense of 'clothe' (p. 165).

[61] Klein, *Triumph of Irony*, p. 55.

38.19). Gamberoni, who agrees that לבש in Judg. 6.34 means 'clothed', classifies the functions of clothing into the following categories: 1. 'without clothing, the individual would be helpless'; 2. clothing identifies social structures and a person's place in society; and 3. 'clothing can express close personal ties'.[62] Citing parallels in other ancient Near Eastern literature, Waldman insists that the imagery of clothing suggests that 'an additional force is added to the wearer' and that 'these qualities, worn by the bearers, add something to their basic natures. They are more than they might have been and are enhanced because of the wrapping of extra power'.[63] The Spirit of Yahweh, as the clothing of Gideon, protects him, empowers him, and identifies him as Yahweh's chosen judge who will lead the Israelites to freedom.[64]

Although the gift of the Spirit authorizes Gideon as a judge and empowers him for leadership, it does not immediately eliminate all of Gideon's weaknesses. Gideon continues to be hesitant and even fearful, as we learn from the further references to the theme of fear (6.27; 7.3, 10; 8.20) and from his repeated requests for assurance from Yahweh.[65] Gideon finally attains faith when he hears the voice of Yahweh speaking through an enemy soldier (Judg. 7.9-11), and he executes a miraculous rout of the Midianites.[66]

The subject of clothing is revisited near the end of the Gideon story when he chooses to commemorate his victories by constructing a golden ephod, which later becomes the object of idolatry (8.27, 33) and a 'snare' to Gideon and his family (8.27, cf. 2.3). The hearer may reflect upon the significance of Gideon's ephod of gold in light of the earlier text where Gideon is clothed by the Spirit. Gideon, it seems, is exchanging one type of clothing for another.

---

[62] Gamberoni, 'לבש', p. 461.

[63] Waldman, 'Imagery of Clothing', p. 163. Waldman cites primarily Sumerian and Akkadian literature, but he points to the same imagery in Syriac texts, Mandaic liturgies, and Aramaic incantation texts. However, according to Waldman, the Gideon text is unique in that other texts in the ANE name 'demons, illness, fear, etc., as the subjects, but there is no mention of a god covering a person' (p. 166). Neve's contention that *labash* registers a 'violent' action is unsubstantiated; see *Spirit of God*, pp. 19-20.

[64] Cf. Gray, *Joshua, Judges, and Ruth*, p. 233, who argues that the clothing of the Spirit signifies Gideon's authority.

[65] It is argued by Webb, *Judges: An Integrated Reading*, p. 150, that Gideon's fear is prominent in the story.

[66] See the discussion of Gideon in Chapter 3 above.

The clothing of the Spirit of Yahweh draws attention to the mission of Yahweh, the power of Yahweh, and to the type of leadership that aspires to the salvation of the community and to the prosperity of the community. Moreover, the clothing of the Spirit is an endorsement of charismatic authority. The ephod, however, is a priestly garment, a sign of institutional authority. Gideon's clothing of gold draws attention to the status and wealth that comes to him as a result of his victories and to the kind of leadership that aspires to personal acclaim and personal prosperity. In spite of the fact that Gideon refuses the offer of kingship, he adopts a lifestyle that is consistent with that of a monarch, multiplying to himself wives and wealth. The early Gideon is a timid man who is enveloped and overwhelmed by the Spirit of 'wonders', but the later Gideon is a confident man (8.1-21) who is enveloped and overwhelmed by a spirit of prestige.[67]

Jephthah: Injudicious Judge

The continuing idolatry of the Israelites signals the beginning of the fifth appearance of the cyclical framework, and Yahweh responds by giving them into the hands of the Philistines and the Ammonites. The Israelites cry out to Yahweh for his aid, but in light of the idolatry surrounding Gideon's ephod, the illegitimate rulership of Abimelech (ch. 9),[68] and two more implied cycles of sin and deliverance (10.1-5), Yahweh speaks directly to the Israelites and angrily declares that he is finished with them. He reminds the Israelites of the numerous times that he has saved them, yet they have continued to forsake him and serve foreign gods. He furiously rebukes them and announces that he will save them no more (10.13).

In the face of Yahweh's refusal to save the Israelites, the elders of Gilead, by their own initiative, seek out a commander to lead them in battle against the Ammonites, and Jephthah is chosen. He

---

[67] Cf. Jacobus Marais, *Representation in Old Testament Narrative Texts* (Biblical Interpretation 36; Leiden: Brill, 1998), p. 114, who writes that Gideon, 'having tasted power, turns on God and becomes his own god'.

[68] Instead of receiving the Spirit of Yahweh (רוח יהוה), Abimelech is undermined by 'an evil spirit' (רוח רעה) that is sent by Yahweh to bring enmity between Abimelech and the people of Shechem (Judg. 9.23).

is 'the son of a prostitute and a mighty warrior' (11.1), who had been driven out of his father's house and has become an outlaw (11.3). Jephthah, the only judge who is not raised up by Yahweh, agrees to lead the Israelites in battle in exchange for the promise of permanent power.

Having been received back into the community, Jephthah attempts diplomatic negotiation with the king of Ammon (11.12). In his communications with the foreign king, Jephthah credits Yahweh as the one who brought the Israelites out of the bondage of Egypt and gave the land to the Israelites (11.23). Moreover, Yahweh is the one to whom Jephthah looks for victory (11.9, 24, 27). Jephthah declares that he will not surrender the land in which he now enjoys a new position of status and a reborn sense of belonging. Having suffered previously the loss of land and the pain of exile, he is not willing to relinquish that which has been restored to him. Jephthah 'seeks to avoid military confrontation if possible, and he defers decisive powers to Yahweh',[69] but his fervent defense of Israel's claim upon the land and his submission of the case to Yahweh as judge (11.27) are not sufficient to convince the Ammonite king to reconsider his attack.

With the Ammonite and Israelite armies assembled for battle (10.17), Yahweh, who had threatened not to help Israel any more (10.13), shows himself once again to be the God of surprising grace and sends his empowering Spirit upon Jephthah (11.29). Although Yahweh does not participate in the selection of Jephthah as a judge, he nevertheless chooses to put his Spirit upon Jephthah. Could it be that Jephthah's recounting of the exodus and his concern for the land awakens Yahweh to action and moves him to put his Spirit upon Jephthah?[70] In any case, the fact that the LORD would put his Spirit upon a leader that had not been divinely chosen demonstrates that his concern for the safety of the community overrides any other considerations.

When the elders of Gilead choose Jephthah, he leads with a negotiated authority, which is centered in his proven abilities as a warrior; but when the Spirit of Yahweh comes upon him, Jephthah leads with a charismatic authority, which is centered in the proven

---

[69] Klein, *Triumph of Irony*, p. 89.
[70] This possibility is entertained as well by Schneider, *Judges*, p. 173.

abilities of Yahweh as Israel's warrior God. When Jephthah is chosen to lead the Gileadites, he makes an offer of peace to the Ammonites. His experience as a warrior would make him fully aware of the pain and death that comes with warfare, and he wisely pursues a peaceful resolution of the conflict. However, when it becomes clear that Jephthah's human attempts at peace have failed and the Ammonite king is intent on going to war against Israel, the Spirit of Yahweh comes upon Jephthah and moves him to attack the enemy and save Israel.[71] Jephthah's actions bear some resemblance to Moses' initial encounters with Pharaoh, in which Moses offers to negotiate the Israelites' peaceful migration out of Egypt. However, when Pharaoh will not allow the Israelites to depart in peace, Yahweh intervenes in a dramatic act of salvation. Similarly, the coming of the Spirit upon Jephthah leaves 'no doubt that Jephthah's victory against the Ammonites was considered to be Yahweh's saving act on behalf of Israel'.[72]

Even though Jephthah departs from the usual pattern for the judges, in that he is not raised up by Yahweh, his Spirit empowerment narrative corresponds in several ways to the narratives of earlier judges. First, the wording of the announcement, 'the Spirit of Yahweh came upon Jephthah', utilizes the same Hebrew phrase that had signaled earlier the Spirit's coming upon Othniel (ותהי על). Second, in the stories of both Gideon and Jephthah, the Spirit is given at a crucial juncture in the narrative when decisive action is required.[73] The Spirit clothes Gideon and he assembles the army; the Spirit comes upon Jephthah and he apparently adds to the already assembled army[74] and launches the attack. The Spirit descends in 'situations of danger in which no escape could be seen … situations of danger in which no hope remained'.[75] Third, as in the case of Gideon, the coming of the Spirit upon Jephthah does not nullify his personal volition nor eliminate all of his doubts. Even after Gideon receives the Spirit, he seeks a reassuring sign from God; and

---

[71] Cf. Gray, *Joshua, Judges, and Ruth*, p. 254. See Olson, 'Judges', who remarks that 'everything up to this point has involved human initiative' (p. 831).
[72] Boling, *Judges*, p. 207.
[73] The brief narrative concerning Othniel includes no details regarding the timing of the Spirit's coming upon him.
[74] Cf. Olson, 'Judges', p. 831.
[75] Welker, *God the Spirit*, p. 52.

after Jephthah receives the Spirit, he makes an unwise vow that he hopes will guarantee his victory.[76] Fourth, both Gideon and Jephthah display knowledge of Israel's deliverance from Egypt, and they manifest a degree of passion regarding Israel's claim to the land. Fifth, after their battles are decided, both Gideon and Jephthah engage in destructive behavior – Gideon builds his golden ephod, and Jephthah sacrifices his daughter.[77] The giving of the Spirit, therefore, does not guarantee that the recipient will pursue righteousness and act always in accordance with God's purposes. God grants even a Spirit-empowered leader the freedom to pursue ruinous behavior that can lead to disastrous consequences. Sixth, both Gideon and Jephthah face intertribal conflict with the Ephraimites. Gideon is able to defuse the tensions peacefully (8.1-3), but Jephthah fights against the Ephraimites and soundly defeats them (12.1-6).

The stories of Gideon and Jephthah seem to demonstrate that the power that flows from the Spirit to initiate and complete Yahweh's salvific mission can produce in the recipient a confidence that continues to manifest itself even after the initial mission has been accomplished. This confidence may then serve the recipient's own desires and purposes, which may be opposed to the purposes of God. Gideon's newfound boldness is registered in his cruel treatment of the people of Succoth and Penuel (8.4-17), and Jephthah's self-assertiveness is evident in his relentless pursuit of the Ephraimites (12.5-6). 'God's Spirit', remarks Dennis Olson, 'does, indeed, give special powers to leaders, but that power may be abused by unfaithful or misguided leaders'.[78]

It has been argued that since Jephthah's rash vow is subsequent to his reception of the Spirit, the Spirit bears some responsibility for Jephthah's unwise act,[79] and the same has been said of Gideon's

---

[76] Commenting on Gideon's and Jephthah's lack of assurance, Welker writes, 'those upon whom the Spirit comes are and remain imperfect, finite, mortal human beings' (*God the Spirit*, pp. 58-59).

[77] Not all interpreters accept that Jephthah actually offered up his daughter, but the text states that Jephthah 'did to her his vow that he had vowed' (11.39). Cf. Soggin, *Judges*, pp. 215-18. In any case, the question of Jephthah's folly is a matter of degree only, since the vow itself was injudicious. The Jephthah story may be within the view of Ps. 106.34-45, especially v. 37, 'they sacrificed their sons and their daughters'.

[78] Olson, 'Judges', p. 768.

[79] Exum, 'The Centre Cannot Hold', pp. 413, 422.

test with the fleece. Such a view, however, requires a degree of Spirit possession that overwhelms the recipient's personal volition, a degree of control that is nowhere indicated in the text.[80] In the book of Judges, the coming of the Spirit immediately produces specific actions. In the case of Othniel, the series of clauses reads: 'the Spirit of Yahweh came upon him, and he judged Israel, and he went out to war' (3.10). Once the Spirit comes upon him, he continues as the subject of the verbs until it is said that 'Yahweh gave' the enemy into his hand. In the case of Gideon, as I noted earlier, the coming of the Spirit is connected syntactically with the subsequent clause, in which Gideon sounds the alarm to assemble the army. In the case of Jephthah, the text reads: 'The Spirit of Yahweh came upon Jephthah, and he passed through Gilead and Manasseh, and he passed on to Mizpah of Gilead and from Mizpah of Gilead he passed over to the Ammonites' (11.29). The next verse, in which Jephthah makes his vow, stands outside the series of events that are directly attributed to the influence of the Spirit. The disjunction at the end of the series is indicated by two grammatical elements: 1. The final verb in the series of four verbs of v. 29 is not a *wayyiqtol*, but is an x-*qatal*, which breaks the series; and 2. The subsequent clause, which registers the vow, restates the named subject: 'And Jephthah vowed a vow to Yahweh' (11.30). The renaming of the subject, when no other subject has intervened in the series of clauses, suggests the beginning of a new series of events. After the episode of the vow, the narrative resumes at the place where it left off in v. 29, with the subject named once more as the signal of a new series of events: 'So Jephthah passed over to the Ammonites to fight against them' (11.32). I contend, therefore, that the undesirable acts of Gideon and Jephthah are not *provoked* by the Spirit but neither are they *prevented* by the Spirit.[81]

---

[80] Cf. Goldingay, *Israel's Gospel*, p. 543, who denies that the Spirit of Yahweh is implicated in the Jephthah's making of the vow. See also, Wong, *Compositional Strategy of the Book of Judges*, pp. 159-63. Wong points to the inconsistency of Exum's argument, in that she wants to attribute Jephthah's vow to the influence of the Spirit, but she does not attribute Gideon's quest for a sign to the same influence.

[81] Cf. Webb, *Judges: An Integrated Reading*, p. 62, who agrees that the vow interrupts the story of Jephthah.

In the story of Jephthah, the narrative continues to display the tension between Yahweh's anger and his compassion. The tension is evident in that, although the Spirit of Yahweh comes upon Jephthah and brings victory, the land is not granted a time of rest, as it is in earlier appearances of the cycle. The land cannot rest because Yahweh defeats only the Ammonites, and he does not remove the threat of the Philistines, who are listed as another enemy in this cycle (10.7). Furthermore, Yahweh does not prevent the sacrifice of Jephthah's daughter; he does not prevent the intertribal battles that follow Jephthah's victory; neither does he speak at any time during the narrative. Apparently, after Yahweh's declaration that he will not save Israel again (10.13), he is determined to intervene as little as possible, yet he is not prepared to allow Israel's complete destruction.[82] Moreover, by their continual idolatry, the Israelites become their own worst enemy, and although the Spirit of Yahweh saves the Israelites from the Ammonites, the Spirit of Yahweh does not save the Israelites from themselves.

Samson: 'Troubled' by the Spirit

For the final time in the book of Judges, the Israelites forsake Yahweh, who hands them over to an oppressive enemy, the Philistines (13.1).[83] The cyclical framework that begins to deteriorate with the Jephthah cycle breaks down completely in the Samson cycle. Although they are given over into the power of the Philistines, the Israelites surprisingly do not cry out for God's help, and they are not saved from the Philistines.

---

[82] For an insightful study of the increasingly ambiguous role of Yahweh in Judges, see Exum, 'The Centre Cannot Hold', pp. 410-31. Exum sees the lack of narrator comment in the final narratives as a failure to expound the theology of Judges, and she observes Yahweh's lack of participation in the stories of Jephthah and Samson. However, she does not make the connection to Yahweh's earlier statement that he will save Israel no more (10.13), and she does not appreciate the importance of the prologue nor recognize the role of the speeches of God within Judges (On the speeches of God, see Martin, *The Unheard Voice of God*). In contrast to Exum, P. Deryn Guest, 'Can Judges Survive without Sources? Challenging the Consensus', *JSOT* 78 (1998), pp. 43-61, denies the need for narrator comment in the final stories of Judges, believing the prologue alone to be sufficient theological explanation of the Judges period.

[83] Actually, the Philistines appear in Judg. 10.7 along with the Ammonites. Jephthah saves Israel from the Ammonites but he does not engage the Philistines.

The foregoing discussion has highlighted the numerous similarities between the judges while acknowledging the uniqueness of each, and Samson's story stands out in numerous ways.[84] Samson is the only judge whom Yahweh prepares from before birth to fill the role of judge. The angel of Yahweh predicts his birth and he is dedicated as a nazirite to God (Judg. 13.3-5). The narrative of Samson's birth classifies him as a person of destiny and creates in the hearer a sense of eager anticipation. Yahweh's unexpected breaking of his silence (after having threatened never to save Israel again) indicates that he may be returning to full engagement with his people, and Samson's miraculous birth might forecast divine blessings upon his life. The calling of Samson to be a nazirite adds to the sense of his purpose and devotion, and the annunciation narrative includes elements that bring to mind the call of Gideon, who was successful in saving the Israelites from their oppressor. Except for the puzzling declaration that Samson will 'begin' to save Israel, everything in ch. 13 indicates that Samson is poised to be the greatest judge of them all.[85]

Samson's early life is described concisely: 'The woman bore a son and called his name Samson. And the boy grew, and Yahweh blessed him. And the Spirit of Yahweh began to trouble him in Mahaneh-dan, between Zorah and Eshtaol' (13.24-25). Samson's potential for greatness is affirmed by the statements, 'the boy grew, and Yahweh blessed him', but the effect of the Spirit upon Samson is stated somewhat ambiguously in the subsequent phrase, 'the Spirit of Yahweh began to trouble him' (פעם). This is the only appearance of the verb פעם in the *qal* stem, and lexicons define it as 'impel, push',[86] or 'to stir, trouble'.[87] It seems likely that this first reference to the Spirit in Samson's life is a foreshadowing of what lies ahead in chs. 14-16, where it is the Spirit, rather than Samson's

---

[84] For a detailed exposition of Samson's uniqueness, see Greenstein, 'The Riddle of Samson', pp. 239-47. In spite of this uniqueness, see Webb, *Judges: An Integrated Reading*, pp. 164-67, who shows numerous comparisons between the Gideon and Samson narratives.

[85] Cf. J. Cheryl Exum, 'Promise and Fulfillment: Narrative Art in Judges 13', *JBL* 99 (1980), pp. 43-59 (49).

[86] *CHALOT*, p. 295.

[87] *HALOT*, II, p. 952.

status as a nazirite or his miraculous birth, that generates his power.[88]

Then again, the verb פעם may foreshadow the Samson story also in a more ominous way, given that in every other appearance in the Hebrew Bible it means 'to be troubled'. The Psalmist writes, 'I am troubled and cannot speak' (Ps. 77.5); Pharaoh's 'spirit was troubled' (Gen. 41.8); and King Nebuchadnezzar says, 'I dreamed a dream, and my spirit was troubled' (Dan. 2.3, also 2.1). Apparently, the stirring of the Spirit could be interpreted as a disconcerting or troubling event in the life of the young Samson. Is it possible that he is not altogether enthusiastic about or comfortable with the Spirit's activity in his life? We might infer from Samson's experience that the coming of the Spirit is not always and altogether a blissful encounter and that we should beware of 'superficial enthusiasm about the Spirit'.[89] Could the *troubling* effect of the Spirit's work in Samson be a clue to his later enigmatic behavior, or could it be a portent of Samson's tragic end, since it is the Spirit that 'sets in motion a process that does not end until Samson's tortured body is brought up from Gaza to be buried'?[90]

Ambiguities notwithstanding, we know that Samson is anointed as the chosen judge of Israel, and his strength flows from the Spirit of Yahweh. The Spirit rests upon Samson and we expect him, like earlier judges, to assemble the army of Israel and engage the enemy, but no such action ensues. The hearer's hopeful expectations regarding Samson go entirely unfulfilled, while Samson pursues his own agenda. Time after time, the Spirit comes upon Samson, but still Samson does not gather the Israelites for battle, and he does not eliminate the Philistine threat. The Spirit enables Samson to tear apart an attacking lion (14.6), to kill 30 Philistines in Ashkelon and take their clothing (14.19) and to break free of his bonds and kill one thousand Philistines with the jawbone of a donkey (15.14).

---

[88] Marc Z. Brettler, *The Book of Judges* (Old Testament Readings; New York: Routledge, 2002), p. 43.

[89] Welker, *God the Spirit*, p. 61. The prophets would agree; cf. Isa. 6.5-7; 49.4; Jer. 4.19; 12.1-3; Ezek. 3.14-15; Hos. 1.2-9; and Jon. 1.1-3; 4.1-2.

[90] Hamlin, *At Risk in the Promised Land*, p. 143. For פעם as a *Leitwort* in the Samson saga (15.3; 16.18, 20, 28), see O'Connell, *The Rhetoric of the Book of Judges*, pp. 44-45.

Each time the Spirit comes upon Samson in chs. 14 and 15, the Hebrew term is צלח, which means to 'succeed'[91] or 'attain',[92] but in some contexts seems to mean 'rush'.[93] For example, 'one thousand men rushed (צלח) to the Jordan ahead of the king' (2 Sam. 19.18); 'seek the Lord and live, lest he rush upon the house of Jacob like fire' (Amos 5.6). Although the Hebrew word may elude precise definition, its usage suggests a forcefulness that exceeds any of the other terms used in Judges to describe the coming of the Spirit. The same terminology describes the experience of Saul when he is engulfed in an ecstatic experience (1 Sam. 10.10). We learn from its use in relation to David, however, that the word does not necessarily include the idea of complete control. When David is anointed by Samuel, the Spirit rushes (צלח) upon him 'from that day forward' (1 Sam. 16.13), and nowhere in the text do we find the suggestion that the Spirit took control of David's body or his will. Consequently, I would argue that Samson is quite overwhelmed every time the Spirit comes upon him but nothing in the text suggests that the Spirit negates Samson's power of volition.[94] In fact, Samson's every act before the Lord departs from him (Judg. 16.20) appears to be driven by his own passions and his own will.

Samson's willfulness and self-centeredness are evident throughout the narratives of chs. 14-16, beginning with his insistence on marrying a Philistine woman despite the objections of his parents (14.1-3). His unruly behavior persists as he breaks his nazirite vows by touching the corpse of a dead lion (14.8-9), and as he visits a prostitute in Gaza (16.1). Because of his roguish conduct, Samson is often used as support for the view that persons in the Old Testament can be empowered by the Spirit but 'not purified', in contrast to the New Testament where it is assumed that purity and power are joined together.[95] In response to the discussions surrounding

---

[91] *HALOT*, II, p. 1026.
[92] J. Hausmann, 'צלח', in *TDOT*, XII, p. 383.
[93] *BDB*, p. 852. Cf. C.J. Goslinga, *Joshua, Judges, Ruth* (Grand Rapids, MI: Regency Reference Library, 1986), p. 422; and Rea, *Holy Spirit*, p. 55.
[94] Cf. Horton, *Holy Spirit*, pp. 40-41.
[95] Hunter, *Spirit-Baptism*, p. 25. On this issue, the New Testament is not as clear as we might assume, and the presence of sin in the lives of believers is a topic that continues to be disputed among Christian theologians.

purity and power, I would offer the following observations.[96] First, the God of Judges is free to distribute power to whomsoever he will, and at times he even empowers unbelievers (e.g. the Canaanites rulers). Second, the charismatic endowment of the Spirit in Judges is not always a sign of spiritual maturity or holy character. Fredricks argues that the same holds true in the New Testament age and in the present age:

> To assume that NT believers live on a higher plane of spirituality is to overlook the sins of division, immorality, and drunkenness in the church at Corinth, the legalism at Galatia, the idleness at Thessalonica as well as the numerous sins present in the Spirit-indwelled church today.[97]

Third, we must beware of constructing a purity and power dichotomy that distorts the message of the book of Judges. Judges is a book that from beginning to end registers Yahweh's exclusive claim upon the people of God. In Judges, sin is not excused, disobedience is not treated lightly, and idolatry does not go unpunished. Yahweh is so angered by the repeated rebellion of the Israelites that upon their single expression of repentance he refuses to forgive them. Fourth, the perspective on sin and idolatry in Judges is more communal than what we find in contemporary theology. The sanctifying work of the Spirit in the life of the individual is not a dominant concern of Judges, rather, the sanctification of the community in covenant takes precedence over the sanctification of the individual. This communal aspect of holiness deserves more attention, especially in this electronic age when humans, in spite of being better connected than ever before, bear little communal responsibility or accountability.[98] Fifth, while it is commonly assumed that the work of the Spirit in Judges is not soteriological (in the theological sense), perhaps our definition of 'soteriology' fails to appreciate the Old

---

[96] Regarding the questionable spiritual value of the judges; see Chapter 7 below.

[97] Fredricks, 'Holy Spirit in the Old Testament', p. 87. We might add to Fredricks' list the strife between Paul and Barnabas (Acts 15.39), the bigotry and hypocrisy of Peter (Gal. 2.11-14), and the sins of the seven churches of Asia Minor (Rev. 2.1-3.22).

[98] For a powerful call to communal holiness, see J. Ayodeji Adewuya, *Holiness and Community in 2 Cor. 6:14-7:1: Paul's View of Communal Holiness in the Corinthian Correspondence* (New York: Peter Lang, 2001).

Testament witness to God's saving acts.⁹⁹ After all, the judges are called 'saviors', and their actions are called 'salvation'. The Israelites are saved from both the physical/political bondage to Canaanite oppressors and from the spiritual bondage to Baal and Asherah, the gods of Canaan. At the end of the Samson saga, Yahweh strengthens Samson so that he might win both a physical and spiritual victory by destroying the temple of the Philistine god Dagon. Furthermore, as demonstrated above, salvation in Judges is cast in the tradition of the exodus, a tradition that is adopted in both the Old Testament and the New Testament as the paradigmatic salvation story.

In Judges the Spirit of Yahweh is given for the purpose of effecting the salvation of Israel, but even with his charismatic endowment Samson 'appears never to have had any concern for the interests of Israel'.¹⁰⁰ Thus, the most obvious discrepancy in the Samson story is his failure to fight for the salvation of Israel, a failure that accounts for the question mark in my title: 'Power to Save!?'. Does Samson, like the previous judges, receive the Spirit as power to save, or does the Spirit in the Samson story fulfill a different role? On the surface, it appears that the Spirit of Yahweh does no more than pull 'Samson out of his scrapes',¹⁰¹ but the Samson story is a complex narrative that operates from beginning to end around the themes of secret knowledge and riddles. It is not surprising, therefore, that the hearers of the story have questions.¹⁰² The actions of the Spirit of Yahweh are clear enough; the Spirit saves Samson from a lion (14.6), moves Samson to kill 30 Philistines and take their clothing (14.19), and saves Samson from being captured while at the same time giving him the strength to kill one thousand Philistines (15.14-

---

⁹⁹ Liberation theologies have heard this Old Testament witness, but the Western theological community has not always welcomed recent global theological insights. On the contribution of Pentecostalism to a broader concept of salvation, see Hollenweger, *The Pentecostals*, pp. 204-17, 246-57, and Richard Schaull, 'La Iglesia, Crisis y Nuevas Perspectivas', *Vida y Pensamiento* 15 (1995), pp. 8-48.

¹⁰⁰ Polzin, *Moses and the Deuteronomist*, p. 181. Cf. Montague, *The Holy Spirit*, p. 18.

¹⁰¹ Klein, *Triumph of Irony*, p. 125.

¹⁰² James L. Crenshaw, *Samson: A Secret Betrayed, a Vow Ignored* (Atlanta: John Knox Press, 1978), pp. 66-69. Cf. Greenstein, 'Riddle of Samson', pp. 246-47; and J. Cheryl Exum, 'Aspects of Symmetry and Balance in the Samson Saga', *JSOT* 19 (1981), pp. 3-29 (4-19).

15). The ultimate goal of Samson's Spirit inspired acts, however, is not easily discerned, because the Israelites do not seem to benefit from Samson's individualistic enterprise. Unlike the earlier judges, Samson never assembles the Israelites for battle against the enemy.

On the one hand, Samson's failure to save Israel might be due to his own disobedience, since the work of the Spirit 'is not effective apart from human participation'.[103] Perhaps he is simply unwilling to gather his people together into a unified force. On the other hand, the absence of salvation might be blamed upon the Israelite people, who do not ask to be saved from the Philistines but who seem content to live under the domination of the enemy. The pattern in the book of Judges is that Yahweh saves the Israelites subsequent to their cry unto him, and without their cry for help, Yahweh is not obligated to save.[104] Moreover, the Israelites' impertinence goes beyond their passive failure to cry out to Yahweh. They actively oppose the work of Samson when they insist that he forego any further attacks upon the Philistines, who, the Israelites say, 'rule over us' (Judg. 15.9-13).[105]

While both Samson and the Israelites bear some responsibility for their continued bondage to the Philistines, it must be acknowledged that Yahweh himself plays a significant role in the story. I have shown that after Yahweh refuses to save Israel again (10.13), he restricts his direct involvement with his people, but his actions in the Samson saga seem to suggest that he may desire to save them once again. Yahweh raises up Samson, promises that he will 'begin to save' the Israelites, blesses him, and endows him with the Spirit. Yahweh is involved both overtly (through the Spirit) and covertly

---

[103] McCann, *Judges*, pp. 65-66.

[104] It should be noted that Yahweh answers the cries that emerge in the Samson narrative. Manoah's prayer is answered (13.8), and so are those of Samson (15.18; 16.28). Wong, *Compositional Strategy of Judges*, pp. 163-64, observes that Samson's fear that he will die of thirst, parallels the doubts of Gideon and Jephthah, which they expressed after the Spirit had come upon them. The cries of Samson, argues Exum, are the goal of the narrative ('Aspects of Symmetry and Balance', pp. 22-24). Cf. J. Cheryl Exum, 'The Theological Dimension of the Samson Saga', *VT* 33 (1983), pp. 30-45 (45). Exum adds, 'The absence of Israel's cry at the beginning of the Samson story perhaps finds compensation in Samson's cry to Yhwh in 16:28-30' ('The Centre Cannot Hold', p. 425).

[105] The words of the Israelites hark back to Gideon's declaration, 'Yahweh will rule over you' (8.23). Cf. also the initial complaint against Moses' efforts of salvation (Exod. 5.15-23).

(manipulating events in the background).[106] Although neither the Israelites nor Samson show any interest in fighting the Philistines, Yahweh seeks 'an occasion against' them (14.4). Still, Israel is not saved, and they are not saved because the Spirit never urges Samson to assemble an army to resist the Philistines.[107] The Spirit comes upon Othniel, Gideon, and Jephthah, prompting them to assemble the troops for battle; but the Spirit never prompts Samson to raise an army. Apparently, Yahweh's intention is not to save the Israelites, but only to 'begin' to save them (13.5).[108]

This aim of partial salvation is acceptable to Yahweh because the Philistines have not yet created unbearable conditions for the Israelites. Although the Philistines oppress Israel, the text does not portray them as an immediate threat to the survival of Israel. Therefore, since Yahweh has determined to limit his involvement with Israel, he does not compel Samson to engage in full-scale war. From the moment that Yahweh refuses to save the Israelites again (10.13), he saves them only from the most imminent danger. Never again in Judges are the Israelites freed completely from oppression.

Yahweh's intention to initiate salvation but not to complete it helps to explain the role of the Spirit in the life of Samson.[109] Although the Spirit does not save all of Israel, the Spirit saves Samson three times. Whenever Samson finds himself in a life-threatening situation, the Spirit of Yahweh comes upon him, enabling him to escape.[110] Twice he is engaging the enemy in battle, and without the aid of the Spirit, he certainly would be defeated. Upon close examination, therefore, we can discern the element of salvation within the work of the Spirit in the life of Samson. When the Spirit comes upon Samson it is to save him from imminent danger. On

---

[106] Exum, 'The Centre Cannot Hold', p. 424, remarks that 'everything is determined by God without the knowledge (or consent?) of those involved'.

[107] Cf. McCann, *Judges*, p. 101.

[108] Contra Crenshaw, *Samson*, pp. 133-34, who writes, 'Eager to deliver Israel from the Philistines, he raises up Samson'.

[109] That the story of Samson represents the story of Israel is argued convincingly by Greenstein, 'Riddle of Samson', pp. 247-55; but Greenstein's assertion (p. 253) that 'Samson does not fight *for* Israel because Samson *is* Israel' holds up only at the figurative level. It is not convincing at the narrative level, which still requires an explanation for the inaction of the judge Samson.

[110] Contra Welker, *God the Spirit*, who denies that Samson's exploits are salvation stories (pp. 66-71).

one occasion the Spirit of Yahweh is responsible both for placing Samson in danger and then for saving Samson from that danger. The Spirit moves Samson to go down to Ashkelon, attack 30 Philistines and steal their clothing (14.19). Without the Spirit, Samson would not have been able to defeat the 30 men and escape from the Philistine city of Ashkelon. The Ashkelon episode is part of the wedding narrative and grows out of the earlier text that states Yahweh's desire to fight against the Philistines (14.4). Yahweh does not intend to deliver Israel, but neither will he permit the Philistines to grow comfortable. Perhaps in the Samson story Yahweh is not so much *for* Israel as he is *against* the Philistines. The conclusion to Yahweh's battle against the Philistines comes when 'Samson tears down not just a local shrine, but the very temple of Dagon ... the *climax* towards which the whole narrative moves'.[111]

It is beyond the scope of this study to examine all the nuances of the Samson saga; and my interpretation, though carefully considered, is provisional and open to modification.[112] The difficulty in defining the role of the Spirit of Yahweh in the Samson story derives from the enigmatic nature of the entire story. It has been

---

[111] Webb, *Judges: An Integrated Reading*, p. 167. Cf. Greenstein, 'Riddle of Samson', p. 252.

[112] Welker, *God the Spirit*, p. 67, argues that 'Samson is chosen as a troublemaker who shall make clear the evil and deviousness of the Philistines, and at the same time show that the strong and clever Israelite can be superior to them'. I commend the efforts of Welker, who, like the rest of us, is scrambling to find a tenable explanation for the Spirit's continued presence in the life of Samson. Welker, however, seems to base his interpretation of Samson as an 'integrative figure' not upon the narrative itself but upon the socio-political situation that stands behind the narrative. At several points Welker's comments are at odds with the biblical narrative. For example, he claims that in the Samson story the Spirit gives 'steadfastness in affliction' (p. 65), but steadfastness is not to be found in Samson or in the Israelites. Welker states further that the Spirit, through Samson, forges in the people of Israel an 'identity of resistance' (p. 68), causing them to 'unite with him in solidarity' (p. 72) and to gather 'behind Samson' (p. 74); but the people never resist the Philistines or unite behind Samson. Welker speaks of the 'power in [Samson'] hair' (p. 70), when in fact his hair is only a symbol of his power. He identifies Samson as a facilitator of Israel's moral 'formation of identity' (p. 73); but at the end of the story, Israel is more de-formed than ever before. He claims that the Philistines are 'an affliction that cannot be removed' (p. 69), but in the world of the text it has been demonstrated through the earlier judges that deliverance is always possible. Finally, I would encourage Welker to consider the views of prominent scholars such as R. Boling, J. Crenshaw, L. Klein, J.C. Exum, and E. Greenstein, none of whom are cited in his study.

argued that the Samson narrative is replete with intentional ambiguity,[113] and it 'epitomizes the paradoxical mode of representation'[114] in Judges and other Old Testament texts by defying all efforts to find a unifying ideology/theology that will explain all of the questions. Moreover, Polzin contends that no 'systematic model of divine mercy and justice' can bring coherence to the Samson cycle.[115] Nevertheless, I perceive a kind of clarity in the incoherence and a certainty in the ambiguity. The Samson saga's narrative clarity/incoherence and certainty/ambiguity find their source and explication in the dynamic relational disposition of Yahweh, who is both angry and compassionate (Judg. 2.14, 18), who both sentences and saves (Judg. 3.8, 10), who both wounds and heals (Judg. 15.18-19), who rejects but then relents (Judg. 16.20, 30), and who is free and yet bound to Israel by his own eternal covenant (Judg. 2.1).

Conclusion

In Judges the Israelites violate their covenant with Yahweh by pursuing other gods, thereby provoking the wrath of Yahweh, who gives his people over to an enemy power. Once in bondage to oppressive forces, they 'cannot evade the superior power, and their powers of resistance are inadequate. The force that is oppressing or threatening the people, the attacking enemy, is simply stronger.'[116] The Israelites, therefore, require a deliverer who is empowered by the Spirit of Yahweh and who will restore hope, build unanimity, and lead them to salvation. Even after their dramatic deliverance from Egypt, the Israelites continue to be tempted and seduced by outside forces, and once the people of God have yielded to those forces, the seducing powers control and threaten to destroy the community. It is Yahweh's saving power, exercised in the giving of his Spirit to the judges, that rescues the community of faith from complete ruin.

My study has shown that the Spirit of Yahweh in Judges functions to authorize and equip God's chosen leaders and to effect

---

[113] Cf. Polzin, *Moses and the Deuteronomist*, p. 185.
[114] Marais, *Representation in Old Testament Narrative Texts*, p. 132.
[115] Polzin, *Moses and the Deuteronomist*, p. 189.
[116] Welker, *God the Spirit*, p. 52.

salvation, even if, as in the case of Samson, it is only the inception of salvation. Clearly, the Spirit proceeds from Yahweh, represents the interests of Yahweh, and serves to highlight the role of Yahweh as savior and creator of new beginnings. Along with Yahweh's participation in the narrative through his actions and his speeches (chs. 2, 6, and 10), the giving of his Spirit assures that he, and not the Israelites, the judges, or the Canaanites is, in control of the progress and direction of the narrative. The workings of the Spirit parallel the other activities of God as he responds to the spiraling decline of Israel's devotion to the covenant. Yahweh's eventual refusal to completely save Israel registers the escalating tension within the passions of Yahweh himself, as he is compelled to distance himself from an increasingly idolatrous Israel.

The series of Spirit endowed judges concludes with Jephthah and Samson whose lives and behavior mirror the collapse of Israel.[117] Despite their charismatic endowments, these judges are unable to control the wandering passions of Israel; in fact, they can not even control themselves. At the end of Judges we are confronted with human frailty, and we are forced to cry out only to God for salvation, because, in the words of James Crenshaw, 'he alone can deliver Israel once and for all time, for he does not sleep on Delilah's knee'.[118]

---

[117] Cf. Exum, 'The Centre Cannot Hold', pp. 410-31, who traces the pattern of decay through the book.
[118] Crenshaw, *Samson*, p. 135.

6

'WHERE ARE ALL HIS WONDERS?': THE EXODUS MOTIF IN THE BOOK OF JUDGES

Introduction

The exodus is the theological crux of the Hebrew Bible. It is fundamental to Israel's self-understanding, and it is the cornerstone of the biblical perceptions of Yahweh, the God of Israel.[1] Traditions regarding the exodus persist as paradigmatic throughout the Former and Latter Prophets, and references to the exodus permeate the Psalms as a principal constituent in Israel's praise and worship of Yahweh.[2] Remembrance of the exodus provokes Israel's deepest longings toward God and his kingdom.

In this examination of the exodus motif in Judges, I am continuing my attempts to hear the text of Judges from within my interpretive location as a Pentecostal.[3] In this chapter, I propose to bring the Pentecostal testimony (and my personal testimony) into

---

[1] Goldingay, *Israel's Gospel*, pp. 288-89, writes, 'Israel's deliverance from Egypt is the real beginning and essential content of the First Testament Gospel'. Cf. Ernest W. Nicholson, *Exodus and Sinai in History and Tradition* (Growing Points in Theology; Richmond, VA: John Knox Press, 1973), pp. 56-57; Brueggemann, *Theology of the Old Testament*, pp. 177-81.

[2] See Rad, *Old Testament Theology*, I, pp. 175-79, and Rolf Rendtorff, *The Canonical Hebrew Bible: A Theology of the Old Testament* (trans. David Orton; Leiden: Deo Publishing, 2005), pp. 71-75.

[3] In part, I am responding to Rickie Moore's challenge that I explicate my 'hearing' of the text with more openness to the critical claims of the Holy Spirit. See Rickie D. Moore, 'Welcoming an Unheard Voice: A Response to Lee Roy Martin's *The Unheard Voice of God*', *JPT* 18.2 (2008), pp. 7-14.

conversation with the book of Judges and its theological witness regarding Israel's exodus tradition, which is one of biblical Israel's most powerful and sustaining memories. I argue here that the exodus tradition serves the narrative of Judges as a witness to Yahweh's power and faithfulness that calls Israel to obedience and encourages their hope in Yahweh's present and future attentiveness.

Testimony of the Exodus

The memory of the exodus pervades the Hebrew Bible, and the book of Judges is no exception to the rule, referring explicitly to the exodus nine times within seven different passages.[4] Although biblical scholarship has devoted significant attention to the exodus tradition, little work has been done to explicate the significance of the exodus within the narrative of Judges. However, two established points of connection between Judges and the exodus deserve mention here. First, as pointed out in Chapter 2, Frederick Greenspahn has shown that Yahweh's acts of deliverance in Judges are based upon the theology of the exodus and the covenant rather than on a theology of repentance.[5] Interpreters have often assumed incorrectly that the cries of Israel are cries of repentance. Julius Wellhausen, for example, characterized Israel's cry as evidence of '*Bekehrung*' ('conversion'),[6] and C.F. Burney declared that one of the lessons of Judges is that 'true repentance is followed by a renewal of the Divine favour',[7] and writers continue to use the terminology of repentance.[8] Michael Welker goes so far as to claim that in Judges the

---

[4] Judges 2.1, 12; 6.8, 9, 13; 10.11; 11.13, 16; and 19.30.

[5] Greenspahn, 'Framework of Judges', pp. 385-96. Building upon Greenspahn's argument, I have insisted that Yahweh's responsive acts in Judges are generated out of his inner passions (anger/compassion). On the one occasion when Israel seems to repent (10.10-15), Yahweh is not responsive.

[6] Wellhausen, *Prolegomena zur Geschichte Israels*, p. 240. As was stated in Chapter 4, for Wellhausen, the four stages of the cycle were '*Abfall Drangsal Bekehrung Ruhe*' (pp. 240-41).

[7] Burney, *The Book of Judges*, p. cxxi.

[8] E.g. Frolov, *The Turn of the Cycle: 1 Samuel 1-8 in Synchronic and Diachronic Perspectives*, pp. 47-48; O'Connell, *The Rhetoric of the Book of Judges*, pp. 40-42; Hughes and Laney, *Tyndale Concise Bible Commentary*, p. 99; Kaiser, *Toward an Exegetical Theology*, p. 136; Pratt, *He Gave us Stories*, p. 135; Finkelstein and Silberman, *The Bible Unearthed*, p. 120; and Matthews, *Judges and Ruth*, p. 53.

Israelites experience 'the forgiveness of sins',[9] apparently overlooking the fact that forgiveness language is entirely absent from Judges.

Rather than being a cry of repentance, Israel's cry in Judges (זעק/ צעק) is reminiscent of the exodus (Exod. 2.23), where the cry is 'a plea to be delivered from oppression'.[10] Just as in the case of the exodus, the cry in Judges is sometimes no more than a groan (נאקה, Judg. 2.18; Exod. 2.24).[11] Israel's suffering under the Egyptian regime is paradigmatic for its later suffering at the hands of the tyrannical Canaanite rulers. The framework of Judges 'thus perceives the period of the judges as continuing the process initiated by the exodus in which Israel's suffering is dealt with by divine salvation'.[12]

The second point of connection between Judges and the exodus is the similarity between Gideon and Moses,[13] a similarity which invests Gideon with divine authority and casts him as a new Moses.[14] A comparison of the stories of Moses and Gideon reveals numerous points of contact, most of which involve the call narratives.[15]

The aforementioned associations between Judges and the exodus demonstrate the importance of the exodus tradition for understanding the theology of the book as a whole.[16] We will now turn

---

[9] Welker, *God the Spirit*, p. 65.

[10] Brueggemann, 'Social Criticism', p. 83.

[11] Guillaume contends that the Israelite's 'groaning' in the prologue reflects an activity different from their 'crying' in the framework (*Waiting for Josiah*, p. 21). To my mind, the parallels in Exod. 2.23-24 and the semantic similarity of the two Hebrew terms suggest that 'groan' and 'cry' describe the same activity spoken of in two different ways. Cf. O'Connell, *The Rhetoric of the Book of Judges*, p. 40; and Wong, *Compositional Strategy of the Book of Judges*, p. 181 n. 13.

[12] Greenspahn, 'Framework of Judges', p. 395.

[13] See pp. 56-57 above and Smith, 'Remembering God', pp. 634-38. Cf. Charles D. Isbell, *The Function of Exodus Motifs in Biblical Narratives: Theological Didactic Drama* (Studies in the Bible and Early Christianity 52; Lewiston, NY: Edwin Mellen Press, 2002), pp. 111-15.

[14] Lindars, 'Gideon and Kingship', p. 317.

[15] For a listing of these similarities, see Martin, *The Unheard Voice of God*, pp. 188-89. In addition to the Moses/Gideon comparison, I have offered a Moses/Deborah comparison in Chapter 3 above.

[16] As I observed in Chapter 1, n. 5, Judges also connects theologically with Exodus 34. We noted the following words and phrases that can be linked directly to the book of Judges: 'I make a covenant' (Exod. 34.10; cf. Judg. 2.1); 'marvels' (Exod. 34.10; cf. Judg. 6.13); the 'work' of Yahweh (Exod. 34.10; cf. Judg. 2.10); 'I am driving out ...' (Exod. 34.11; cf. Judg. 6.9); 'beware lest you make a covenant with the inhabitants of the land' (Exod. 34.12; cf. Judg. 2.2); 'lest it be for a snare' (Exod. 34.12; cf. Judg. 2.3); 'you shall destroy their altars' (Exod. 34.13; cf. Judg. 2.2); 'you shall worship no other god' (Exod. 34.14; cf. Judg. 3.6; 6.10); 'lusting

our attention to the passages in Judges where the exodus is mentioned explicitly.

YHWH's Self-testimony through the Angel of YHWH (Judges 2.1-5)

The book of Judges first mentions the exodus at the beginning of ch. 2:

> Now the angel of the Yahweh went up from Gilgal to Bochim, and said, 'I brought you up from Egypt, and brought you into the land that I had promised to your ancestors. I said, "I will never break my covenant with you. For your part, do not make a covenant with the inhabitants of this land; tear down their altars". But you have not obeyed my command. See what you have done!' (Judg. 2.1-2, NRSV)[17]

In light of Israel's failure to complete the conquest (as related in Judges 1), the angel of Yahweh appears in order to deliver a stern rebuke.[18] He begins with a testimony of the exodus tradition, which serves as a powerful reference and poses a certain characterization of Yahweh. The description of Yahweh as the one who brought Israel up from Egypt is 'probably the earliest and at the same time the most widely used'[19] of Israel's confessions.

The testimony that is highlighted by his statement, 'I brought you up out of Egypt',[20] affirms that Yahweh is a benevolent God who delivered them from slavery. In addition, he is a powerful God, who overthrew the mighty armies of Egypt. His appearance,

---

after their gods' (Exod. 34.15; cf. Judg. 2.17); and '[do not] take their daughters to marry your sons' (Exod. 34.16; cf. Judg. 3.6); 'you shall make no molded gods' (Exod. 34.17; cf. Judg. 17.3, 4; 18.14-18).

[17] I discuss this passage in detail in Martin, *The Unheard Voice of God*, pp. 105-60.

[18] Heinz-Dieter Neef argues that even the mention of the angel of Yahweh harks back to the exodus (Exod. 14.19 and 23.20). See Heinz-Dieter Neef, '"Ich Selber bin in Ihm" (Ex 23,21): Exegetische Beobachtungen zur Rede vom "Engel des Herrn" in Ex 23,20-22; 32,34; 33,2; Jdc 2,1-5; 5,23', *BZ* 39 (1995), p. 69. Daniel Block agrees, linking the angel to the events of Exod. 23.20-33; 32.34; 33.2; and 34.11-15. See Block, *Judges, Ruth*, p. 110. Cf. Moore, *Judges*, p. 57, who associates Judg. 2.1 with Exod. 32.20.

[19] Rad, *Old Testament Theology*, I, pp. 121, 179. Cf. Brueggemann, *Theology of the Old Testament*, pp. 173-75.

[20] On the anomalous yiqtol verb here (אעלה), see Martin, *The Unheard Voice of God*, pp. 120-22, 238-39.

therefore, would inspire awe. Furthermore, he is the God of the Sinai covenant, which begins: 'I am Yahweh your God, who brought you out of the land of Egypt, out of the house of slavery' (Exod. 20.2). Israel's covenant with Yahweh is founded upon his act of salvation. Because of his gracious salvation, he is Israel's covenant God and deserves their allegiance. Therefore, his appearance should awaken Israel's sense of gratitude and obligation.

Yahweh's declaration, 'I brought you up out of Egypt', assumes his claim to an essential disposition of grace toward Israel. Thus, the Israelites are reminded that Yahweh saved them from the slavery of Egypt not because they deserved salvation, but because he chose them to be his people. Just as their salvation was based not upon their commitment to Yahweh but on his commitment to them, his present posture toward them continues to rest upon the same foundation – his grace and love.

The testimony of the exodus recalls Yahweh's election of Israel, his mighty acts of judgment in the land of Egypt and his overthrowing of Pharaoh in the Red Sea. Israel's salvation from Egypt was a manifestation of God's power, and the God of the exodus even now has the ability to overthrow the Canaanites and to negate every power that would shackle Israel. The exodus tradition, as Brueggemann writes, 'enunciates Yahweh's resolved capacity to intervene decisively against every oppressive, alienating circumstance and force that precludes a life of well-being'.[21] Although Israel's many failures are recited at the end of Judges 1, the people may have hope that Yahweh will prevail in spite of their failures.

In addition to Yahweh's grace and his power, another important theme is conveyed by the exodus story – the theme of Yahweh's purpose. Brueggemann's testimony to 'Yahweh's resolved capacity' illuminates the integration of Yahweh's purposes and his power, because purpose is prerequisite to resolve.[22] Yahweh's overall purpose in the exodus is to liberate Israel for himself, to free them from the land of Egypt in order that they may live in the land of promise and to bring them out of the household of bondage that they might be the household of God. The mention of the exodus, therefore, might suggest their plight 'as continuing the process initiated by the

---

[21] Brueggemann, *Theology of the Old Testament*, p. 174.
[22] Brueggemann, *Theology of the Old Testament*, p. 174.

exodus in which Israel's suffering is dealt with by divine salvation'.[23] Yahweh aspires to liberate Israel from Egypt, from Canaan, and from every other power, in order that they may be his special possession (Exod. 19.5).

From a narrative perspective, it seems significant that the angel first draws attention to the faithfulness of Yahweh before he addresses Israel's failure. Yahweh said that he would bring them out from the land of Egypt, and he did so. He swore to the patriarchs that he would bring them into the land of Canaan, and he fulfilled his oath. He promised that he would never break his covenant, and he was patient enough not to break it. After testifying to his own fidelity, Yahweh, in three brief statements, sharply rebukes the Israelites for their infidelity: 1. He had told them, 'You shall make no covenant with the inhabitants of this land;' and 2. 'You shall tear down their altars;' 3. Thus he concludes, 'But you have not obeyed My voice' (Judg. 2.2). The Israelites are disloyal on all counts. Consequently, a crucial theme for Judg. 2.1-5 is the contrast between the covenant loyalty of Yahweh and the disloyalty of Israel.[24] Brevard Childs observes, 'In stark contrast to Israel's faithlessness is God's faithfulness'.[25]

The Narrator's Testimony (Judges 2.11-12)

Since an initial theme of Judges 2 is Yahweh's faithfulness as opposed to Israel's faithlessness, the hearer of Judges might be inclined to anticipate further development of this theme as the narrative progresses. As expected, the theme is continued later in ch. 2 when the narrator explains that after the death of Joshua and his faithful generation a new generation arose (2.10) who were unfaithful:

> Then the Israelites did what was evil in the sight of the LORD and worshiped the Baals; and they abandoned the LORD, the

---

[23] Greenspahn, 'Framework of Judges', p. 395. As we read further into the book of Judges, we will observe the continued prominence of the salvation theme. The Hebrew root ישע (to save) is used 21 times in Judges, and the word נצל (deliver) is found 6 times.

[24] Cf. Carlos R. Sosa, 'Análisis Exegético y Literario de Jueces 2:1-5', *Kairós* (Guatemala) 43 (July-Dec. 2008), pp. 9-38.

[25] Brevard S. Childs, *Biblical Theology of the Old and New Testaments: Theological Reflection on the Christian Bible* (Minneapolis, MN: Fortress Press, 1st Fortress Press edn, 1993), p. 420.

God of their ancestors, who had brought them out of the land of Egypt; they followed other gods, from among the gods of the peoples who were all around them, and bowed down to them; and they provoked the LORD to anger (Judg. 2.11-12, NRSV).

The idolatry of the Israelites is punished by the LORD when he hands them over to their enemies. After a time of oppression, the Israelites cry out to Yahweh for his help, and he raises up a judge who delivers them. Soon, however, the Israelites return to their idolatry, and thus begins the long recognized cyclical pattern of the book of Judges.

This testimony of the exodus calls attention to Israel's lack of gratitude and lack of loyalty. Israel abandoned the God who had saved them from bondage in Egypt. Yahweh is deserving of gratitude, loyalty, and devotion, but Israel is unwilling to remain faithful. Yahweh's aforementioned speech (2.1-5) had rebuked the Israelites for their failure to tear down the altars of Canaan, but here the disobedience goes a step further – they are actively engaged in worship at those altars. Instead of steadfastly worshiping Yahweh who had saved them, they turn to the gods of Canaan, the very gods whose altars the Israelites where tasked to destroy.

Yahweh's Self-testimony through a Prophet (Judges 6.7-10)

The next testimony of the exodus comes from Yahweh through the mouth of his prophet. Once again, Yahweh begins his address with a reminder of the exodus:

> The Israelites cried to the LORD on account of the Midianites, and the LORD sent a prophet to the Israelites; and he said to them, 'Thus says the LORD, the God of Israel: I led you up from Egypt, and brought you out of the house of slavery; and I delivered you from the hand of the Egyptians, and from the hand of all who oppressed you, and drove them out before you, and gave you their land; and I said to you, "I am the LORD your God; you shall not fear the gods of the Amorites, in whose land you dwell". But you have not obeyed my voice' (Judg. 6.7-10).[26]

---

[26] I discuss this passage briefly in Chapter 3 above.

Some four generations have passed since Yahweh's first testimony (2.1-5), and the exodus is now an even more distant event than it had been when the angel of the Lord spoke of it. During that interim God has saved the Israelites from three enemies, demonstrating that 'the God of the exodus continues to effect a series of new exoduses throughout the book of Judges'.[27] Nevertheless, the situation of the Israelites has deteriorated significantly, and this testimony of the exodus serves as reassurance that Yahweh 'acts powerfully on behalf of Israel when Israel is helpless and has no power of her own',[28] and that the power of Yahweh 'is more than a match for the powers of oppression',[29] powers which are embodied in the Midianite encampments.

The Israelites who are 'brought very low (דלל) because of Midian' (6.6, NASB),[30] are now reminded of the time when Yahweh brought them up (עלה) out of Egypt (6.8). By the oppressive acts of the Midianites, the Israelites are brought 'low', but they can be brought 'up' by the power of Yahweh, who brought them up from Egypt.

The exodus theme is expanded further by Yahweh's second affirmation: 'I brought you out (ואציא) from the house of bondage' (6.8). The Israelites had been slaves in Egypt; they had belonged to the household of bondage; but Yahweh had brought them out. The reference to slavery may cause the Israelites to compare their current extreme situation to the earlier Egyptian bondage. Is it possible that they had been brought so low by the Midianites that their condition was as woeful to them as slavery? Even so, Yahweh, who had brought them out from the house of bondage, is able to bring them out from their enslavement to the Midianites.

Yahweh continues his speech with a third reference to the exodus: 'I delivered you (ואצל) from the hand of Egypt and from the hand of all your oppressors (לחציכם)' (6.9).[31] Yahweh not only reiterates his act of delivering the Israelites from Egypt, but he

---

[27] McCann, *Judges*, p. 63.
[28] Walter Brueggemann, *The Bible Makes Sense* (Atlanta: John Knox Press, 1977), p. 64.
[29] Brueggemann, *Theology of the Old Testament*, p. 174.
[30] Cf. *BDB*, p. 195.
[31] The phrase 'from the hand of the Egyptians' (מיד מצרים) precedes Judg. 6.9 only in Exod. 3.8; 14.30; 18.9; and 18.10.

expands that deliverance to include his rescue from their enemies subsequent to the exodus. Because the two objects are predicated upon only one verb, the hearer might infer that the exodus serves as the paradigm for Yahweh's subsequent saving acts.

It is from the 'hand' (יד) of Egypt and subsequent enemies that Yahweh has delivered Israel. Forty-nine times in the book of Judges the word 'hand' serves as a metaphor for 'power'.[32] On one occasion the enemy is subdued under (תחת) the hand of the Israelites (3.30), and ten times a reversal of power is signified by either Israel or the Canaanites being sold (מכר) or given (נתן) into the hand of the other. Furthermore, the metaphorical use of the hand to signify power (6.9) combines with the term 'oppressors' (לחציכם) to form a graphic depiction of Israel's plight. Since 'oppressors' is a participle of the Hebrew לחץ, which means to 'squeeze',[33] the image is that of Israel being squeezed in the hand of the Midianites, causing both 'physical and psychological oppression'.[34] God, however, affirms that he has delivered the Israelites from the hand of the Egyptians and from the hand of all other oppressors,[35] with the implication that he is now able to deliver them from the hand of the Midianites.

The interval between the exodus and Judges 6 includes numerous episodes of divine intervention in which Yahweh saves the Israelites by the agency of Joshua, Othniel, Ehud, Shamgar, and Deborah; but this is the first use in Judges of the word 'deliver' (נצל).[36] The term is used 14 times in the book of Exodus, for example: 'I have come down to deliver them from the hand of the Egyptians' (Exod. 3.8). The verb נצל is quite forceful, as Brueggemann explains, 'This verb references an abrupt physical act of grasping or

---

[32] Judges 1.2, 4, 35; 2.14, 15, 16, 18, 23; 3.8, 10, 28, 30; 4.2, 7, 9, 14, 24; 6.1, 2, 9, 36, 37; 7.2, 7, 9, 11, 14, 15; 8.3, 7, 22, 34; 9.17, 29; 10.7, 12; 11.21, 30, 32; 12.2; 13.1, 5; 15.12, 13, 18; 16.23, 24; 18.10; 20.28. Also, the word 'palm' (כף) means 'power' in Judg. 6.13, 14; 8.6, 15; and 12.3. Cf. BDB, p. 389; CHALOT, p. 128; and HALOT, I, p. 888.

[33] BDB, p. 537. Cf. DCH, IV, p. 539.

[34] I. Swart, 'לָחַץ', in NIDOTTE, II, p. 792.

[35] The most recent enemy who is called an 'oppressor' of Israel is Jabin, king of Canaan (Judg. 4.3).

[36] In chs. 1-5, the idea of Yahweh's rescue is indicated by the phrases 'Yahweh saved (ישׁע) Israel' (2.16, 18; 3.9, 15, 31) and 'Yahweh subdued (כנע) the enemy' (3.30; 4.23).

seizing – often, as here, grasping or seizing in order to pull out of danger ... Israel is 'snatched' out of the danger of Egyptian slavery in a forceful, physical gesture by Yahweh'.[37] The Israelites are now languishing in the 'hand of the Midianites' (6.1), but the same God who had snatched them from the 'hand of the Egyptians and from the hand of all' their oppressors (6.9) can now snatch them away from the power of the Midianites.

Yahweh completes his self-testimony with one more word. He declares, 'I am Yahweh your God; you shall not fear the gods of the Amorites' (6.10). The first appearance of the phrase 'I am Yahweh your God (אני יהוה אלהיכם)'[38] is connected to the exodus: 'Then I will take you to be My people, and I will be your God; and you shall know that I am Yahweh your God, who brought you out from under the burdens of the Egyptians' (Exod. 6.7). Yahweh claims the Israelites as his people, and he gives himself to them to be their God. In light of the covenantal connections of Yahweh's claim to be Israel's God, his renewal of that claim through the word of the prophet in Judges 6 serves as a condemnation of the Israelites' idolatry that is implied in their doing of 'the evil' (Judg. 6.1), and it serves as a fitting prerequisite to the prohibition 'You shall not fear the gods of the Amorites' (6.10), in which Yahweh and the Amorite gods are set in juxtaposition.

The prophet's appeal to the exodus affirms both Yahweh's might and his mercy. It is not enough that Yahweh defeats the gods of Egypt and shows himself superior in strength; his acts go beyond a simple demonstration of power. Yahweh's power is exercised toward salvific purpose in bringing the Israelites out of slavery, and the covenant is founded not upon the abstract notion of divine power but upon the concrete expressions of divine care. Therefore, Yahweh insists that his awesome acts of grace toward the Israelites are deserving of the joint responses of fear and love. Thus, when Yahweh says, 'I am Yahweh your God, you shall not fear the gods of the Amorites', he is insisting that his acts of salvation and his giving of the covenant establish him as the only deity who is

---

[37] Brueggemann, *Theology of the Old Testament*, p. 174. Cf. *HALOT*, I, p. 717, who offers the translation 'to tear from'.

[38] Previous to Judg. 6.10, the Hebrew phrase אני יהוה אלהיכם is used 22 times in Leviticus, and it is found in Exod. 6.7; 16.12; Num. 10.10; 15.41; and Deut 29.5.

deserving of the worship of the Israelites. His manifest love for the Israelites calls for their reciprocation, and his gracious acts of salvation require the Israelites' exclusive reverence.

The Testimony Disputed (Judges 6.13)

Immediately following the prophet's speech (6.7-10), we are introduced to Gideon, who is threshing wheat in the wine press in order to hide his grain from the marauding Midianites. He is greeted by the angel of Yahweh who declares, 'Yahweh is with you' (6.12). Gideon replies dubiously (sarcastically?) with a question that makes reference to the exodus testimony:

> [I]f Yahweh is with us, then why has all this happened to us? And where are all his wonders that our ancestors recounted to us saying, 'Did not Yahweh bring us up from Egypt?' But now Yahweh has abandoned us and handed us over to the Midianites (Judg. 6.13).

Until now, the hearer of Judges has not been informed of the Israelites' inner attitudes and feelings toward Yahweh and toward their situation in Canaan. Gideon's dialogue with the angel is the first disclosure of these inner thoughts. The perspective of Gideon may represent that of the Israelites throughout Judges, a perspective that stands in conflict with the perspective of Yahweh. Yahweh speaks of the deliverance from Egypt as a point of assurance, but Gideon sees the same tradition as a point of suspicion. Gideon has heard testimonies of the exodus and Yahweh's faithfulness in the past, but he has not experienced Yahweh's wonders (נפלאת). He is one of the 'new generation ... who did not know Yahweh nor the works that he had done for Israel' (Judg. 2.10).

The angelic proclamation affirmed Yahweh's presence – 'Yahweh is with you' – but Gideon has experienced only Yahweh's absence. Gideon asks, 'If Yahweh is with us, then why have all these things happened to us?' The question reveals Gideon's unfulfilled expectations, his disappointment with the theology handed down to him. Gideon is not satisfied with a divine word of mere affirmation or a vague promise of comfort in the time of affliction. Specifically, Gideon asks, 'Where are all his wonders that our elders told us about?' He demands that the God of the exodus show himself to be God in the midst of the present crisis. In effect, Gideon is asking, 'I have heard the testimonies of what the LORD has done in the past, but where is he now, in this desperate time?'

Gideon's question, therefore, may indicate that he is skeptical of the testimony that he has heard from his ancestors (his elders). When we come to the Gideon cycle, the exodus testimony has been recited three times already (2.1; 2.11; 6.8), but Gideon questions that testimony. He admits that he has heard the testimony of the exodus but he does not profess to believe it. Gideon does not say, 'Yahweh brought us up out of Egypt'; instead he remarks, *'they said*, "Yahweh brought us up"'. Gideon knows the testimony and cites it, but he falls short of confessing agreement with his elders. Perhaps he doubts that the testimony of the exodus is reliable and relevant and that the testimony of the elders can be trusted.

Gideon remembers the testimony of the exodus, but his remembrance of Yahweh's presence in the past serves only to bring attention to Yahweh's absence in the present. Gideon believes that theological reflection on past memories should carry relevance for the present. He wants to believe in a God who is reliable across generations, but he has his doubts. For Gideon, Yahweh is no longer the God who saves.

Bernon Lee observes that Gideon's response is the beginning of 'an ongoing conflict' between Gideon and Yahweh.[39] Lee maintains that the narrative 'provides ample opportunity for hearer participation in the suspension of belief in divine fidelity;'[40] it allows the hearer to have 'a measure of sympathy for Gideon'[41] in his complaint. According to Lee, the hearer and Gideon are united in the question of 6.13b, 'where are all his wonders that our fathers told us about?'[42] The hearer of the narrative might wonder if Gideon's protest is his way of motivating Yahweh to action[43] or if it is a foreshadowing of Gideon's pessimistic outlook that continues throughout the story.[44]

It is appropriate that Gideon should inquire about the 'wonders' of Yahweh because the word 'wonders' (נפלאת), often translated

---

[39] Lee, 'Fragmentation', p. 70.
[40] Lee, 'Fragmentation', p. 70.
[41] Lee, 'Fragmentation', p. 86.
[42] Lee, 'Fragmentation', p. 86.
[43] Webb, *Judges. An Integrated Reading*, pp. 147-48.
[44] O'Connell, *The Rhetoric of the Book of Judges*, p. 149.

'miracles', is used several times in the Hebrew Bible to describe the mighty acts of Yahweh that accompanied the exodus. In the call narrative of Moses, Yahweh promised, 'I will stretch out my hand and strike Egypt with all my *wonders* that I will do in it; then he will let you go' (Exod. 3.20). After the deliverance at the Red Sea, Moses sang, 'Who is like you, O LORD, among the gods? Who is like you, majestic in holiness, awesome in splendor, doing *wonders*?' (Exod. 15.11). When Moses is upon Mt. Sinai, Yahweh points forward to the conquest of Canaan with this promise: 'Before all your people I will perform *wonders*, such as have not been performed in all the earth or in any nation; and all the people among whom you live shall see the work of the LORD; for it is an awesome thing that I will do with you' (Exod. 34.11).[45] Upon the eve of their crossing into Canaan, Joshua charges Israel, 'Sanctify yourselves; for tomorrow the LORD will do *wonders* among you' (Josh. 3.5). Other texts in the Hebrew Bible use the word 'wonder' with reference to the exodus: 'I will call to mind the deeds of the LORD; I will remember your *wonders* of old' (Ps. 77.11); 'He sent signs and *wonders* into your midst, O Egypt, against Pharaoh and all his servants' (Ps. 135.9); and 'You showed signs and *wonders* in the land of Egypt ...' (Jer. 32.20). Salvation from Egypt is accomplished through the wonders of Yahweh; entering the promised land is accompanied by the wonders of Yahweh, and deliverance from oppression is a wonder for which Gideon now yearns.

The narrative offers at least two reasons for Gideon's reticence to accept the testimony of his elders. First, the objective data seem to contradict the testimony. To Gideon, the Midianite oppression is a sign that Yahweh has abandoned Israel. If the testimony about the exodus is true, Gideon reasons, Yahweh would act and bring deliverance. Gideon's question implies either that the testimony of the elders may be less than truthful or that God has changed in his relationship to the Israelites. The testimonies of the distant past do not seem to be sufficient in the face of Gideon's present reality of daily suffering and crushing oppression. Yahweh's failure to save is

---

[45] Exodus 34.10-16 contains a number of verbal connections to Judges 2–3, including the reference to the making of the covenant (v. 10), the warning that the Canaanites will be a snare (v. 12), the injunction to tear down the altars of Canaan (v. 13), the prohibition against entering into covenant with the Canaanites (v. 15), and the prohibition against intermarriage with the Canaanites (v. 16).

to Gideon a violation of the settled and stable theology that he has been taught.[46] Israel's covenant with Yahweh should grant to them a position of privilege and entitlement in regard to Yahweh's protection, but that protection has not been forthcoming. The Midianites continue to plunder the Israelites, devastate their crops and terrorize their villages. Human reason suggests to Gideon that, for whatever reason, Yahweh is inactive.

In our current context, modern biblical scholarship often presents a challenge to the testimony of our Pentecostal elders. Young women and men enroll in seminary or university graduate programs in religion, and they find immediately that the academy does not appreciate the testimony of the elders. Like the Midianites, the academy is an irresistible force that leaves the children impoverished (Judg. 6.6). Critical scholarship points to the 'objective' data and dismisses the wonders of Yahweh as ancient mythology that must be abandoned.[47] Julius Wellhausen (the Moses of historical criticism) acknowledged as much when he resigned his theology post at Greifswald. Making reference to his 'scientific treatment of the Bible', as he called it, he confessed, '[D]espite all caution on my own part I make my hearers unfit for their office' as ministers in the Protestant church.[48]

Well-known biblical scholar, Daniel Patte, has acknowledged that his training in the biblical studies academy taught him to

---

[46] Niditch, *Judges*, p. 90, observes the similarity between Gideon's complaint and Israel's national laments in Psalms 74 and 77. Unlike the usual lament form, however, and in contrast to Pss. 74.12-17 and 77.11-20, Gideon does not give voice to a prayer, nor does he confess confidence in Yahweh.

[47] It is a fundamental assumption of historical criticism that the accuracy of Scripture's testimony of events can be judged according to the analogy of present, empirically verifiable experience. For the flaws in this assumption and for an extensive Pentecostal critique of the historical critical method, see Kenneth J. Archer, *A Pentecostal Hermeneutic: Spirit, Scripture and Community* (JPTSup 28; London: T&T Clark, 2004). I will cite the CPT Press edition (Cleveland, TN, 2009), pp. 200-208. Despite my objections to historical criticism, however, I am not arguing for a return to pre-critical exegesis (see Martin, *The Unheard Voice of God*, pp. 19-59). Among historical criticism's many helpful gains, we might include its exposing of the human dimension in the Bible's creation and transmission.

[48] Alfred Jepsen, 'Wellhausen in Greifswald', in *Festschrift zur 500-Jahrfeier der Universität Greifswald* (Greifswald: Ernst Moritz-Arndt-Universität, 1956), pp. 47-56; cited in Rudolf Smend, 'Julius Wellhausen and his Prolegomena to the History of Israel', *Semeia* 25 (1982), p. 6.

disregard the testimony of his elders. Speaking of his entrance into the Protestant Institute (Montpellier, France), he writes:

> We were entering a programme supposed to prepare us for a ministry of the Word and sacraments. But, ironically, it demanded that we ignore and reject as sentimental, emotional, naïve and childish the very *pro me* and *pro nobis* interpretations of the Bible that had convinced us to pursue theological studies, with, of course, a major focus on biblical studies. In my case, critical biblical studies demanded that I disregard the transforming religious power of the biblical text upon me, upon others and upon society! ... As an evangelical descendant of Huguenots, these powerful biblical teachings defined my identity as a member of my family and of my small Protestant community.[49]

A similar story comes from Rickie D. Moore, whose experience at Vanderbilt University included a challenge to the testimony of his elders:

> There I was directed once again to the first words of the book of Deuteronomy, but now a mountain of scholarship stood before these words and yielded a very different reading, namely, 'these are *not* the words of Moses' ... This towering fortress of scholarship, with its formidable conclusions about the text and methods used to read them, was a far cry from the ethos and impulses of my Pentecostal confession ... In a way that went against my deepest and mostly unconscious longings, I was being relentlessly conditioned to experience criticism and confession as mutually exclusive opposites.[50]

Like Gideon, Patte and Moore were overwhelmed by the power of those who opposed the testimony of their elders; but as in the case of Gideon, they found their way back to a place of confidence in God's power to save and transform.

Gideon, however, has a second and even more compelling reason for his skepticism regarding the testimony of his elders, and

---

[49] Daniel Patte, 'The Guarded Personal Voice of a Male European-American Biblical Scholar', in I.R. Kitzberger (ed.), *Personal Voice in Biblical Interpretation* (London: Routledge, 1999), pp. 13-14.

[50] Rickie D. Moore, 'Deuteronomy and the Fire of God: A Critical Charismatic Interpretation', *JPT* 7 (1995), pp. 13-14.

that is the disloyalty of the elders themselves. They testify of Yahweh's wondrous works, but all the while their idolatrous practices contradict their testimony. Gideon's father may have believed that Yahweh brought up Israel from Egypt, but his construction of an altar for the worship of Baal (Judg. 6.25) reveals his lack of devotion to Yahweh. Most likely, the entire community was committed to the worship of numerous gods (Judg. 6.28-32) in violation of their covenant with Yahweh. The vacillation of the elders contradicts their own testimony. Can the children believe the testimony of elders who have come to depend upon idols?

As the Pentecostal church in the West gives birth to the third, fourth, and even fifth generations of Pentecostal adherents, we are faced with the same contradiction. We hear the testimony that encourages trust and faithfulness, but we see numerous idols that are set up in the Church. Many of our children are cynical and distrustful of leaders who seem to major in ecclesiastical politics and manipulation. Will our children believe the testimony of elders who have come to depend upon the gods of status, materialism, human ingenuity, and ambition? I hope that God will soon raise up a new Gideon, who will obey God's call to tear down our altars to Baal.[51]

The irony in Gideon's story is that while he is skeptically questioning the truth of what he has heard, Yahweh is already preparing to intervene in a way that is consistent with the elders' testimony. He has heard the cries of Israel (6.6), and he sends his angel to commission Gideon, proving that he is indeed the God of the exodus testimony, the God who never ceases to act on behalf of those who suffer. Thus, even as Gideon is yearning for salvation, Yahweh is moving to revisit Israel with 'all his wonders', and he has chosen Gideon as the new Moses, who will bring his people out of bondage.

---

[51] A colleague, Kevin Spawn, suggested still another factor that could have fueled Gideon's distrust of his elders, namely, their selectivity in appropriating their traditions. While the elders affirm the exodus tradition, they violate other traditions by later inviting Gideon to rule over them. The move toward monarchy is itself questionable, but doubly so in light of the fact that Gideon is from the tribe of Manasseh. Tradition appears to specify that Israel's eventual king should come from Judah. Furthermore, in reflecting upon their victory, the elders prefer to glorify Gideon rather than Yahweh. They say to Gideon, 'you delivered us' (8.22). Cf. Susanne Gillmayr-Bucher, 'Framework and Discourse in the Book of Judges', *JBL* 128 (2009), pp. 687-702 (695–96).

Yahweh's Third Self-testimony (Judges 10.11-13)

The sixth cycle of rebellion begins when the Israelites again 'did what was evil in the sight of Yahweh' (10.6).[52] In this cycle, the idolatry of the Israelites seems to have increased: 'they served the Baals and the Ashtartes, the gods of Aram, the gods of Sidon, the gods of Moab, the gods of the Ammonites, and the gods of the Philistines. And they forsook Yahweh and did not serve him' (10.6). When compared to the earlier cycles, the appearance of such an array of foreign gods in Judg. 10.6 raises the intensity level of the Israelites' idolatry and heightens their guilt.[53] It appears that the Israelites have strengthened their ties to the foreign gods, while at the same time they have drifted farther away from Yahweh. The Israelites' allowing of Canaanite worship to continue is despicable to Yahweh (2.2), and their adoption of other gods alongside Yahweh is forbidden by the Decalogue (Exod. 20.3). Moreover, their complete abandonment of Yahweh cannot be tolerated.

Yahweh's response to rejection is vehement: 'The anger of Yahweh was hot against Israel, and he sold them into the hand of the Philistines and into the hand of the Ammonites' (10.7-8). These enemies crushed and oppressed Israel for 18 years, and 'Israel was greatly distressed' (10.9).[54] The shattering and crushing oppression causes the Israelites to cry out to Yahweh once again (10.10).[55] On this occasion, they not only beg for deliverance, but they also confess, 'We have sinned against you, in that we have forsaken our God and we have served the Baals' (10.10). Never before in Judges is the content of their cry supplied to the hearer, and never before do the Israelites confess any sin.[56] It would appear that, in this case, they are expressing genuine repentance toward God.

In light of the apparent repentance of the Israelites and the previous mercies of Yahweh, the hearer of Judges would likely expect

---

[52] This refrain appears once in the introduction (2.11), then it serves as the beginning of every major judge cycle (3.7; 3.12; 4.1; 6.1).
[53] Cf. Webb, *Judges. An Integrated Reading*, p. 44; and Block, *Judges, Ruth*, p. 344.
[54] The phrase, 'the anger of Yahweh', has not been used since Judg. 3.8.
[55] The same Hebrew word (זעק) is used for 'cry' in 3.9, 15; 6.6, 7; 10.10 and 10.14. In 4.3 the word is צעק, which is a variant spelling of the same root. Cf. BDB, p. 858.
[56] That the previous 'cries' of Israel do not include genuine repentance is the view of most interpreters, including Exum, 'The Centre Cannot Hold', pp. 411-12; and Polzin, *Moses and the Deuteronomist*, p. 155.

Yahweh to respond by raising up a judge who would bring salvation to the Israelites (cf. 3.9; 3.15; 4.4; and 6.11). God, however, does not respond as expected. Surprisingly, Yahweh says to the Israelites:

> Was it not from the Egyptians and from the Amorites and from the Ammonites and from the Philistines – and when the Sidonians and Amalek and Maon oppressed you, you cried unto me, and I saved you from their power? But you have forsaken me and served other gods; therefore, I will not save you again. Go and call upon the gods that you have chosen. They will save you in the time of your distress (Judg. 10.11-13).

Yahweh once again reminds the Israelites of his faithfulness, mercy, and salvation in the past. Once again he points back all the way to the exodus from Egypt and then lists six more enemies from which he had saved them.[57] It seems significant that only here in Judges does Yahweh himself respond verbally to the Israelites' cries. In previous rebukes of the Israelites, Yahweh employs an angel (2.1) and a prophet (6.8). The immediacy of the dialogue is accentuated by the lack of a mediating angel or prophet. The tone of the rebuff is quite sarcastic, 'Go cry to the gods you have chosen',[58] perhaps alluding ironically to Joshua's covenant renewal ceremony where the Israelites 'chose' to serve Yahweh (Josh. 24.22). The Lord seems to be completely unresponsive to the Israelites' cries and unconcerned about their suffering. Pressler reads this rebuff as 'the passionate, pained response of a lover whose love is betrayed one too many times'.[59] God's response here is not only unprecedented but also completely unexpected.[60] In Yahweh's earlier speeches (2.1-5 and 6.7-10), it is Israel who will not hear; but now, Yahweh will not hear. Consequently, he advises the Israelites to cry out to the gods they have chosen; perhaps those gods will hear and save.

---

[57] The list of nations in Judg. 10.11-12 corresponds to previous deliverances. Amorites (Num. 21; Josh. 24.8); Ammonites (Judg. 3.13); Philistines (Judg. 3.31); Sidonians (Josh. 13.6; Judg. 3.3); Amalekites (Judg. 6.3, 33; 7.12); Maon (Josh. 15.55. The LXX has Midian in the place of Maon, which would point to Judges 6).

[58] Cf. Webb, *Judges. An Integrated Reading*, p. 45.

[59] Pressler, *Joshua, Judges, and Ruth*, p. 198.

[60] The cyclical pattern disintegrates because Yahweh becomes frustrated with Israel's unfaithful behavior (cf. Chapter 4 above).

As before (2.2; 2.11; and 6.8), Yahweh's self-testimony affirms his covenant faithfulness in saving the Israelites from their enemies. The exodus is presented as the first in a series of Yahweh's mighty acts of deliverance. Also as before, the faithfulness of Yahweh is contrasted to the unfaithfulness of Israel, who, in violation of the covenant with Yahweh, has chosen to pursue other gods. There can be little doubt that Yahweh is justified in his decision to punish Israel's idolatry.

The Testimony Appropriated (Judges 11.15-24)

Jephthah is a 'mighty warrior and the son of a prostitute' (11.1), and he is a man displaced and marginalized, having been disinherited by his family and expelled from his community (11.2-3). When the elders of Gilead decide to seek Jephthah as military leader against the invading Ammonites, he is not even living in Gilead, so they go 'to fetch him from the land of Tob' (11.5). Having been received back into the community, he subsequently lays claim to the land in his diplomatic letter to the king of Ammon in which Jephthah writes, 'Why have you come against me to fight in *my land*?' (11.12, emphasis added). The Ammonite king responds to Jephthah with his own claim to the land, saying, 'Because Israel, on *coming from Egypt*, took away my land from the Arnon to the Jabbok and to the Jordan; now therefore restore it peaceably' (11.13, emphasis added).[61] The Ammonite ruler knows of the exodus, but he does not credit Yahweh with deliverance. Jephthah responds with a lengthy, detailed accounting of Israel's journey through the wilderness. He writes,

> Israel did not take away the land of Moab or the land of the Ammonites, but when *they came up from Egypt*, Israel went through the wilderness to the Red Sea and came to Kadesh. Israel then sent messengers to the king of Edom, saying, 'Let us pass through your land'; but the king of Edom would not listen. They also sent to the king of Moab, but he would not consent. So Israel remained at Kadesh. Then they journeyed through the wilderness, went around the land of Edom and the land of Moab, arrived on the east side of the land of Moab, and camped on the other side of the Arnon. They did not enter the territory of

---

[61] This testimony from a foreigner functions in the narrative to add credibility to the exodus tradition. Cf. the testimony of Rahab in Josh. 2.8-11.

Moab, for the Arnon was the boundary of Moab. Israel then sent messengers to King Sihon of the Amorites, king of Heshbon; and Israel said to him, 'Let us pass through your land to our country'. But Sihon did not trust Israel to pass through his territory; so Sihon gathered all his people together, and encamped at Jahaz, and fought with Israel. Then Yahweh, the God of Israel, gave Sihon and all his people into the hand of Israel, and they defeated them; so Israel possessed all the land of the Amorites, who inhabited that country. They possessed all the territory of the Amorites from the Arnon to the Jabbok and from the wilderness to the Jordan. So now Yahweh, the God of Israel, has dispossessed the Amorites from before his people Israel. Do you intend to take their place? Should you not possess what your god Chemosh gives you to possess? So whatever the LORD our God takes possession of before us, we will possess (Judg. 11.15-24, emphasis added).

Jephthah argues that all lands east of the Jordan were taken by the Israelites in self-defense when they were on their journey from Egypt to Canaan and the inhabitants refused to allow them to pass through peaceably (11.20-21); therefore, the Israelites 'possessed all the land of the Amorites' (11.21). Furthermore, Jephthah credits Yahweh as the one who dispossessed the Amorites and gave the land to the Israelites (11.23), and Yahweh is the one to whom Jephthah looks for victory (11.9, 24, 27). Consequently, Jephthah will not surrender the land in which he now enjoys a new position of status and a reborn sense of belonging. Having suffered previously the loss of land and the pain of exile, he is not willing to relinquish that which has been restored to him.

The extent of Jephthah's knowledge of the exodus/wilderness tradition is surprising to the hearer of the narrative, given the fact that Jephthah has lived outside the community for most of his life. The hearer is also surprised to learn that immediately after Jephthah's fervent defense of Israel's claim and his submission of the case to Yahweh as judge (11.27); Yahweh, who had threatened not to help Israel any more (10.12), shows himself once again to be the God of surprising grace and sends his empowering Spirit upon Jephthah (11.29). Could it be that Jephthah's recitation of the tradition awakens Yahweh to action and moves him to put his Spirit upon Jephthah?[62]

The Testimony and Israel's Origin (Judges 19.30)

The final chapters of Judges recount the unspeakable atrocities that are inflicted upon a Levite's secondary wife (19.25-30), who is raped, murdered, and dismembered, and upon the women of Jabesh-gilead and Shiloh, who are kidnapped and forced to become wives to the Benjaminite remnant (21.12, 20-23). It is in the midst of these cruelties that we hear Judges' final testimony to the exodus. A certain Levite and his *pilagesh* (פילגש),[63] or secondary wife, find lodging in the home of a Gibeonite man. When night falls certain worthless men of the city surround the house and demand that the Levite be given to them for their pleasure. Instead, the Levite pushes his concubine outside, and the men rape and murder her. The next morning, the Levite puts her dead body upon his donkey and carries her home. Then he divides her corpse into 12 pieces and sends them out to the tribes of Israel as a way of demanding justice, asking that the men of Gibeah be punished for their crimes. When the Israelites receive the gruesome message, everyone says, 'Nothing like this has been done or seen from the day that the Israelites came up from the land of Egypt until this day. Consider it, take counsel, and speak up' (Judg. 19.30).

The reference to the exodus harks back to Israel's founding moment, a moment marked by Yahweh's grace that delivered his people from oppression and bondage. It is a moment that brings to mind hopeful expectations of a future free of abuse and fear, expectations that apparently remain unfulfilled given the crimes against this helpless and unprotected woman. Thrown to the mob to be raped and murdered, she is victimized twice, the second time by her husband when he dismembers her dead body and sends it throughout the land.[64] Israel's exodus, the high point in its history, stands in stark contrast to this low point in Judges, when freedom is turned into anarchy and the oppressed become the oppressor.

---

[62] This possibility is entertained as well by Schneider, *Judges*, p. 173.

[63] Often translated 'concubine', a פילגש is a second wife who is of lower status than the primary wife. Victor P. Hamilton, 'פלגש', *TWOT*, II, p. 724. Cf. BDB, p. 811; and *CHALOT*, p. 292.

[64] Cf. Niditch, *Judges*, p. 194.

To hear this testimony is to admit that we have fallen far short of the promise of saving grace. The testimony points to the exodus as a founding moment when Yahweh's saving power created a new people, called and united under the covenant. The God of the exodus is the God who stands on the side of the weak, the slave, the abused. It is only when we choose the same stance that we become the holy people that we were meant to be.

The Exodus Motif and the Original Audience of Judges

I have shown that the exodus tradition serves the narrative of Judges as a witness to Yahweh's saving power and faithfulness that calls Israel to obedience and encourages their hope in Yahweh's present and future attentiveness. This means that because of his gracious salvation, he is Israel's covenant God and deserves their allegiance, their worship, and their loyalty. The exodus testimony also means that even now he has the might to overthrow the Canaanites and to negate every power that would shackle Israel. Yahweh's overall purpose in the exodus is to liberate Israel for himself, to bring them out of the household of bondage that they might be the household of God.

The original audience, along with every audience until now, would observe the contrast between the covenant loyalty of Yahweh and the disloyalty of Israel. In light of Israel's continual unfaithfulness, there can be little doubt that Yahweh is justified in his decision to punish Israel, eventually sending them into the Babylonian exile. Like Gideon, the hearers of Judges would experience times when the testimony of God's attentiveness would be challenged. The exile is one of those times. During and after the exile, however, the testimony of the exodus would serve as a point of hope that God is able to deliver his people.

The Pentecostal Testimony

The universal Pentecostal testimony is that God never ceases to be intensely active; that is, he continues to speak and work through and among his people for the sake of his kingdom in the world.[65] From

---

[65] Cf. Steven J. Land, *Pentecostal Spirituality: A Passion for the Kingdom* (JPTSup 1; Sheffield: Sheffield Academic Press, 1993). I will cite the CPT Press edition (Cleveland, TN, 2010), pp. 60-61. William Faupel, *The Everlasting Gospel: The*

Azusa Street until now, Pentecostals everywhere have insisted upon the present reality of God's presence to save, sanctify, fill with the Holy Spirit, heal, and reign as coming king.[66] The emphasis is not that God saved (past tense) but that God saves (present tense). Pentecostals long to see and hear what God is doing now, both among the elders and among the younger generations.

While past efforts to connect Gideon and Pentecostalism have centered on Gideon's reception of the Spirit, I see also an association between Pentecostalism and Gideon's use of the exodus tradition. I hear in Gideon's question, 'where are all his wonders?', an analogy to the aforementioned Pentecostal theme, namely, the urgent longing for a new manifestation of God's saving presence. The exodus testimony discloses a God who intervenes for those who suffer,[67] and Gideon yearns for divine intervention on behalf of his people who are suffering acutely at the hands of the merciless Midianites.

A Personal Testimony

It was during a personal crisis that I began to hear the yearning and the anguish in Gideon's voice. On May 17, 2007, I awoke suddenly because of a sharp, crushing pain in the center of my chest. I should have called an ambulance, but instead I took two aspirin and sat in a recliner until the pain subsided to a dull ache. I struggled through the morning and early afternoon, praying and believing God for healing. I recited to God all of the healing testimonies from

---

Significance of Eschatology in the Development of Pentecostal Thought (JPTSup 10; Sheffield: Sheffield Academic Press, 1996), pp. 22-43; and Archer, *A Pentecostal Hermeneutic*, pp. 174-77.

[66] *The Apostolic Faith* 1.1 (Sept. 1906), p. 1 and *passim*. Writing in the first issue of *PNEUMA*, William MacDonald, 'Temple Theology', *PNEUMA* 1.1 (1979), insists, 'Unless we dare claim that Christianity was fossilized in the first century, we must contend that the Spirit is still speaking to the churches' (p. 48). On the five-fold Gospel, see Faupel, *Everlasting Gospel*, p. 39; Land, *A Passion for the Kingdom*, pp. 55-56; and Donald W. Dayton, *The Theological Roots of Pentecostalism* (Studies in Evangelicalism 5; Metuchen, NJ: Scarecrow Press, 1987). Dayton recognizes the five-fold pattern (p. 20); however, he points out that the four-fold Gospel characterizes all Pentecostals while the five-fold pattern is adopted only by the holiness Pentecostals.

[67] Cf. Goldingay, *Israel's Gospel*, pp. 313-17. Brueggemann, *Theology of the Old Testament*, pp. 180-81.

Scripture, and I reminded him of the healings that I had witnessed and experienced. When faced with death, the doctrine of healing is not a point for theoretical debate, and the belief in God's present willingness to intervene on our behalf is not a dusty tradition. During that time of wrestling with God, I became convinced that God had kept me alive through the day and that I would 'not die, but live, and declare the works of the Lord' (Ps. 118.17). Nevertheless, with the pain continuing, I went to the hospital emergency room and underwent tests that showed a 99 per cent blockage in the left descending cardiac artery (but no heart damage). After four arterial grafts (bypasses) and five days of recovery, I returned home with a good prognosis.

In the wake of my near-death experience, I came back to the study of Judges with a new perspective; and when I read the question of Gideon, I heard in his plaintive voice my own yearning, my own craving for the authentic reality of God's saving presence. I experienced a rekindling of my passion for the manifestation of 'all his wonders' as reflected in the cry of Gideon and in the testimonies of my elders in the Pentecostal family.

Final Reflections

From my interpretive location as a Pentecostal, I hear in Yahweh's stern warning (Judg. 10.11-13) that his patience has its breaking point. At what point does our continued rebellion call for radical judgment on the part of God? The message of Jesus to the seven churches of Asia Minor suggests that the Church is not excused from the requirements of faithfulness. He warns the church at Ephesus, 'Remember therefore from where you have fallen; repent and do the first works, or else I will come to you quickly and remove your lampstand from its place – unless you repent' (Rev 2.5). Judges' call for faithfulness on the part of Israel resonates with Pentecostals and their demand for holiness of heart and life. Obedience issues from the gratitude of a saved and transformed life.

Furthermore, I hear in Jephthah's testimony (Judg. 11.15-24) the longing of one who had been marginalized, excluded, outcast, now laying claim to his place in the community based upon his testimony of the exodus. The exodus demonstrates that Yahweh embraces the outsider and the ostracized. Similarly, to hear the testimony of Judg. 19.30 is to believe that the God of the exodus is the God who stands on the side of the weak, the slave, the abused. It is only when we choose the same stance that we become the holy people that we were meant to be.

For Pentecostals, who often testify of God's saving power, the exodus is paradigmatic for salvation.[68] This soteriology declares that God's power is available and sufficient to deliver us from any power that binds or oppresses. In some contexts salvation might mean liberation from political and social oppression. In others, salvation might be a spiritual work, for just as Yahweh delivered Israel from Egyptian bondage, he delivers us from the bondage of sin. Still another possibility is that salvation can mean deliverance from the power of drugs, alcohol, and other life-controlling substances and addictions.

To hear the question of Gideon is to hunger for a fresh display of Yahweh's 'wonders'. The question of Gideon mirrors our own yearning that the God of the exodus will manifest himself in the work of saving, sanctifying, filling with his Spirit, healing the sick, and reigning as coming king. If we hear Gideon's question, we will turn to the Lord, forsake all of our idols, and destroy our altars to Baal so that our children and grandchildren will receive our testimony with joy.

---

[68] I preached one of my first sermons, at the age of 19, on the text that reads, 'Fear not, but stand still, and see the salvation of the LORD, which he will show to you this day' (Exod. 14.13).

7

JUDGING THE JUDGES: SEARCHING FOR VALUE IN THESE PROBLEMATIC CHARACTERS

Introduction

'Time would fail me', declares the writer of Hebrews,

> to tell of Gideon, Barak, Samson, Jephthah, of David and Samuel and the prophets – who through faith conquered kingdoms, administered justice, obtained promises, shut the mouths of lions, quenched raging fire, escaped the edge of the sword, won strength out of weakness, became mighty in war, put foreign armies to flight'(Heb. 11.32-34; NRSV).

With these words the judges of the Old Testament are forever enshrined as heroes of the faith, and consequently they have served as examples to Christian believers from the first century until now. Careful hearers of the book of Judges, however, might suggest a few changes to Hebrews 11, so that the text would read: 'Time would fail me to tell of the judges ... who through unbelief tested God, committed murders, pursued pleasure, enabled idolatry, and turned Israel into a land of anarchy'.

As these hypothetical changes to Hebrews show, we are faced with paradoxical depictions of the judges; for although the book of Hebrews applauds the faith of the judges, the book of Judges records the obvious flaws and failings of those same judges.[1] Both Jephthah and Samson are particularly unfit for the designation 'heroes', given their apparently immoral character. Jephthah is an outlaw who makes a rash vow that results in the sacrifice of his daughter, and Samson is a divinely chosen nazirite who breaks his sacred vows, marries a forbidden foreigner, sleeps with a prostitute, and loses his God-given power while asleep on the lap of Delilah.

Pre-critical interpreters as a rule are either unwilling or unable to wrestle with the tensions presented by the judges.[2] John Wesley, for example, maintaining that Jephthah did not kill his daughter but only devoted her to life-time tabernacle service, furiously rebukes Matthew Henry for even entertaining the possibility that Jephthah, a chosen leader, would actually sacrifice his daughter.[3] Although I would by no means exonerate Jephthah, I would suggest that he might be no more sinful than other biblical characters, such as the venerable David, who commits adultery and premeditated murder, motivated solely by self-interest.[4] Although Wesley included the book of Judges in his notes on the Bible, he apparently did not preach from Judges.[5] Perhaps Wesley would have agreed with

---

[1] Interpreters from a number of traditions have questioned how it is possible for God to use these judges who seem to be morally deficient. E.g. Wolf, 'Judges', p. 381, calls this tension a 'problem'; and McCann, *Judges*, p. 1, admits that Judges is 'an embarrassment to most church folk'.

[2] On the pre-critical exegesis of Judges, see Chapter 2 of Martin, *The Unheard Voice of God*. Most interpreters prior to the reformation resorted to allegory and typology as the way to make sense of the judges. Cf. David M. Gunn, *Judges* (Blackwell Bible Commentaries; Malden, MA: Blackwell Pub, 2005), who traces the reception history of the entire book of Judges.

[3] John Wesley and G. Roger Schoenhals, *Wesley's Notes on the Bible* (Grand Rapids, MI: Francis Asbury Press, 1987), p. 171. One stream of the Jewish tradition asserts that God's choosing of the judges is evidence of their spiritual qualifications. Cf., for example, Scherman, *Joshua/Judges*, p. xiv, who writes, 'The judges were chosen by God as individuals of outstanding merit'.

[4] One of my former teachers, Jerome Boone, suggested that the brevity of the stories of the judges makes their flaws more conspicuous than those of David, whose failures are a small part of a longer story.

[5] Neither the Scripture index nor the subject index in John Wesley, *The Works of John Wesley* (14 vols.; Grand Rapids, MI: Zondervan, 1958), XIV, pp. 367-532, contains any reference to the book of Judges.

esteemed commentator C.F. Burney, who declares that Judges lacks 'spiritual appeal'.[6]

In my monograph on the book of Judges, I point out that the human characters of Judges have received the primary attention of biblical scholars while the character of Yahweh has not been sufficiently treated. I argue that considerable theological insight can be mined from Judges by paying attention to the previously unappreciated speeches of God in the book.[7] It remains to be seen, however, if anything good can be salvaged when it comes to the actions and attitudes of the judges themselves. Biblical scholarship has doubted that the lives of Barak, Gideon, Jephthah, and Samson can offer any positive theological models for righteousness, holiness, or faithful leadership. Recent interpreters, however, have constructed a theological view of the book of Judges that promises hope for redeeming the judges from the hands of their judges.[8]

In this chapter, I will examine the place of the judges within the argument of the book of Hebrews, and I will evaluate the judges as they are characterized in the narrative of Judges. I will attempt to discover the ways in which the judges may serve as positive figures, and I will suggest connections between the biblical portrait of the judges and our own integrity crisis in contemporary Christian leadership.

The Role of the Judges in Hebrews 11

The book of Hebrews is an elaborately constructed literary masterpiece that speaks to a number of theological, ethical, and social issues that are of concern to its intended audience. Although the complexity of the book continues to defy biblical scholarship's quest for consensus regarding its purpose, the text suggests, on one level at least, that Hebrews is an encouragement to Christian

---

[6] Burney, *The Book of Judges*, p. cxxi. While pre-critical writers and holiness interpreters have struggled primarily with the personal immorality of the judges, it is the violence in Judges that offends many contemporary interpreters.
[7] See Chapter 1 of Martin, *The Unheard Voice of God*.
[8] E.g. Brueggemann, 'Social Criticism', pp. 73-90; McCann, *Judges*, pp. 14-20; and Birch *et al.*, *A Theological Introduction to the Old Testament*, pp. 181-89.

faithfulness in the face of severe opposition.[9] The nature of Hebrews as exhortation is registered in the frequency of hortatory subjunctives: 'Let us fear ... lest anyone fall short' (4.1); 'let us strive' (4.11); 'let us hold fast to our confession' (4.14); 'let us approach with confidence' (4.16); 'let us go on toward perfection' (6.1); 'let us approach with a true heart' (10.22); 'let us hold fast' (10.23); 'let us consider one another' (10.24); 'let us lay aside every weight ... and let us run the race' (12.1); and so forth. Christian believers are enjoined to hold fast, to run their race patiently, and to encourage each other, because Christianity is the better way. Christ is better than the angels (1.4), better than Moses (3.3), better than Joshua (4.8), and better than the Old Testament priesthood (7.1-28). Christians have a better hope (7.19), based on a better covenant (7.22), with better promises (8.6). They offer better sacrifices (10.1), have a better future (10.34), in a better country (11.16), because God has 'provided something better for us' (11.40).

The Christian audience of Hebrews, therefore, is enjoined to do better than the Israelites of the Old Testament; that is, they should go forward and not turn back (Heb. 3.7-4.13). They are exhorted to beware, lest there be found in them 'an evil heart of unbelief' (3.12). They should be steadfast (3.14), unlike the Israelites in the wilderness, who heard God's word but did not have 'faith' (4.2). The audience should not fall into 'unbelief' (4.11), but should believe the living word of God (4.12), and should, in times of struggle, approach the throne of grace through Jesus, the faithful high priest (4.16).

The importance of faith to Christian perseverance, a topic introduced in Hebrews 3, is revisited in ch. 10 in a text which, along with 12.1-3, serves to bracket ch. 11 with calls for steadfastness. Thus, before we are presented with the hero list of ch. 11, we hear, 'the just shall live by faith, but if he should hesitate my soul takes

---

[9] Kimberly F. Baker, 'Hebrews 11 – the Promise of Faith', *RevExp* 94.3 (1997), p. 439, writes that the purpose of Hebrews is 'to call believers to remain steadfast and to take courage'. Cf. David A. Renwick, 'Hebrews 11:29-12:2', *Int* 57.3 (2003), pp. 300-301. See also Harold W. Attridge, 'Paraenesis in a Homily (λόγος παρακλήσεως): The Possible Location of, and Socialization in, the "Epistle to the Hebrews"', *Semeia* 50 (1990), p. 217; William L. Lane, *Hebrews: A Call to Commitment* (Peabody, MA: Hendrickson Publishers, 1988), pp. 472-75; and Paul Ellingworth, *The Epistle to the Hebrews: A Commentary on the Greek Text* (Grand Rapids, MI: Eerdmans, 1993), p. 58.

no pleasure in him. But we are not people of hesitation that leads to destruction, but people of faith[10] that leads to the preserving of the soul' (10.38-39). This faithful endurance is then exemplified in the biblical characters who are presented in Hebrews 11. The kind of faith practiced by these Old Testament believers is more than saving faith;[11] it is 'persevering faith';[12] it is 'active' faith.[13] By faith they obey God; by faith they overcome insurmountable odds; by faith they continue walking with God when contextual forces stand in opposition to his promises.[14] However, even though the heroes of ch. 11 are 'witnesses'[15] to God's faithfulness and are examples of

---

[10] Although the genitives ὑποστολῆς and πίστεως are often translated as if they were plural participles (e.g. 'we are not of those who shrink back ... but of those who believe' [NIV]), they are in fact singular nouns and could be translated, 'we are not of hesitation ... but of faith'. As genitives of relationship, their function is to describe the subject and could be paraphrased, 'we are not characterized by hesitation ... but by faith' (Cf. BDF, §162).

[11] Baker, 'Hebrews 11 – The Promise of Faith', p. 440.

[12] Steven M. Baugh, 'The Cloud of Witnesses in Hebrews 11', WTJ 68.1 (2006), p. 119.

[13] Baker, 'Hebrews 11 – The Promise of Faith', p. 440. Discussions regarding the Christian content of faith within the epistle are not directly germane to my argument; nevertheless, cf. Michael R. Cosby, *The Rhetorical Composition and Function of Hebrews 11: In Light of Example Lists in Antiquity* (Macon, GA: Mercer, 1988), pp. 34-40; and Pamela Michelle Eisenbaum, *The Jewish Heroes of Christian History: Hebrews 11 in Literary Context* (Atlanta, GA: Scholars Press, 1997), p. 144, n. 43 for a list of works that address πίστις in Hebrews. Eisenbaum agrees (as do I) with the leading view that 'Hebrews is continuous with the Jewish understanding of faith as fidelity, firmness, and trust in God' (p. 144), a view that in my mind does not exclude Jesus as the object of saving faith for New Testament believers. So also, Victor Rhee, 'Christology and the Concept of Faith in Hebrews 5:11-6:20', *JETS* 43.1 (2000), p. 93.

[14] On the rhetorical significance of the anaphoric use of 'by faith', see Cosby, *Rhetorical Composition and Function of Hebrews 11*), pp. 41-55; and Michael R. Cosby, 'The Rhetorical Composition of Hebrews 11', *JBL* 107.2 (1988), pp. 258-61.

[15] Baugh, 'The Cloud of Witnesses in Hebrews 11', pp. 118-21. Regarding the function of Hebrews 11, Baugh argues that the heroes are not so much examples whose faith 'we are to emulate' as they are 'recipients of divine testimony to the coming eschatological realities, and thence by faith they became participants in and witnesses to the world to come' (p. 113). Although I am unconvinced of Baugh's primary thesis, he offers a number of helpful observations. E.g. he argues for the cruciality of the repeated motif of seeing the unseen (pp. 121-22), a motif that I also emphasized when I suggested that the faith of Hebrews 11 can 'See the Invisible, Obey the Incomprehensible, Accomplish the Impossible, and Endure the Intolerable' (Lee Roy Martin, 'What Faith Can Do' [Sermon, Cleveland, TN: Prospect Church of God, 28 Jan. 1996]). Baugh's argument is weakened by the fact that he limits his detailed study to only Abel, Enoch, Noah, and Abraham.

endurance, the most important example is Jesus himself. Following the list of prominent Old Testament characters, we hear another call to perseverance, 'Therefore, let us run with endurance the race that is set before us, looking unto Jesus the founder and perfecter of faith ... consider him lest you grow weary and lose heart' (12.1-3).[16]

The bracketing of Hebrews 11 with exhortations to steadfastness,[17] suggests that the function of ch. 11 is to give hope to those who are struggling,[18] by demonstrating the genuine possibility of faithful endurance.[19] These Old Testament characters persevered; they ran faithfully 'on the same field, in the same arena of life, in the name of the same God, as the present readers'.[20] Both of the bracketing texts contain the word 'faith' (Heb. 10.38, 39; 12.2). Thus, the writer of Hebrews argues that the just shall live by faith, and we are people of faith (10.38-39). This faith is exemplified in the heroes of the Old Testament (11.1-40), but Jesus is the greatest example. In fact, he is more than an example; he is the founder and perfecter of faith (12.2).

Having established that at least one purpose of the hero list of Hebrews 11 is to offer hope and encouragement to the hearers of the epistle, let us now examine the place of the four judges within the list. The hero list begins with Abel and proceeds to name

---

[16] For Jesus as an example of endurance, see Victor Rhee, 'Chiasm and the Concept of Faith in Hebrews 11', *BSac* 155.619 (1998), pp. 274-75.

[17] A contextual factor that is recognized by R. Alan Culpepper, 'A Superior Faith: Hebrews 10:19-12:2', *RevExp* 82.3 (1985), pp. 375-80; and Eisenbaum, *Jewish Heroes*, p. 137. This bracketing is not acknowledged by Robert L. Brawley, 'Discoursive Structure and the Unseen in Hebrews 2:8 and 11:1: A Neglected Aspect of the Context', *CBQ* 55.1 (1993), pp. 81-98, whose emphasis is, ironically, on the context of Heb. 11. Cosby, *Rhetorical Composition and Function of Hebrews 11*, pp. 40, 85-89, notes the introductory function of 10.35-39 but does not observe the concluding function of 12.1-3.

[18] Furthermore, in Heb. 11, 'faith and hope are immediately linked', declares Baker ('Hebrews 11 – The Promise of Faith', p. 440). Gerhard Dautzenberg, 'Der Glaube Im Hebraerbrief', *BZ* 17 (1973), pp. 167-68, goes so far as to assert that in Hebrews faith and hope are interchangeable.

[19] Assurance is desperately needed by the intended hearers, argues Renwick, who writes, 'Their strength had been so sapped that the community as a whole could not help its members meet their present difficulties with any enthusiasm, let alone with any longing to persevere' ('Hebrews 11:29-12:2', p. 300).

[20] Renwick, 'Hebrews 11:29-12:2', p. 301. Eisenbaum concludes, 'Calling on the names of so many great biblical individuals and describing their accomplishments is intended as inspiration as well as argumentation' (*Jewish Heroes*, p. 136).

Enoch, Noah, Abraham, Sarah, Isaac, Jacob, Joseph, Moses' parents, Moses, the Israelites, and Rahab in chronological order. In each case, at least one event from the life of the hero is presented as an example of trust in the promises of God. At v. 32, however, the writer expresses a need to conserve time, and the pattern of reportage changes.[21] The faith of the judges, David, and the prophets is described in general terms, without reference to specific events and out of sequence chronologically. Commendation of the judges, David, Samuel, and the prophets is given for the following praiseworthy actions: they 'conquered kingdoms, administered justice, obtained promises, shut the mouths of lions, quenched raging fire, escaped the edge of the sword, won strength out of weakness, became mighty in war, put foreign armies to flight' (Heb. 11.33-34; NRSV). For the purposes of this chapter, we need not connect each action to a particular Old Testament figure, but we should consider a few general observations:[22] 1. All of these actions are interpreted by the writer as expressions of faith, even though the word 'faith' is not found in the book of Judges;[23] 2. All of these actions are related closely to strength and victory in warfare, except for the four phrases in the middle of the list ('administered justice, obtained promises, shut the mouths of lions, quenched raging fire'); 3. The phrase 'obtained promises' is a motif that is prominent in

---

[21] The rhetorical features of Heb. 11.32-34 are detailed by Cosby, *Rhetorical Composition and Function of Hebrews 11*, pp. 57-71.

[22] Surprisingly, the Greek phrases in Heb. 11.32-34 have no verbal parallels in the LXX. Words like 'lion', 'righteousness', 'fire', 'sword', and 'armies' are found in the Old Testament, but not in combination with the verbs used in Hebrews 11.

[23] On the hermeneutics of the writer of Hebrews, see Luke Timothy Johnson, 'The Scriptural World of Hebrews', *Int* 57.3 (2003), pp. 237-50. See also Eisenbaum, *Jewish Heroes*, pp. 89-134, who argues that, as a reinterpretation of Jewish history for a Christian audience, Hebrews 11 displays these attributes: 1. Hebrews 11 removes the nationalism from the Old Testament story; 2. The exploits of the characters in Hebrews 11 are diminished so that their fame will not challenge that of Jesus; and 3. Characters in Hebrews 11 are praised for actions that differ from the actions for which they are praised in the Old Testament. Eisenbaum's is a helpful study, but her selective use and misinterpretation of evidence make her conclusions applicable only to a few of the persons named in Hebrews 11, while her arguments are unconvincing when applied to the whole list. F.F. Bruce, *The Epistle to the Hebrews* (NICNT 58; Grand Rapids: Eerdmans, 1964), pp. 318-21, explicates what he considers to be evidence of faith in Barak, Gideon, Jephthah, and Samson. However, my purpose in this chapter is not to show explicit correspondence between Hebrews and Judges.

Hebrews;[24] 4. The phrases, 'shut the mouths of lions' and 'quenched raging fire', suggest escape from dangers that may not be directly related to warfare; 5. The judges are not venerated for moral virtues, except that they 'administered justice' (εἰργάσαντο δικαιοσύνην), which can mean 'did what was right',[25] but which, coming after 'conquered kingdoms', more likely means that they restored order and justice after vanquishing enemy forces. The administering of justice is lauded by the Old Testament prophets as a quality of godly rule and as a mark of the eschatological kingdom of God.[26] As will become evident when we examine the book of Judges, the mention in Hebrews 11 of the administering of justice reveals a point of agreement between the perspectives of Hebrews and Judges.

Therefore, we might observe that in Hebrews 11 the judges are not commended for their holiness, compassion, generosity, meekness, or self-control.[27] This observation is not surprising, however, when we compare the writer's treatment of the other Old Testament heroes. In fact, none of the heroes of Hebrews 11 are praised for their moral purity and few are presented in the Old Testament as blameless.[28] Noah begins well, but then succumbs to drunkenness and ends up cursing his son. Abraham's life is a series of ups and downs, checkered with lies and doubts. When Sarah hears God's promise, she laughs incredulously. Moses is a murderer; Rahab is a prostitute; David is an adulterer and a premeditated murderer. By faith the Israelites passed through the Red Sea (Heb. 11.29), but the next day they grumbled against Moses (Exod. 15.24). By faith the walls of Jericho fell down (Heb. 11.30); but in their next battle, the Israelites were soundly defeated because of disobedience (Josh. 7.1-15). Samuel was nearly perfect, but he failed in the end by installing his unscrupulous and immoral sons as judges (1 Sam. 8.1-

---

[24] The Greek word ἐπαγγελία is found 14 times in Hebrews (4.1; 6.12, 15, 17; 7.6; 8.6; 9.15; 10.36; 11.9, 13, 17, 33, 39).

[25] *BAGD*, p. 389.

[26] Among many texts, cf. 2 Sam. 8.15; 1 Kgs 10.9; Isa. 9.7; and Jer. 23.5. On this point I am indebted to my friend and colleague William Lyons.

[27] By no means, however, should this detract from the numerous ethical injunctions in Hebrews, e.g. 'Pursue peace with everyone, and holiness without which no one will see the Lord' (12.14).

[28] Of all the characters in Hebrews 11, only Abel, Enoch, and Moses' parents are without fault in the Old Testament narrative.

4). As examples of endurance, therefore, the Old Testament characters are acceptable; but as an example of victory over sin, only Jesus is sufficient (Heb. 4.15).[29]

In spite of their sins, however, the heroes of Hebrews 11 embraced the promises of God and pressed forward beyond their encumbering circumstances and their personal flaws. I contend that the inclusion of the judges in the list of heroes is not a blanket approval of their every act; it does not exonerate them from their crimes.[30] The book of Hebrews, by highlighting the positive qualities of Old Testament characters, provides examples of heroic acts that are worthy of appreciation and emulation.[31]

Although the writer of Hebrews does not choose to point out the failures of the Old Testament characters,[32] those failures are not ignored in the Old Testament, and they would be well-known by the original audience of the book of Hebrews. The Old Testament, by showing both the positive and negative qualities of its characters, is able to utilize these characters in complex and realistic events that register a variety of subtle theological messages. The book of Judges, as narrative, is able to paint a picture of the judges that is more holistic than is possible within the confines of an epistle. Hebrews, therefore, focuses only on the positive characteristics of the judges that might encourage the early Christians to endure faithfully.

In spite of its commendation of the judges, then, Hebrews 11 does not provide justification to disregard the moral and ethical

---

[29] However, we might point to Moses, who chooses suffering instead of 'transitory sinful pleasure' (11.25).

[30] For examples of how interpreters have failed to let stand the tension between Judges and Hebrews 11, see Gunn, *Judges*, pp. 134, 169, and 171.

[31] We could expand the conversation to include famous leaders throughout Christian history. The divisive argument between Barnabus and Paul in Acts 15 does not erase their praiseworthy and sacrificial accomplishments of the previous chapters. The hypocrisy of Peter (Gal. 2.11) does not diminish his role in the inclusion of the Gentile believers (Acts 10-11). Martin Luther's anti-Semitism does not eliminate his courage and steadfastness in leading the Reformation; and the smoke that arises from the burning of Michael Servetus does not blot out the light that shines from John Calvin's commentaries.

[32] Outside of Hebrews 11, however, Old Testament characters can serve negatively as warnings; cf. the Israelites (Heb. 3.7-19) and Esau (Heb. 12.16).

problems that are reflected in the book of Judges.³³ For example, it is not legitimate for us to assume, on the basis of his presence in Hebrews 11, that Jephthah would not have sacrificed his daughter. Nevertheless, the inclusion of the judges among the heroes of faith suggests that our search for something of value in these problematic characters is canonically legitimate.³⁴ We move now to the book of Judges to continue that search.

The Role of the Judges In The Book of Judges

The judges do not appear in a vacuum; rather, they emerge as characters within the narrative of the book of Judges. Consequently, I would argue that the value of the judges must be discerned in light of their place in the narrative and message of the book of Judges. The judges are mentioned first in the prologue of the book (2.6-3.6), which outlines the cyclical framework for the series of stories to come in Judges 3-16. The cycle begins when the Israelites forget Yahweh and engage in idolatry. The behavior of the Israelites provokes Yahweh to anger, and he disciplines them by handing them over to an oppressive enemy. The Israelites then cry out to Yahweh for deliverance, and Yahweh is moved with compassion because of their suffering. Finally, Yahweh raises up a judge who saves the Israelites from their enemy, and the land enjoys a time of peace. Although each appearance of the cycle incorporates a unique combination of elements,³⁵ the cycle can be reduced to two basic movements. First, the Israelites rebel and Yahweh punishes them; and

---

³³ Gunn, *Judges*, pp. 106-109, shows how popular character studies have downplayed the flaws of the judges.

³⁴ It might be argued that Hebrews 11 has already identified the value of the judges – their value is in their faith. Such an argument has merit; but as I pointed out above, the writer of Hebrews characterizes the judges in a way that advances the argument of Hebrews. I hope to discern the value of the judges as they are portrayed in the book of Judges. I accept, with some limitations, the contention of Robby Waddell, *The Spirit of the Book of Revelation* (JPTSup 30; Blandford Forum: Deo Publishing, 2006), p. 78, that the intertextual reading of an interpretive text (Hebrews) will cause us to reconsider and revise our readings of the interpreted text (Judges).

³⁵ The variations are charted in detail by O'Connell, *The Rhetoric of the Book of Judges*, pp. 22-25.

second, the Israelites cry to Yahweh and Yahweh saves them.[36] Both of these movements hinge on the responsiveness of Yahweh, who acts out of both judgment (sin/punishment) and mercy (cry/salvation) to preserve Yahweh's covenant relationship to Israel.

Although the actions of the judges relate on the surface to the second movement of the cycle (cry and salvation), at a symbolic level the lives of the judges intersect with the first movement (sin and punishment) as well. That is, the sin of Israel is reflected in the flaws of the judges. This symbolism develops out of the perspective toward Israel's sin that is conveyed by the book of Judges. The besetting sin of the Israelites is breaking the covenant, forsaking Yahweh, and worshiping foreign gods – in a word: idolatry. Furthermore, the book of Judges presents Yahweh's relationship to his people in corporate terms. The unfaithfulness of the Israelites, therefore, incurs Yahweh's punishment of the entire people; and the cries of the Israelites elicit Yahweh's compassion toward the entire body.[37] Finally, the behavior of the Israelites grows worse throughout Judges (2.19); therefore, the repeated pattern represents more than a cyclical repetition; it is a downward spiral.[38]

This corporate downward spiral into unfettered idolatry is paralleled in the narrative by the problematic behavior of the judges themselves. The increasingly negative characterization of the judges mirrors the increasingly disobedient character of the Israelites and the overall spiritual decline within the book.[39] Othniel is the ideal judge, a mighty warrior, who saves Israel from the oppressive king

---

[36] Cf. Beyerlin, 'Gattung und Herkunft', pp. 1-29; and Brueggemann, 'Social Criticism', pp. 73-90. See also Chapter 4 of this work.

[37] The book of Judges uses the term ישראל or בני ישראל, 'Israelites' (154 times) even when only one or two tribes are in view (e.g. Abimelech rules Shechem only, but the narrative says he 'ruled Israel' [9.22], and Jephthah leads Gilead alone, but the text says he 'judged Israel' [12.7]). Although the judges and their battles may be limited in scope, the narrative (by using 'Israelites') invests each episode with national significance, a feature observed as well by von Rad, *Old Testament Theology*, I, pp. 331-32; Gottwald, *The Tribes of Yahweh*, p. 149; Pietro Alberto Kaswalder, 'Le Tribù in Gdc 1,1-2,5 e in Gdc 4-5', *LA* 43 (1993), p. 89; and Goldingay, *Israel's Gospel*, pp. 531-33. Cf. Adewuya, *Holiness and Community in 2 Cor. 6:14-7:1*, whose work is an important challenge to the Church's rampant individualism.

[38] Lilley, 'A Literary Appreciation of the Book of Judges', pp. 98-99.

[39] Cf. Exum, 'The Centre Cannot Hold', pp. 410-31, who traces the pattern of decline through the book.

Cushan-rishathaim (3.7-11). The progression from the ideal (Othniel) to the worst of the judges (Samson) begins subtly with the second judge Ehud, who has no major flaws; but his left-handedness makes him less than ideal (3.15). Deborah is also without fault, but her gender may have presented her with distinct challenges in the male-dominated society. Barak is the first judge to show a hint of weakness, when he hesitates to follow the instructions of Deborah (4.6).[40] Gideon, the next judge, is a full-fledged coward (6.27), who requires repeated assurances from God and who unwittingly leads Israel back into idolatry (8.27). Jephthah, the son of a prostitute, is an outcast from society who is chosen not by God, but by the elders of Gilead. Jephthah foolishly vows to offer up as a whole burnt offering the first person (or thing) who comes out to greet him on his safe return from battle (11.30-31). Jephthah saves the Israelites from only one of the two nations who threaten the Israelites (10.7), thus being the first judge who fails to bring complete deliverance. Finally, Samson does not save Israel at all; he only 'begin[s] to save' them from the Philistines (13.5) through the limited impact of his brief skirmishes.[41] Samson is the only judge who does not raise an army of Israelites and inspire a rebellion against their oppressor. Samson is the only judge who is captured by the enemy. The story of Samson, however, ends with a ray of hope, as he cries out to Yahweh who restores his strength, enabling him to destroy the temple of Dagon, thus striking at the very heart of the enemy's god.[42] In spite of Samson's final individual effort, however, the downward spiral is complete, as the Israelites are content to live under the domination of the Philistines (15.11). Samson serves as a paradigmatic figure, whose feeble response to divine gifting represents the inability of all Israel to remain loyal to the covenant.[43] At the end of Judges anarchy and immorality reign supreme, and the Israelites do as they please because there is no king – neither human nor divine – in Israel (17.6; 18.1; 19.1; 21.25).

---

[40] Cf. Gunn, *Judges*, pp. 68-69.

[41] See my discussion of Samson in Chapter 5 of this work.

[42] Cf. Webb, *Judges: An Integrated Reading*, p. 167; and Greenstein, 'The Riddle of Samson', p. 252.

[43] That the story of Samson represents the story of Israel is argued convincingly by Greenstein, 'The Riddle of Samson', pp. 237-60.

The foregoing sketch of Judges suggests that the flaws of Barak, Gideon, Jephthah, and Samson are essential to the theological message of the book of Judges and carry a significant spiritual warning. The increasingly problematic character of the judges parallels the increasingly disobedient character of the Israelites. If the writer of Judges had chosen to downplay the failures of these final judges, the narrative impact of the book would have been greatly diminished. The sin of the judges, in conjunction with the sin of Israel, registers a valuable spiritual message, though a *negative* one.

A more positive role for the judges is their participation in the second movement of the cycle – cry and salvation. In Judges the Israelites violate their covenant with Yahweh by pursuing other gods, thereby provoking the wrath of Yahweh, who gives his people over to an enemy power. These enemies are the Canaanite city-states, small kingdoms that are ruled by autocratic monarchs, who dispense tyranny from within fortified cities. Many of these kings and their city-states are listed among the conquests of Joshua (Josh. 12). Like the Egyptians, the Canaanites represent oppressive forces that undermine the liberating nature of the Mosaic covenant. In the Canaanite system, the gods are an integral part of the royal power structure, bound to the king and his ruling elite. In the Mosaic covenant, however, God is free and stands as judge over the political structure. In the Canaanite system, human rights are afforded only to the wealthy landowners; but in the Mosaic covenant, even the poor, the widow, the orphan, and the alien are given human rights. McCann argues that the Canaanites symbolize the 'ways of organizing social life that perpetuate injustice and ultimately produce oppressive inequalities that threaten human life'.[44]

The suffering of the oppressed Israelites is portrayed vividly in the accounts of Judges. King Jabin of Hazor, the enemy in the Barak story, 'mightily oppressed' the Israelites for 20 years (Judg. 4.3). The Philistines and the Ammonites, the foes of Jephthah, 'vexed and oppressed the Israelites 18 years' and the Israelites were 'sore distressed' (10.8-9). It is said that the Philistines, against whom Samson struggled, ruled over the Israelites 40 years (13.1). The most extensive description of Israel's suffering is found in ch. 6, where the violence of the Midianites is described:

---

[44] McCann, *Judges*, p. 19.

> The hand of Midian prevailed over Israel; and because of Midian the Israelites provided for themselves hiding places in the mountains, caves and strongholds. For whenever the Israelites put in seed, the Midianites and the Amalekites and the people of the east would come up against them. They would encamp against them and destroy the produce of the land, as far as the neighborhood of Gaza, and leave no sustenance in Israel, and no sheep or ox or donkey. For they and their livestock would come up, and they would even bring their tents, as thick as locusts; neither they nor their camels could be counted; so they wasted the land as they came in. Thus Israel was greatly impoverished because of Midian; and the Israelites cried out to the LORD for help (Judg. 6.2-5; NRSV).

Once in bondage to these oppressive forces, the Israelites 'cannot evade the superior power, and their powers of resistance are inadequate. The force that is oppressing or threatening the people, the attacking enemy, is simply stronger'.[45] Jabin, for example, has iron chariots (4.3), and the Midianites have a vast army riding on camels (6.5).

Under the burden of tyranny and in the face of hopelessness, Gideon laments, 'where are the wonders that our ancestors recounted to us?' (6.13). The Israelites cry out to Yahweh, and he hears their cries and is moved with compassion. Yahweh's response belongs to the paradigm of the exodus in which Yahweh reveals himself as Israel's savior, and to the Mosaic covenant in which he reveals himself as Israel's king, her suzerain, who guarantees freedom from the human structures of authority that seek to dominate and enslave.[46] Yahweh, therefore, is a new kind of Ancient Near Eastern God who is not bound to human political systems and, therefore, is not beholden to human centers of power. Yahweh is the God who is free to bestow his saving power upon whomsoever he will, who is faithful to his covenant people, who passionately

---

[45] Welker, *God the Spirit*, p. 52. It must be remembered that God, not the judge, is the hero of the story. Any reading of the Bible that attends to the roles of human characters to the exclusion of the role of God will be theologically deficient.

[46] The exodus is mentioned in nine verses of Judges (2.1, 12; 6.8, 9, 13; 10.11; 11.13, 16 and 19.30) and seems to be in the background of Judg. 5.5 and 21. On the importance of these references to the exodus, see Chapter 6 above.

embraces those who suffer, and who suffers with them. Because of his covenant loyalty, Yahweh determines to deliver Israel from the oppressive powers of the Canaanites.

When Yahweh decides to move on behalf of Israel, he 'raises up' (2.16; 3.9; 3.15; etc.) judges who will mobilize the people and lead them to freedom from bondage. Yahweh recruits human partners who serve in an active role of leadership, human partners who 'succeed in restoring loyalty, solidarity, and the capacity for communal action among the people'.[47] In spite of their weaknesses, even the most troubling of the judges are able to accomplish amazing and inspiring deeds as they pursue salvation and justice for their communities. The judges, therefore, are more than a reflection of the spiraling decline of Israel's relationship to Yahweh; they are active participants in God's work of salvation. As human agents who are raised up by Yahweh to bring deliverance to the Israelites, the judges register Yahweh's response to the Israelites' cries for help and his intervention on their behalf.[48]

The ministry of the judges, therefore, witnesses to the 'important role of human agency in partnership with the redeeming activity of God'.[49] In this role the judges are called 'saviors' (3.9; 3.15), who 'save' Israel (2.16; 3.9; 3.31; 6.14; 10.1; and 13.5). These saviors, however, do not act alone; they are Spirit-empowered leaders who challenge the community to action. At the behest of Deborah, Barak gathers a fighting force of 10,000 men. The Spirit of Yahweh clothes Gideon who subsequently sounds the trumpet and assembles an army (6.34). The Spirit of Yahweh comes upon Jephthah who travels throughout the region, calling the people together for battle. The judges are able to create a 'renewal of the people's unanimity and capacity for action, a renewal of the people's power of resistance in the midst of universal despair'.[50] What is commendable in the judges is their willingness to surrender themselves to God and to his saving mission, even when striving against overwhelming opposition. The judges respond in obedience to God's

---

[47] Welker, *God the Spirit*, p. 53; cf. p. 56.
[48] See Chapter 5 above.
[49] Birch *et al.*, *A Theological Introduction to the Old Testament*, p. 122.
[50] Welker, *God the Spirit*, p. 53.

call; and with God's promise as their only assurance, they place themselves at risk in the battle to deliver Israel.

Theologically, the battle of the judges against the Canaanites represents resistance to oppression and life-negating forces of evil. The judges encourage us to pursue God's continuing mission of liberation, equality, justice, and peace (cf. Isaiah 11). The stories of the judges compel us to participate enthusiastically and sacrificially in God's work of salvation. The mission of the judges is not far from that of Jesus the Messiah, who declared, 'The Spirit of the Lord is upon me, because he has anointed me to bring good news to the poor. He has sent me to proclaim release to the captives and recovery of sight to the blind, to let the oppressed go free' (Lk. 4.18; NRSV).[51]

While I am arguing that the primary spiritual value of the judges is to be found in their dedication to God's mission of deliverance, I would suggest as well that the charismatic nature of their leadership continues to offer an important model for the Church. The Old Testament people of Israel existed under two primary models of organization – tribal leadership and monarchy. Each of these paradigms has distinct benefits and clear drawbacks, and we could argue for the advantage of one over the other. While it is true that charismatic leadership finds more acceptance within egalitarian tribal organization than within hierarchical structures, the biblical narrative seems to bear witness to the value of charismatic leadership as a continuing element in the government of God's people.[52]

---

[51] It is not that we have lost our will to fight, but that we, like the Israelites at the end of Judges, fight among ourselves rather than fighting against the oppressor. We fight over ecclesiastical politics; we fight over budgets; we fight over recognition; we fight over personal rights; we fight over fine points of theology; we fight over church programs; we fight over denominational pride; we fight over music styles. Our energy is expended by internal strife, so that we have no strength to fight for the weak, the poor, and the disenfranchised. We should be treading on serpents and scorpions, casting out devils, and laying hands on the sick. If the Church serves Baal, who is left to offer hope to the alcoholic, the drug addict, the prostitute, the pornographer, the laid-off factory worker, the abandoned child, the widow, and the single mother?

[52] A vast literature has developed around the sociology of charismatic leadership; and while I appreciate the insights of sociology, I would argue that sociological studies do not account for the theological content of the biblical model of charismatic leadership. On charismatic leadership in Judges, see Timothy M. Willis, 'The Nature of Jephthah's Authority', *CBQ* 59 (1997), pp. 33-44; Abraham Malamat, 'Charismatic Leadership in the Book of Judges', in F. Cross, W. Lemke,

Pre-monarchic Israel is structured around tribes, elders, and local chieftains; and although God often chooses to utilize established leaders (e.g. Num. 11.16; Judg. 3.9), he also raises up leaders who held no previously recognized authority (Judg. 6.11; 11.1-11). Once Israel becomes a centralized monarchy, the entire social structure is reordered; and the king has power to authorize, commission, and empower leaders.[53] Even under the monarchy, however, God continues to raise up charismatic leaders, leaders who do not come to their position by inheritance, leaders who do not arrive through political campaigns, leaders who do not gain their positions through violent overthrow of their predecessors, leaders who are raised up by God, authorized and empowered by the Spirit of God. The history of the church is in part a struggle for a biblical system of ecclesial polity that is just, equitable, and effective in governing the Church and in facilitating the Church's mission. As the Pentecostal movement grows and is challenged by forces of institutionalization, it is important that we retain the biblical appreciation for charismatic leadership.[54]

The Judges Are Among Us

I have shown that due to the tension between Hebrews 11 and the book of Judges we have struggled to find an appropriate interpretation of and response to the judges. On the one hand, the judges can be helpful as examples of charismatic leaders who devote

---

and P. Miller (eds.), *Magnalia Dei, the Mighty Acts of God: Essays on the Bible and Archaeology in Memory of G. Ernest Wright* (Garden City, NY: Doubleday, 1976), pp. 293-310; Peter A. Munch, 'The "Judges" of Ancient Israel: An Exploration in Charismatic Authority', in W. Swatos (ed.), *Time, Place, and Circumstance: Neo-Weberian Studies in Comparative Religious History* (New York: Greenwood Press, 1990), pp. 57-69; Ze'eb Weisman, 'Charismatic Leaders in the Era of the Judges', *ZAW* 89 (1977), pp. 399-411.

[53] King David himself is a charismatic leader, but most of the charismatics in the monarchic period are prophets.

[54] On the role of charismatic leadership in the Pentecostal movement, see Margaret M. Poloma, *The Assemblies of God at the Crossroads: Charisma and Institutional Dilemmas* (Knoxville, TN: University of Tennessee Press, 1989); Margaret M. Poloma, 'Charisma, Institutionalization and Social Change', *PNEUMA* 17.2 (1995), pp. 245-52; and Margaret M. Poloma, 'The Future of American Pentecostal Identity: The Assemblies of God at a Crossroad', in Michael Welker (ed.), *The Work of the Spirit* (Grand Rapids, MI: Eerdmans, 2006), pp. 147-68.

themselves to the saving mission of God; on the other hand, their reputations are stained by moral flaws. I would suggest that our struggle with the judges parallels in some ways the contemporary integrity crisis in Christian leadership. The Holiness-Pentecostal movement is mired in a culture that is unable to deal effectively with issues of discipline. We rightly affirm the Wesleyan tradition of Christian perfection, but we have unwittingly created an idealized view of leadership, which tends to follow one of two extremes. Either ministers are not held accountable for their sins because it is believed that the 'success' of their ministry is proof that they are in good standing with God; or ministers are forced out of their pastorates because of sins that might demand disciplinary action, but which should not disqualify the person for ministry.[55] Either we refuse to require accountability for moral failings (even when the person is convicted for criminal behavior), or we demonize any leader who is suspected of a moral lapse.

It is clear that the endowment of the Spirit does not grant infallibility to humans. It is also clear that Spirit-filled leaders should not be immune from the demands of biblical holiness. Barak is celebrated for his victory, but he is rebuked for his hesitancy (Judg. 4.9). Gideon is praised for leading 300 brave soldiers against a mighty army of Midianites, but he is reprimanded for constructing a golden ephod (Judg. 8.27).[56] I am not suggesting that the Church should use the Old Testament as the primary resource for the development of a theology of leadership, but I am suggesting that our uncertain response to the judges is symptomatic of our uncertain response to contemporary leadership failure. In a nutshell, when leaders fail, we do not know what to do!

Conclusion

The positive representation of the judges in Hebrews 11 must not be seen as a blanket endorsement of their lives and character, but neither should the Old Testament's portrayal of the negative

---

[55] Assuming, of course, that the person was willing to submit to discipline.
[56] Neither Jephthah nor Samson is rebuked directly in the text of Judges, partly because their sins are obvious and partly because God withdraws and does not speak.

qualities of the judges cause us to doubt the appropriateness of the judges inclusion in Hebrews 11. Pre-critical interpreters, who come to the text with a predisposed sympathy toward biblical characters, tend to be unable or unwilling to wrestle with difficult texts that expose the spiritual inadequacies of those characters. Thus, pre-critical commentators often minimize the undesirable aspects of Old Testament characters while focusing upon their heroic traits. Critical interpreters, however, with no vested interest in defending the biblical characters, often highlight their shortcomings and flaws. I would argue that neither approach fully appreciates the richly textured portrayals of the biblical characters and neither does justice to the biblical text as narrative theology.

We find similar inappropriate polarizing responses when faced with contemporary leadership failures. Church leaders who stumble are either demonized as worthless hypocrites or their sins are minimized through the uncritical use of the clichés: 'nobody's perfect' or 's/he is only human'. On the one hand, even a small error can lead to complete ruin, or on the other hand, a gross moral failure can result in no more than a brief embarrassment, depending upon the prevalent mood of the public. Unfortunately, genuine dialogue, reflection, and discernment are rarely employed as responses to leadership transgressions.

Early holiness and Pentecostal Christians are well known for their devotion to the mission of God in the world; but the contemporary Church, much like Israel, is tempted to accommodate itself to the dominant culture, to be seduced by the idols of the powerful, and to abandon God's mission of salvation for the poor and oppressed. In many places, the Church itself is in bondage to the Canaanites. Like Israel, the Church has settled down with the Canaanites, intermarried with the Canaanites, and served the gods of the Canaanites (Judg. 3.5-6). Let us cry out to God for deliverance, trusting that he will raise up Spirit-filled leaders who will sound a call that mobilizes the Church to repentance, renewal, and mission.

BIBLIOGRAPHY

Ackerman, Susan, *Warrior, Dancer, Seductress, Queen: Women in Judges and Biblical Israel* (AB Reference Library; New York: Doubleday, 1998).
Adewuya, J. Ayodeji, *Holiness and Community in 2 Cor. 6:14-7:1: Paul's View of Communal Holiness in the Corinthian Correspondence* (New York: Peter Lang, 2001).
Alexander, Kimberly Ervin, and R. Hollis Gause, *Women in Leadership: A Pentecostal Perspective* (Cleveland, TN: Center for Pentecostal Leadership & Care, 2006).
Allen, R.B., 'עמל', in R. Laird Harris, Gleason L. Archer and Bruce K. Waltke (eds.), *Theological Wordbook of the Old Testament* (2 vols.; Chicago: Moody Press, 1980), II, p. 675.
Amit, Yairah, *The Book of Judges: The Art of Editing* (trans. Jonathan Chipman; Biblical Interpretation 38; Leiden: Brill, 1999).
Archer, Kenneth J., *A Pentecostal Hermeneutic: Spirit, Scripture and Community* (Cleveland, TN: CPT Press, 2009). First published: (JPTSup 28; London: T&T Clark, 2004).
Assis, Elie, 'Man, Woman, and God in Judg 4', *Scandinavian Journal of the Old Testament* 20.1 (2006), pp. 110-24.
Attridge, Harold W., 'Paraenesis in a Homily (λόγος παρακλήσεως): The Possible Location of, and Socialization in, the "Epistle to the Hebrews"', *Semeia* 50 (1990), pp. 211-26.
Auld, A. Graeme, 'Gideon: Hacking at the Heart of the Old Testament', *Vetus Testamentum* 39 (1989), pp. 257-67.
Auzou, Georges, *La Force de l'Esprit, Étude du 'Livre des Juges'* (Paris: Éditions de l'Orante, 1966).
Baker, Kimberly F., 'Hebrews 11 – the Promise of Faith', *Review & Expositor* 94.3 (1997), pp. 439-45.
Bal, Mieke, *Death & Dissymmetry: The Politics of Coherence in the Book of Judges* (Chicago Studies in the History of Judaism; Chicago: University of Chicago Press, 1988).
Baugh, Steven M., 'The Cloud of Witnesses in Hebrews 11', *Westminster Theological Journal* 68.1 (2006), pp. 113-32.
Benson, Alphonsus, 'The Spirit of God in the Didactic Books of the Old Testament' (STD Diss., Catholic University of America, 1949).
Bernhardt, Karl, 'אין', in G.J. Botterweck and H. Ringgren (eds.), *Theological Dictionary of the Old Testament* (trans. D.E. Green; 18 vols.; Grand Rapids, MI: Eerdmans, 1973-), I, pp. 140-47.
Beyerlin, Walter, 'Gattung und Herkunft des Rahmens im Richterbuch', in Ernst Würthwein and Otto Kaiser (eds.), *Tradition und Situation: Studien zur alttestamentlichen Prophetie. Artur Weiser zum 70 Geburtstag* (Göttingen: Vandenhoeck & Ruprecht, 1963), pp. 1-29.

—'Geschichte und heilsgeschichtliche Traditionsbildung im alten Testament: Ein Beitrag zur Traditionsgeschichte von Richter 6-8', *Vetus Testamentum* 13 (1963), pp. 1-25.

Birch, Bruce C. et al., *A Theological Introduction to the Old Testament* (Nashville: Abingdon Press, 1999).

Block, Daniel I., 'Deborah among the Judges: The Perspective of the Hebrew Historian', in A. Millard, J. Hoffmeier and D. Baker (eds.), *Faith, Tradition, and History* (Winona Lake, IN: Eisenbrauns, 1994), pp. 229-53.

—*Judges, Ruth* (New American Commentary 6; Nashville, TN: Broadman & Holman Publishers, 1999).

—'Why Deborah's Different', *Bible Review* 17.3 (2001), pp. 34-40, 49-52.

Boling, Robert G., *Judges: A New Translation with Introduction and Commentary* (AB; Garden City, NY: Doubleday, 1975).

Boogaart, Thomas A., 'Stone for Stone: Retribution in the Story of Abimelech and Shechem', *Journal for the Study of the Old Testament* 32 (1985), pp. 45-56.

Brawley, Robert L., 'Discoursive Structure and the Unseen in Hebrews 2:8 and 11:1: A Neglected Aspect of the Context', *Catholic Biblical Quarterly* 55.1 (1993), pp. 81-98.

Brettler, Marc Z., *The Book of Judges* (Old Testament Readings; New York: Routledge, 2002).

Bruce, F.F., *The Epistle to the Hebrews* (New International Commentary on the New Testament 58; Grand Rapids: Eerdmans, 1964).

Brueggemann, Walter, *The Bible Makes Sense* (Atlanta: John Knox Press, 1977).

—'Social Criticism and Social Vision in the Deuteronomic Formula of the Judges', in Patrick D. Miller (ed.), *A Social Reading of the Old Testament: Prophetic Approaches to Israel's Communal Life* (Minneapolis, MN: Fortress Press, 1981), pp. 73-90.

—*Theology of the Old Testament: Testimony, Dispute, Advocacy* (Minneapolis: Fortress Press, 1997).

—'The Recovering God of Hosea', *Horizons in Biblical Theology* 30.1 (2008), pp. 5-20

Burney, C.F., *The Book of Judges, with Introduction and Notes* (London: Rivingtons, 1918).

Childs, Brevard S., *Biblical Theology of the Old and New Testaments: Theological Reflection on the Christian Bible* (Minneapolis, MN: Fortress Press, 1st Fortress Press edn, 1993).

Claassens, L. Juliana M., 'The Character of God in Judges 6-8: The Gideon Narrative as Theological and Moral Resource', *Horizons in Biblical Theology* 23.1 (2001), pp. 51-71.

Cosby, Michael R., *The Rhetorical Composition and Function of Hebrews 11: In Light of Example Lists in Antiquity* (Macon, GA: Mercer, 1988).

—'The Rhetorical Composition of Hebrews 11', *Journal of Biblical Literature* 107.2 (1988), pp. 257-73.

Crenshaw, James L., *Samson: A Secret Betrayed, a Vow Ignored* (Atlanta: John Knox Press, 1978).

Culpepper, R. Alan, 'A Superior Faith: Hebrews 10:19-12:2', *Review & Expositor* 82.3 (1985), pp. 375-90.
Dautzenberg, Gerhard, 'Der Glaube im Hebraerbrief', *Biblische Zeitschrift* 17 (1973), pp. 161-77.
Dayton, Donald W., *The Theological Roots of Pentecostalism* (Studies in Evangelicalism 5; Metuchen, NJ: Scarecrow Press, 1987).
Eichrodt, Walther, *Theology of the Old Testament* (2 vols.; Philadelphia: Westminster Press, 1961).
Eisenbaum, Pamela Michelle, *The Jewish Heroes of Christian History: Hebrews 11 in Literary Context* (Atlanta, GA: Scholars Press, 1997).
Ellingworth, Paul, *The Epistle to the Hebrews: A Commentary on the Greek Text* (Grand Rapids, MI: Eerdmans, 1993).
Even-Shoshan, Avraham, *A New Concordance of the Old Testament* (Jerusalem: Kiryat Sefer, Baker/Ridgefield edn, 1983).
Exum, J. Cheryl, 'Promise and Fulfillment: Narrative Art in Judges 13', *Journal of Biblical Literature* 99 (1980), pp. 43-59.
—'Aspects of Symmetry and Balance in the Samson Saga', *Journal for the Study of the Old Testament* 19 (1981), pp. 3-29.
—'The Theological Dimension of the Samson Saga', *Vetus Testamentum* 33 (1983), pp. 30-45.
—'The Centre Cannot Hold: Thematic and Textual Instabilities in Judges', *Catholic Biblical Quarterly* 52 (1990), pp. 410-31.
Faupel, William, *The Everlasting Gospel: The Significance of Eschatology in the Development of Pentecostal Thought* (JPTSup 10; Sheffield: Sheffield Academic Press, 1996).
Fee, Gordon D., *God's Empowering Presence: The Holy Spirit in the Letters of Paul* (Peabody, MA: Hendrickson Publishers, 1994).
Fiddes, Paul S., *The Creative Suffering of God* (New York: Clarendon Press, 1988).
Finkelstein, Israel, and Neil Asher Silberman, *The Bible Unearthed: Archaeology's New Vision of Ancient Israel and the Origin of Its Sacred Texts* (New York: Free Press, 2001).
Fokkelman, J.P., 'Structural Remarks on Judges 9 and 19', in M. Fishbane, E. Tov and W. Fields (eds.), *Sha'arei Talmon* (Winona Lake, IN: Eisenbrauns, 1992), pp. 33-45.
Fredricks, Gary, 'Rethinking the Role of the Holy Spirit in the Lives of Old Testament Believers', *Trinity Journal* 9.1 (1988), pp. 81-104.
Fretheim, Terence E., *The Suffering of God: An Old Testament Perspective* (Overtures to Biblical Theology 14; Philadelphia: Fortress Press, 1984).
—'Salvation in the Bible vs Salvation in the Church', *Word & World* 13 (1993), pp. 363-72.
Freytag, Gustav, *Die Technik des Dramas* (Leipzig: S. Hirzel, 1897).
Frolov, Serge, *The Turn of the Cycle: 1 Samuel 1-8 in Synchronic and Diachronic Perspectives* (New York: Walter de Gruyter, 2004).
—'Rethinking Judges', *Catholic Biblical Quarterly* 71 (2009), pp. 24-41.

Gamberoni, J., 'לבשׁ', in G.J. Botterweck and H. Ringgren (eds.), *Theological Dictionary of the Old Testament* (trans. D.E. Green; 18 vols.; Grand Rapids, MI: Eerdmans, 1973-), VII, pp. 457-68.

Gerstenberger, Erhard, *Theologies in the Old Testament* (trans. John Bowden; Minneapolis: Fortress Press, Fortress Press edn, 2002).

Gesenius, Wilhelm, E. Kautzsch, and A.E. Cowley, *Gesenius' Hebrew Grammar* (Oxford: The Clarendon Press, 2d English edn, 1910).

Gillmayr-Bucher, Susanne, 'Framework and Discourse in the Book of Judges', *Journal of Biblical Literature* 128 (2009), pp. 687-728.

Goldingay, John, 'The Breath of Yahweh Scorching, Confounding, Anointing: The Message of Isaiah 40-42', *Journal of Pentecostal Theology* 11 (1997), pp. 3-34.

—*Old Testament Theology: Israel's Gospel* (Downers Grove, IL: InterVarsity Press, 2003).

—*Old Testament Theology: Israel's Faith* (Downers Grove, IL: InterVarsity Press, 2006).

Gooding, D.W., 'The Composition of the Book of Judges', in *Eretz-Israel, Archeological Historical and Geographical Studies XVI* (Jerusalem: Israel Exploration Society, 1982), pp. 70-79.

Goslinga, C.J., *Joshua, Judges, Ruth* (Grand Rapids, MI: Regency Reference Library, 1986).

Gottwald, Norman K., *The Tribes of Yahweh: A Sociology of the Religion of Liberated Israel, 1250-1050 B.C.E.* (Maryknoll, NY: Orbis Books, 1979).

Gray, John, *Joshua, Judges, and Ruth* (New Century Bible; Greenwood, SC: Attic Press, rev. edn, 1977).

Green, Chris E.W., *Sanctifying Interpretation: Vocation, Holiness, and Scripture* (Cleveland, TN: CPT Press, 2015).

Green, Michael, *I Believe in the Holy Spirit* (I Believe 1; Grand Rapids, MI: Eerdmans, 1975).

Greenspahn, Frederick E., 'The Theology of the Framework of Judges', *Vetus Testamentum* 36 (1986), pp. 385-96.

Greenstein, Edward L., 'The Riddle of Samson', *Prooftexts* 1.3 (1981), pp. 237-60.

Guest, P. Deryn, 'Can Judges Survive without Sources? Challenging the Consensus', *Journal for the Study of the Old Testament* 78 (1998), pp. 43-61.

Guillaume, Philippe, *Waiting for Josiah: The Judges* (JSOTSup 385; New York: T & T Clark, 2004).

Gunn, David M., *Judges* (Blackwell Bible Commentaries; Malden, MA: Blackwell Pub, 2005).

Hamilton, Victor P., 'פלג', in R. Laird Harris, Gleason L. Archer and Bruce K. Waltke (eds.), *Theological Wordbook of the Old Testament* (2 vols.; Chicago: Moody Press, 1980), II, pp. 724.

Hamlin, E. John, *At Risk in the Promised Land: A Commentary on the Book of Judges* (International Theological Commentary; Grand Rapids, MI: Eerdmans, 1990).

Harris, J. Gordon, Cheryl Anne Brown, and Michael S. Moore, *Joshua, Judges, Ruth* (New International Biblical Commentary; Peabody, MA: Hendrickson Publishers, 2000).

Hausmann, J., 'צלח', in G.J. Botterweck and H. Ringgren (eds.), *Theological Dictionary of the Old Testament* (trans. D.E. Green; 18 vols.; Grand Rapids, MI: Eerdmans, 1973-), XII, pp. 382-85.
Herr, Denise Dick, and Mary Petrina Boyd, 'A Watermelon Named Abimelech', *Biblical Archaeology Review* 28.1 (2002), pp. 34-37, 62.
Herzberg, Bruce, 'Deborah and Moses', *Journal for the Study of the Old Testament* 38.1 (2013), pp. 15–33.
Heschel, Abraham Joshua, *The Prophets* (2 vols.; New York: Harper & Row, 1962).
Hildebrandt, Wilf, *An Old Testament Theology of the Spirit of God* (Peabody, MA: Hendrickson Publishers, 1995).
Hollenweger, Walter J., *The Pentecostals* (trans. R.A. Wilson; Minneapolis, MN: Augsburg Pub. House, 1st US edn, 1972).
Horton, Stanley M., 'The Holy Spirit in the Book of Judges', *Paraclete* 3 (1969), pp. 9-14.
—*What the Bible Says About the Holy Spirit* (Springfield, MO: Gospel Pub. House, 1976).
Hughes, Robert B., and J. Carl Laney, *Tyndale Concise Bible Commentary* (The Tyndale Reference Library; Wheaton, IL: Tyndale House Publishers, 2001).
Hunter, Harold D., *Spirit-Baptism: A Pentecostal Alternative* (Lanham, MD: University Press of America, 1983).
—*Spirit Baptism: A Pentecostal Alternative* (Eugene, OR: Wipf & Stock, 2009).
Isbell, Charles D., *The Function of Exodus Motifs in Biblical Narratives: Theological Didactic Drama* (Studies in the Bible and Early Christianity 52; Lewiston, NY: Edwin Mellen Press, 2002).
Janzen, J. Gerald, 'A Certain Woman in the Rhetoric of Judges 9', *Journal for the Study of the Old Testament* 38 (1987), pp. 33-37.
Jepsen, Alfred, 'Wellhausen in Greifswald', in *Festschrift zur 500-Jahrfeier der Universität Greifswald* (Greifswald: Ernst Moritz-Arndt-Universität, 1956), pp. 47-56.
Johnson, Luke Timothy, 'The Scriptural World of Hebrews', *Interpretation* 57.3 (2003), pp. 237-50.
Joüon, Paul, and T. Muraoka, *A Grammar of Biblical Hebrew* (Subsidia Biblica 14; 2 vols.; Roma: Editrice Pontificio Instituto Biblico, 1991).
Kaiser, Walter C., *Toward an Exegetical Theology: Biblical Exegesis for Preaching and Teaching* (Grand Rapids, MI: Baker, 1981).
Kaswalder, Pietro Alberto, 'Le Tribù in Gdc 1,1-2,5 e in Gdc 4-5', *Liber Annuus* 43 (1993), pp. 89-113.
Kittel, Rudolf *et al.*, *Biblia Hebraica Stuttgartensia* (Stuttgart: Deutsche Bibelgesellschaft, 3rd emended edn, 1987).
Klein, Lillian R., *The Triumph of Irony in the Book of Judges* (Bible and Literature 14; Sheffield: Almond, 1988).
Knierim, R., 'און', in Ernst Jenni and Claus Westermann (eds.), *Theological Lexicon of the Old Testament* (trans. Mark E. Biddle; 3 vols.; Peabody, MA: Hendrickson Publishers, 1997), I, pp. 60-62.
Köhler, Ludwig, *Old Testament Theology* (trans. A.S. Todd; Philadelphia: Westminster Press, 1957).

—*The Hebrew and Aramaic Lexicon of the Old Testament* (2 vols.; Leiden: Brill, Study edn, 2001).
Köhler, Ludwig, and Walter Baumgartner, *Lexicon in Veteris Testamenti Libros* (Leiden: Brill, 1958).
Kutsch, E., 'ברית', in Ernst Jenni and Claus Westermann (eds.), *Theological Lexicon of the Old Testament* (trans. Mark E. Biddle; 3 vols.; Peabody, MA: Hendrickson Publishers, 1997), I, pp. 256-66.
Land, Steven J., *Pentecostal Spirituality: A Passion for the Kingdom* (Cleveland, TN: CPT Press, 2010). First published: (JPTSup 1; Sheffield: Sheffield Academic Press, 1993).
Lane, William L., *Hebrews: A Call to Commitment* (Peabody, MA: Hendrickson Publishers, 1988).
Lee, Bernon, 'Fragmentation of Reader Focus in the Preamble to Battle in Judges 6:1-7:14', *Journal for the Study of the Old Testament* 25 (2002), pp. 65-86.
Liddell, Henry George *et al.*, *A Greek-English Lexicon* (Oxford: Clarendon Press, 1940).
Lieberman, David, *The Eternal Torah: A New Commentary Utilizing Ancient and Modern Sources in a Grammatical, Historical, and Traditional Explanation of the Text* (River Vale, NJ: Twin Pines Press, 1979).
Lilley, J.P.U., 'A Literary Appreciation of the Book of Judges', *Tyndale Bulletin* 18 (1967), pp. 94-102.
Lindars, Barnabas, 'Gideon and Kingship', *Journal of Theological Studies* 16 (1965), pp. 315-26.
—*Judges 1-5: A New Translation and Commentary* (Edinburgh: T&T Clark, 1995).
Longacre, Robert E., *An Anatomy of Speech Notions* (Lisse: Peter de Ridder Press, 1976).
MacDonald, William, 'Temple Theology', *PNEUMA* 1.1 (1979), pp. 39-48.
Malamat, Abraham, 'Charismatic Leadership in the Book of Judges', in F. Cross, W. Lemke and P. Miller (eds.), *Magnalia Dei, the Mighty Acts of God: Essays on the Bible and Archaeology in Memory of G. Ernest Wright* (Garden City, NY: Doubleday, 1976), pp. 152-68.
Marais, Jacobus, *Representation in Old Testament Narrative Texts* (Biblical Interpretation 36; Leiden: Brill, 1998).
Maré, Leonard P., 'Some Remarks on the Spirit of God in the Life of David', *Ekklesiastikos Pharos* 88 (2006), pp. 30-41.
Martin, James D., *The Book of Judges: A Commentary* (New York: Cambridge University Press, 1975).
Martin, Lee Roy, *The Unheard Voice of God: A Pentecostal Hearing of the Book of Judges* (JPTSup 32; Blandford Forum, UK: Deo Publishing, 2008).
Matthews, Victor H., *Judges and Ruth* (New Cambridge Bible Commentary; Cambridge: Cambridge University Press, 2004).
McCann, J. Clinton, *Judges* (Interpretation: A Bible Commentary for Teaching and Preaching; Louisville, KY: John Knox Press, 2002).
Mendenhall, George E., 'Hebrew Conquest of Palestine', *Biblical Archaeologist* 25 (1962), pp. 66-87.

Moltmann, Jürgen, *The Crucified God: The Cross of Christ as the Foundation and Criticism of Christian Theology* (Minneapolis: Fortress Press, 1993).
Montague, George T., *The Holy Spirit: Growth of a Biblical Tradition* (An Exploration Book; New York: Paulist Press, 1976).
Moody, Dale, *Spirit of the Living God: The Biblical Concepts Interpreted in Context* (Philadelphia: Westminster Press, 1968).
Moore, George F., *A Critical and Exegetical Commentary on Judges* (ICC; New York: Charles Scribner's Sons, 1895).
Moore, Rick Dale, *God Saves: Lessons from the Elisha Stories* (JSOTSup 95; Sheffield: JSOT Press, 1990).
—'Deuteronomy and the Fire of God: A Critical Charismatic Interpretation', *Journal of Pentecostal Theology* 7 (1995), pp. 11-33.
—'Welcoming an Unheard Voice: A Response to Lee Roy Martin' *The Unheard Voice of God*', *Journal of Pentecostal Theology* 18.2 (2008), pp. 7-14.
Munch, Peter A., 'The "Judges" of Ancient Israel: An Exploration in Charismatic Authority', in W. Swatos (ed.), *Time, Place, and Circumstance: Neo-Weberian Studies in Comparative Religious History* (Contributions to the Study of Religion 24; New York: Greenwood Press, 1990), pp. 57-69.
Neef, Heinz-Dieter, '"Ich Selber bin in Ihm" (Ex 23,21): Exegetische Beobachtungen zur Rede vom "Engel des Herrn" in Ex 23,20-22; 32,34; 33,2; Jdc 2,1-5; 5,23', *Biblische Zeitschrift* 39 (1995), pp. 54-75.
Neve, Lloyd R., *The Spirit of God in the Old Testament* (Centre for Pentecostal Theology Classics Series; Cleveland, TN: CPT Press, 2011).
Niccacci, Alviero, *The Syntax of the Verb in Classical Hebrew Prose* (trans. Wilfred G.E. Watson; JSOTSup 86; Sheffield: JSOT Press, 1990).
Nicholson, Ernest W., *Exodus and Sinai in History and Tradition* (Growing Points in Theology; Richmond, VA: John Knox press, 1973).
Niditch, Susan, *Judges: A Commentary* (Old Testament Library; Louisville, KY: Westminster John Knox Press, 2008).
Noll, K.L., 'Deuteronomistic History or Deuteronomic Debate? (A Thought Experiment)', *Journal for the Study of the Old Testament* 31 (2007), pp. 311-45.
Noth, Martin, *Überlieferungsgeschichtliche Studien* (Halle: M. Niemeyer, 1943).
O'Connell, Robert H., *The Rhetoric of the Book of Judges* (VTSup 63; Leiden: Brill, 1996).
Olson, Dennis, 'Judges', in *The New Interpreter's Bible: Numbers-Samuel* (12 vols.; Nashville, TN: Abingdon Press, 1994), II, pp. 721-888.
Patte, Daniel, 'The Guarded Personal Voice of a Male European-American Biblical Scholar', in I.R. Kitzberger (ed.), *Personal Voice in Biblical Interpretation* (London: Routledge, 1999), pp. 12-24.
Payne, J. Barton, 'רוח', in R. Laird Harris, Gleason L. Archer and Bruce K. Waltke (eds.), *Theological Wordbook of the Old Testament* (2 vols.; Chicago: Moody Press, 1980), II, pp. 836-37.
Penchansky, David, *Twilight of the Gods: Polytheism in the Hebrew Bible* (Louisville, KY: Westminster John Knox Press, 2005).
Pinnock, Clark H., 'Divine Relationality: A Pentecostal Contribution to the Doctrine of God', *Journal of Pentecostal Theology* 5 (2000), pp. 3-26.

Poloma, Margaret M., *The Assemblies of God at the Crossroads: Charisma and Institutional Dilemmas* (Knoxville, TN: University of Tennessee Press, 1989).
—'Charisma, Institutionalization and Social Change', *PNEUMA* 17.2 (1995), pp. 245-52.
—'The Future of American Pentecostal Identity: The Assemblies of God at a Crossroad', in Michael Welker (ed.), *The Work of the Spirit* (Grand Rapids, MI: Eerdmans, 2006), pp. 147-68.
Polzin, Robert, *Moses and the Deuteronomist: A Literary Study of the Deuteronomic History* (New York: Seabury Press, 1980).
—*Samuel and the Deuteronomist: A Literary Study of the Deuteronomic History: Part Two: 1 Samuel* (San Francisco: Harper & Row, 1989).
Pratt, Richard L., *He Gave Us Stories: The Bible Student's Guide to Interpreting Old Testament Narratives* (Brentwood, TN: Wolgemuth & Hyatt, 1990).
Pressler, Carolyn, *Joshua, Judges, and Ruth* (Westminster Bible Companion; Louisville, KY: Westminster John Knox Press, 2002).
Rad, Gerhard von, *Old Testament Theology* (2 vols.; New York: Harper, 1962).
Rea, John, *The Holy Spirit in the Bible: All the Major Passages About the Spirit: A Commentary* (Lake Mary, FL: Creation House, 1990).
Rendtorff, Rolf, *The Canonical Hebrew Bible: A Theology of the Old Testament* (trans. David Orton; Leiden: Deo Publishing, 2005).
Renwick, David A., 'Hebrews 11:29-12:2', *Interpretation* 57.3 (2003), pp. 300-302.
Rhee, Victor, 'Chiasm and the Concept of Faith in Hebrews 11', *Bibliotheca Sacra* 155.619 (1998), pp. 327-45.
—'Christology and the Concept of Faith in Hebrews 5:11-6:20', *Journal of the Evangelical Theological Society* 43.1 (2000), pp. 83-96.
Scherman, Nosson, *The Prophets: Joshua/Judges. The Early Prophets with a Commentary Anthologized from the Rabbinic Writings* (Artscroll; Brooklyn, NY: Mesorah Publications, 1st Rubin edn, 2000).
Schneider, Tammi J., *Judges* (Berit Olam; Collegeville, MN: Liturgical Press, 2000).
Schult, H., 'שמע', in Ernst Jenni and Claus Westermann (eds.), *Theological Lexicon of the Old Testament* (trans. Mark E. Biddle; 3 vols.; Peabody, MA: Hendrickson Publishers, 1997), II, pp. 1375-80.
Schwertner, Siegfried, 'עמל', in Ernst Jenni and Claus Westermann (eds.), *Theological Lexicon of the Old Testament* (trans. Mark E. Biddle; 3 vols.; Peabody, MA: Hendrickson Publishers, 1997), II, pp. 924-26.
Shaull, Richard, 'La Iglesia, Crisis Y Nuevas Perspectivas', *Vida y Pensamiento* 15 (1995), pp. 8-48.
Shaull, Richard, and Waldo A. Cesar, *Pentecostalism and the Future of the Christian Churches: Promises, Limitations, Challenges* (Grand Rapids, MI: Eerdmans, 2000).
Shiveka, Avi, '"Watiqzar Nafsho Ba'amal Yisrael": A New Understanding', *Beth Mikra* 172 (2002), pp. 77-86.
Smith, Mark S., 'Remembering God: Collective Memory in Israelite Religion', *Catholic Biblical Quarterly* 64.4 (2002), pp. 631-51.
Soggin, J. Alberto, *Judges: A Commentary* (Old Testament Library; Philadelphia: Westminster Press, 1981).

—*Judges: A Commentary* (Old Testament Library; London: SCM Press, 2nd edn, 1987).
Solivan, Samuel, *The Spirit, Pathos and Liberation: Toward an Hispanic Pentecostal Theology* (JPTSup 14; Sheffield: Sheffield Academic Press, 1998).
Sosa, Carlos R., 'Análisis Exegético y Literario de Jueces 2:1-5', *Kairós* (Guatemala) 43 (July-Dec. 2008), pp. 9-38.
Stoebe, H.J., 'נחם', in Ernst Jenni and Claus Westermann (eds.), *Theological Lexicon of the Old Testament* (trans. Mark E. Biddle; 3 vols.; Peabody, MA: Hendrickson Publishers, 1997), II, pp. 734-39.
Stone, Lawson Grant, 'From Tribal Confederation to Monarchic State: The Editorial Perspective of the Book of Judges' (PhD Diss., Yale University, 1988).
Swart, I., 'לחץ', in Willem Van Gemeren (ed.), *New International Dictionary of Old Testament Theology and Exegesis* (5 vols.; Grand Rapids, MI: Zondervan, 1997), II, pp. 792–93.
Tanner, J. Paul, 'The Gideon Narrative as the Focal Point of Judges', *Bibliotheca Sacra* 149 (1992), pp. 146-61.
Thompson, David, 'עמל', in Willem Van Gemeren (ed.), *New International Dictionary of Old Testament Theology and Exegesis* (5 vols.; Grand Rapids, MI: Zondervan, 1997), III, pp. 435-37.
Turco, Lewis, *The Book of Literary Terms: The Genres of Fiction, Drama, Nonfiction, Literary Criticism, and Scholarship* (Hanover, NH: University Press of New England, 1999).
Van der Merwe, Christo H.J., J.A. Naudé, and Jan H. Kroeze, *Biblical Hebrew Reference Grammar* (Biblical Languages: Hebrew 3; Sheffield: Sheffield Academic Press, 1999).
Waddell, Robby, *The Spirit of the Book of Revelation* (JPTSup 30; Blandford Forum: Deo Publishing, 2006).
Waldman, Nahum M., 'The Imagery of Clothing, Covering and Overpowering', *Journal of the Ancient Near Eastern Society* 19 (1989), pp. 161-70.
Waltke, Bruce K., and Michael Patrick O'Connor, *An Introduction to Biblical Hebrew Syntax* (Winona Lake, IN: Eisenbrauns, 1990).
Webb, Barry G., 'The Theme of the Jephthah Story (Judges 10.6-12.7)', *Reformed Theological Review* 45 (1986), pp. 34-43.
—*The Book of the Judges: An Integrated Reading* (JSOTSup 46; Sheffield: JSOT Press, 1987).
Weisman, Ze'eb, 'Charismatic Leaders in the Era of the Judges', *Zeitschrift für die alttestamentliche Wissenschaft* 89 (1977), pp. 399-411.
Welker, Michael, *God the Spirit* (trans. John F. Hoffmeyer; Minneapolis, MN: Fortress Press, 1994).
Wellhausen, Julius, *Prolegomena zur Geschichte Israels* (Berlin: Georg Reimer, 1883).
—*Prolegomena to the History of Israel* (trans. J. Sutherland Black and Allan Menzies; Edinburgh: Adam & Charles Black, 1885).
Wesley, John, *The Works of John Wesley* (14 vols.; Grand Rapids, MI: Zondervan, 1958).

Wesley, John, and G. Roger Schoenhals, *Wesley's Notes on the Bible* (Grand Rapids, MI: Francis Asbury Press, 1987).
Wilcock, Michael, *The Message of Judges: Grace Abounding* (Downers Grove, IL: InterVarsity Press, 1992).
Willis, Timothy M., 'The Nature of Jephthah's Authority', *Catholic Biblical Quarterly* 59 (1997), pp. 33-44.
Wolf, Herbert, 'Judges', in F.E. Gaebelein (ed.), *The Expositor's Bible Commentary* (Grand Rapids: Zondervan, 1992), III, pp. 375-508.
Wong, Gregory T.K., *Compositional Strategy of the Book of Judges: An Inductive, Rhetorical Study* (VTSup 111; Leiden: Brill, 2006).
Wright, Walter C., 'The Use of *Pneuma* in the Pauline Corpus with Special Attention to the Relationship between *Pneuma* and the Risen Christ' (PhD Diss., Fuller Theological Seminary, 1977).

CREDITS

Permission is gratefully acknowledged for republication of material included in the following chapters of this book:

Chapter 2: *Old Testament Essays* 18.3 (2005), pp. 722-40.

Chapter 3: S.J. Land, R.D. Moore, and J.C. Thomas (eds.), *Passover, Pentecost, and Parousia: Studies in Celebration of the Life and Ministry of R. Hollis Gause* (JPTSup 36; Blandford Forum, UK: Deo Publishers, 2010), pp. 33-53.

Chapter 4: *Old Testament Essays* 22.2 (2009), pp. 356-72.

Chapter 5: *Journal of Pentecostal Theology* 16.2 (2008), pp. 21-50.

Chapter 6: *Journal of Biblical and Pneumatological Research* 2 (Fall 2010), pp. 87-109.

Chapter 7: *Verbum et Ecclesia* 29.1 (2008), pp. 110-29.

Index of Biblical References

Genesis		16.12	118	35.31	80, 91
2.18	30	17.8-13	44		
3.21	92	17.8	45	Numbers	
6.3	80, 81	17.9	44	10.10	118
6.6	32	17.14	44	11.16	84, 150
23.13	17	18.9	116	11.17-29	80, 81, 86
31.52	17	18.10	116	11.25	84
38.19	92	18.13-26	42	11.29	81
41.8	100	19.5	114	13.26	50
41.38	91	20.2-3	47	14.21	17
42.38	80	20.2	112	15.41	118
50.20	80	20.3	125	20.11-12	89
		23.20-33	112	21	15, 126
Exodus		23.20	112	24.2	80
1.13-14	78	23.32-33	6	27.18	80, 84, 86, 91
2.23-24	63, 111	28.3	80, 91	31.1-12	45
2.23	63, 78, 111	31.3	80, 91	32.20	17
2.24	63, 111	32.2-4	89		
3.1	88	32.20	112	Deuteronomy	
3.2	89	32.34	112	4.23-26	61
3.4	89	33.2	112	4.25	61
3.7	32	33.15	43	4.26	61
3.8	116, 117	34	66	7.2	6
3.10	89	34.6-7	4, 5, 22, 77	9.18-21	61
3.11	89	34.6	66	9.18	61
3.12	49, 81, 89	34.9	4	11.16	47
3.20	49, 121	34.10	4	13.6	47
4.2-8	89	34.11	4	17.2-3	61
4.2-3	89	34.12	4	17.2	17
4.18	89	34.13	4	18.15	41
5.15-23	104	34.14	4	24.1	17
5.21	89	34.16	4	25.17-19	45
6.7	118	34.17	4	28.1-14	2
10.13	79	34.10-16	121	28.7	2
10.19	79	34.10	17, 66	28.15-68	2
14.13	133	34.11-15	112	28.25	2
14.19	112	34.11	66, 121	28.33	2
14.21	79	34.12	6, 66	28.36-68	3
14.30	116	34.13	66	29.5	118
15.11	49, 88, 121	34.14	66	29.21	17
15.20	44	34.15	6, 66	30.17-18	2
15.24	142	34.16	66	31.8	43

Index of Biblical References 167

31.16	2, 40	1.14	50	2.15-22	45
31.20	2, 61	1.15	50	2.15	117
31.29	61	1.16	29	2.16-17	11, 58
34.9	80, 84, 86, 91	1.19-22	82	2.16	17, 42, 82, 117, 148, 149
		1.20	50		
Joshua		1.35	117	2.17	4, 10, 11, 40, 41, 60, 66, 77
1.1	36	2-3	20, 121		
2.8-11	127	2	22, 38, 66, 108, 114	2.18	4, 11, 17, 26, 52, 59, 63, 64, 81, 86, 107, 111, 117
3.5	49, 88, 121				
3.7	36	2.1-5	vii, 2, 3, 38, 39, 44, 47, 48, 59, 61, 65, 67, 72, 76, 112-15, 126		
4.1	36			2.19	11, 59, 61, 77, 145
4.8	36				
4.15	36			2.20-23	59
5.2	36			2.20-22	39
5.2	36				
6.2	36	2.1-2	27, 82, 112	2.20	4, 11, 23, 39-41, 61, 65
7.1-15	142	2.1	4, 15, 17, 22, 23, 38, 48, 52, 66, 67, 70, 82, 107, 110, 112, 120, 126, 148		
7.10	36			2.21	40
8.1	36			2.22	40
8.18	36			2.23	117
9.15	6			3-16	59, 60, 67, 144
10.8	36				
11.6	36	2.2	4, 6, 10, 37-39, 41, 50, 56, 61, 66, 67, 72, 114, 125, 127	3-9	71, 72
12	147			3	16
13.6	15, 126			3.1-6	40
15.55	15, 126			3.3	15, 126
20.1	36			3.4	11
23.2	37	2.3	4, 66, 76, 93	3.5-6	153
24.8	15, 126	2.5	82	3.7-16.31	10, 11, 76
24.15	28, 47	2.6-3.6	39, 40, 76, 144	3.6	4, 66
24.22	52, 126			3.7-11	52, 77-87, 145
24.24	38	2.6	11		
		2.10	viii, 4, 49, 114, 119	3.7	13, 14, 59, 60, 125
Judges					
1.1-3.6	10, 76	2.11-19	26	3.8	4, 61, 107, 117
1.1-2.5	10, 39, 40, 76	2.11-13	40, 60		
1.1-31	39	2.11-12	60, 114-15	3.9	4, 11, 15, 50, 52, 59, 62, 83, 87, 117, 125, 126, 148, 149, 150
1	37, 112, 113	2.11	11, 13, 58, 59, 120, 125, 127		
1.1-2	54, 69				
1.1	36				
1.2	36-37, 54, 69, 117	2.12	4, 22, 48, 110, 148	3.10	12, 59, 75, 81, 84, 87, 97, 107, 117
		2.13	40		
1.4	82, 117	2.14-15	3, 11, 58		
1.7	3, 82	2.14	4, 11, 26, 58, 61, 82, 107, 117	3.11	12, 59
1.11-15	83			3.12-30	41, 52
1.12	50				
1.13	41, 50				

3.12	13, 59, 61, 86, 125	6.1-6	87	6.28-32	90, 124
		6.1	13, 45, 59, 61, 89, 117, 118, 125	6.33	15, 126
3.13	15, 126			6.34	12, 59, 75, 82, 89, 91, 92, 149
3.14	62				
3.15	4, 11, 15, 52, 59, 117, 125, 126, 145, 148, 149	6.2-5	147		
		6.2	117	6.35	89
		6.3	15, 126	6.36	117
		6.5	148	6.37	117
3.19	60	6.6	4, 15, 62, 116, 122, 124, 125	7.1	51
3.26	60			7.2	117
3.28	117			7.3	50, 92
3.30	12, 59, 117	6.7-10	vii, 3, 65, 115-19, 126	7.7	117
3.31	15, 41, 117, 126, 149			7.9-11	51, 92
		6.7	11, 15, 59, 61, 62, 125	7.9	43, 117
4-5	50			7.10	92
4	18	6.8	15, 17, 48, 110, 116, 120, 126, 127, 148	7.11	51, 117
4.1-5.31	52			7.12	15, 126
4.1	13, 59, 61, 125			7.14	117
				7.15	51, 117
4.2	61, 117	6.9	4, 17, 48, 66, 110, 116, 117, 118, 148	8.1-21	93
4.3	4, 11, 14, 15, 59, 62, 125, 147, 148			8.1-3	96
				8.3	117
		6.10	4, 11, 41, 45-48, 60, 66, 118	8.4-17	96
4.4-5	41, 42			8.6	117
4.4	15, 52, 126			8.7	117
4.6-8	67	6.11-24	44	8.15	117
4.6-7	41-45	6.11	15, 52, 87, 88, 126, 150	8.20	89, 92
4.6	145			8.22-23	68
4.7	43, 117	6.12	48-51, 88, 119	8.22	17, 117, 124
4.9	117, 152			8.23	104
4.14	43, 117	6.13	4, 17, 48, 49, 61, 88, 89, 110, 117, 119-24, 148	8.24-27	89
4.23	117			8.27	60, 89, 93, 145, 152
4.24	117			8.28	12, 59, 86
5	18				
5.5	48, 148	6.14	17, 49, 89, 117, 149	8.33	60, 61, 93
5.7-8	42			8.34	117
5.8	61	6.15	89	9	12, 22, 93
5.9-23	44	6.16	49, 88, 89	9.17	17, 117
5.21	48, 148	6.17	89	9.22	145
5.23	44	6.21	89	9.23	93
5.31	12, 45, 59	6.22	49	9.29	117
6-9	13	6.23	49	9.56-57	13
6-8	12, 87-93	6.25-32	60, 89	9.56	3
6	15, 108, 117, 118, 147	6.25-26	50	10-12	93-98
		6.25	88, 124	10	9, 10, 16, 18, 19, 20, 21, 22, 23, 24,
6.1-8.28	52	6.27	50, 92, 145		

Index of Biblical References 169

Reference	Pages
	25, 26, 27, 68, 70, 71, 72, 108, 117
10.1-5	21, 93
10.1	13, 149
10.2	86
10.3	13, 86
10.6-16	vii, 3, 9-34, 52, 67
10.6	13, 14, 18, 22, 59, 60, 68, 125
10.7-16	70
10.7-9	14
10.7-8	125
10.7	4, 22, 61, 98, 99, 117, 146
10.8-9	147
10.8	2
10.9	125
10.10-16	62, 65
10.10-15	110
10.10-14	60
10.10	4, 11, 15, 59, 62, 125
10.11-16	48, 51
10.11-14	15
10.11-13	9, 52, 125-27, 132
10.11-12	15, 17, 18, 62, 125-27
10.11	16, 17, 28, 48, 62, 148
10.12	17, 117, 128
10.13-14	62
10.13	4, 5, 51-52, 53, 56, 64, 67, 70, 94, 98, 105
10.14	15, 29, 56, 125
10.15	18
10.16	4, 5, 18, 19, 22, 23, 24, 26, 64, 70
10.17	94
11-16	70
11.1-11	150
11.1	94, 127
11.2-3	127
11.3	94
11.5	127
11.9	94, 128
11.12	94, 127
11.13	17, 48, 110, 127, 148
11.15-24	127-29, 132
11.16	17, 48, 110, 148
11.20-21	128
11.21	117, 128
11.23	94, 128
11.24	94, 128
11.27	94, 128
11.29	12, 59, 75, 94, 97, 128
11.30-31	145
11.30	97, 117
11.32	98, 117
11.39	96
12.1-6	96
12.2	117
12.3	117
12.5-6	96
12.7	86, 145
12.9	86
12.11	86
12.14	86
13-16	98-107
13	19
13.1	59, 61, 99, 117, 147
13.2-23	44
13.3-5	53, 99
13.5	17, 52-54, 68, 105, 117, 146, 149
13.8	104
13.24-25	99
13.25	12, 59, 75
14-16	100, 101
14-15	101
14.1-3	101
14.4	54, 105, 106
14.6	12, 59, 75, 101, 104
14.8-9	101
14.19	59, 75, 101, 104, 106
15.3	100
15.9-13	104
15.11	68, 146
15.12	117
15.13	117
15.14-15	104
15.14	12, 59, 75, 101
15.18-19	54, 107
15.18	104, 117
15.20	86
16.1	101
16.18	100
16.20	86, 100, 101, 107
16.23	117
16.24	117
16.28	54, 56, 100, 104
16.30	107
16.31	86
17.1-21.25	10, 12, 13, 70
17	12
17.2	54, 68
17.3	4, 54, 68
17.4	4
17.6	38, 54, 68, 69, 146
17.13	54, 68
18	12
18.1	68, 146
18.10	117
18.14-18	4
18.25	11
18.27-30	68
18.30	3
19-21	12
19.1	68, 146
19.25-30	68, 129
19.25	11
19.30	48, 110, 129-30, 133, 148

20.3	11	51.11	86	5.11	91
20.18	54-55, 69	74	122	10.5	91
20.22	54, 69	74.12-17	122	12.6	91
20.28	55, 69, 117	77.5	100		
21.1-7	69	77	122	Hosea	
21.12	69, 129	77.11-20	122	1.2-9	100
21.20-23	69, 129	77.11	121		
21.25	38, 54, 68, 69, 146	78.38	32	Amos	
		106.34-45	96	2.10	47
		118.17	132	5.6	101
1 Samuel		135.9	121		
3.1	5, 54			Jonah	
8.1-4	142	Proverbs		1.1-3	100
10.5	44	31.7	25	4.1-2	100
10.10	101	31.21	91		
10.18	47			Micah	
16.13	101	Isaiah		3.8	91
16.14	86	6.5-7	100		
17.5	91	9.7	142	Haggai	
18.10	44	11	149	1.6	92
23.4	43	45.1	86		
		49.4	100	Zechariah	
2 Samuel		63.9	32	2.12	32
1.24	92			3.3	91
8.15	142	Jeremiah			
19.18	101	4.19	100	Matthew	
22.4	17	12.1-3	100	9.36	32
24.14	18	23.5	142	25.45	32
		32.20	121		
1 Kings				Luke	
10.9	142	Ezekiel		4.18	149
22.10	91	2.2	91	12	32
		3.14-15	100	24.26	32
1 Chronicles		9.2	91		
2.55	50	9.11	91	John	
25	44	10.2	91	11.35	32
		10.6	91	14.16	85
Job		23.6	91	15.18-19	32
3.20	24	23.12	91	20.27	32
11.16	24	38.4	91		
15.35	25			Acts	
29.14	91	Daniel		5.3-11	85
		2.1	100	9.4	32
Psalms		2.3	100	10-11	143
10.7	25	4.8	91	10.44	85
30.5	56	4.9	91	13.9-11	85
46.1	32	4.18	91	15	143

15.39	102	4.14	138	11.17	141
16.16-18	85	4.15	32, 142	11.25	142
		4.16	138	11.29	142
1 Corinthians		6.1	138	11.30	142
13	31	6.12	141	11.32-34	135, 141
		6.15	141	11.32	140
Galatians		6.17	141	11.33-34	141
2.11-14	102	7.1-28	138	11.33	141
2.11	143	7.6	141	11.39	141
3.28	42	7.19	138	11.40	138
		7.22	138	12.1-3	138, 139, 140
Philippians		8.6	138, 141	12.1	138
2	32	9.15	141	12.2	140
		10	138	12.14	142
Hebrews		10.1	138	12.16	143
1.4	138	10.22	138		
2.18	32	10.23	138	1 Peter	
3	138	10.24	138	5.7	32
3.3	138	10.34	138		
3.7-4.13	138	10.35-39	140	James	
3.7-19	143	10.36	141	2.19	31
3.12	138	10.38-39	138, 140		
3.14	138	11	135, 137-43,	Revelation	
4.1	138, 141		150, 152	2.1-3.22	102
4.2	138	11.1-40	140	2.5	132
4.8	138	11.9	141	2.10	33
4.11	138	11.13	141	12.5-6	32
4.12	138	11.16	138	21.3-4	33

Index of Authors

Ackerman, S.   43
Adewuya, J.A.   103, 145
Alexander, K.E.   42
Allen, R.B.   25
Amit, Y.   78, 81
Archer, K.J.   122, 131
Assis, E.   41, 42, 43, 44
Attridge, H.W.   137
Auld, A.G.   89
Baker, K.F.   137
Bal, M.   41
Baugh, S.M.   139
Benson, A.   79, 81
Bernhardt, K.   24
Beyerlin, W.   50, 57, 60, 77, 144
Birch, B.C.   83, 86, 137, 149
Block, D.I.   14, 17, 20, 21, 28, 41, 42, 61, 68, 112, 125
Boling, R.G.   17, 20, 27, 95, 107
Boogaart, T.A.   21
Boyd, M.P.   13
Brawley, R.L.   140
Brettler, M.Z.   100
Brown, C.A.   19, 21, 27
Bruce, F.F.   141
Brueggemann, W.   2, 4, 7, 57, 63, 65, 77, 78, 81, 109, 111, 112, 113, 116, 117, 118, 131, 137, 144
Burney, C.F.   62, 110, 136
Cesar, W.A.   71
Childs, B.S.   114,
Claassens, L.J.M.   46
Crenshaw, J.L.   103, 105, 107, 108
Culpepper, R.A.   140
Dautzenbert, G.   140
Dayton, D.W.   131
Eichrodt, W.   6, 45
Eisenbaum, P.M.   139, 140, 141
Ellingworth, P.   137
Even-Shoshan, A.   24
Faupel, W.   130, 131

Fee, G.D.   80
Fiddes, P.S.   29, 30, 31
Finkelstein, I.   63, 110
Fokkelman, J.P.   21
Fredricks, G.   87, 102
Fretheim, T.E.   10, 27, 29, 30, 31, 32, 71
Freytag, G.   39
Gamberoni, J.   91, 92
Gause, R.H.   42
Gerstenberger, E.S.   47
Gillmayr-Bucher, S.   124
Goldingay, J.   6, 7, 47, 75, 79, 80, 97, 109, 131, 145
Gooding, D.W.   10, 21
Goslinga, C.J.   101
Gottwald, N.K.   45, 46, 145
Gray, J.   4951, 92,
Green, C.E.W.   5
Green, M.   80
Greenspahn, F.E.   6, 57, 58, 60, 61, 63, 65, 66, 110, 111, 113
Greenstein, E.L.   61, 99, 103, 105, 106, 107, 146
Guest, P.D.   98
Guillaume, P.   60, 63, 111
Gunn, D.M.   136, 143, 145
Hamilton, V.P.   129
Hamlin, E.J.   85, 100
Harris, J.G.   19, 21, 27
Hausmann, J.   101
Herr, D.D.   13
Herzberg, B.   44
Heschel, A.J.   19, 23, 29, 30, 31, 70
Hildebrandt, W.   35, 75, 80
Hollenweger, W.   71, 103
Horton, S.M.   35, 75, 82, 84, 86, 101
Hughes, R.B.   63, 110
Hunter, H.D.   79, 102
Isbell, C.D.   111
Janzen, J.G.   21

Jepsen, A. 122
Johnson, L.T. 141
Joüon, P. 17
Kaiser, W.C. 63, 110
Kaswalder, P.A. 145
Kittel, R. 16
Klein, L.R. 46, 89, 91, 94, 103, 107
Knierim, R. 25
Köhler, L. 79
Kroeze, J.H. 17
Kutsch, E. 6
Land, S.J. 130, 131
Lane, W.L. 137
Laney, J.C. 63, 110
Lee, B. 120
Lieberman, D. 45
Lilley, J.P.U. 67, 145
Lindars, B. 47, 50
Longacre, R.E. 39
MacDonald, W. 131
Malamat, A. 150
Marais, J. 93, 107
Maré, L.P. 85
Martin, J.D. 11, 17, 36
Matthews, V.H. 63, 110
McCann, J.C., Jr 45, 104, 105, 116, 136, 137, 147
Mendenhall, G.E. 83
Moltmann, J. 27, 28, 30, 31
Montague, G.T. 35, 75, 103
Moody, D. 75, 79, 80, 82
Moore, G.F. 17, 21, 23, 62, 63, 112
Moore, M.S. 19, 21, 27
Moore, R.D. 43, 109, 123
Munch, P.A. 150
Muraoka, T. 17
Naudé, J.A. 17
Neef, H.-D. 112
Neve, L.R. 80
Niccacci, A. 89
Nicholson, E.W. 109
Niditch, S. 60, 122, 129
Noll, K.L. 19, 65
Noth, M. 57
O'Connell, R.H. 17, 59, 63, 76, 100, 110, 111, 120, 144

Olson, D. 46, 48, 95, 96, 97, 109
Patte, D. 122, 123
Payne, J.B. 79
Penchansky, D. 47
Pinnock, C.H. 5, 27
Poloma, M.M. 151
Polzin, R. 58, 61, 63, 64, 66, 103, 107, 125
Pratt, R.L. 63, 110
Pressler, C. 15, 16, 17, 19, 23, 26, 29, 37, 46, 66, 67, 126
Rad, G. von 6, 72, 109, 112, 145
Rea, J. 35, 75, 87, 101
Rendtorff, R. 109
Renwick, D.A. 137, 140
Rhee, V. 139
Scherman, N. 29, 36, 37, 45, 136
Schneider, T. 14, 17, 94, 129
Schult, H. 10
Schwertner, S. 24, 25
Shaull, R. 71, 103
Shiveka, A. 23, 24, 26
Smith, M.S. 50, 88, 111
Soggin, J.A. 17, 37, 96
Solivan, S. 31, 71, 83
Sosa, C.R. 114
Stoebe, H.J. 26, 64
Stone, L.G. 41, 78
Swart, I. 117
Tanner, J.P. 85
Thompson, D. 24, 25
Turco, L. 39
Van der Merwe, C.H.J. 17
Waddell, R. 144
Waldman, N.M. 91, 92
Waltke, B.K. 17
Webb, B.G. 14, 15, 17, 21, 26, 29, 45, 52, 82, 92, 98, 99, 106, 120, 125, 126, 146
Weisman, Z. 150
Welker, M. 63, 75, 76, 77, 78, 81, 83, 86, 90, 96, 100, 106, 107, 110, 111, 148, 149, 150
Wellhausen, J. 62, 76, 77, 84, 110, 122
Wesley, J. 136

Wilcock, M. 17, 20, 45
Willis, T.M. 150
Wolf, H. 42, 45, 81, 135

Wong, G.T.K. 60, 63, 67, 97, 104, 111
Wright, W.C. 79

www.ingramcontent.com/pod-product-compliance
Lightning Source LLC
Chambersburg PA
CBHW071710090426
42738CB00009B/1732